For Rita
So nice to have met you...
Hope to do so again sometime
Best wishes

A.K.A *Geoff Sleeman* Geoff

D1824648

Too Many Goodbyes

Written By
Geoff Sleeman

Little School
Publishing

www.littleschoolpublishing.co.uk

Little School Publishing
22A Main Street
Greetham
Oakham
Rutland LE15 7NL

www.littleschoolpublishing.co.uk

British Library Cataloguing in Publication Data:
A catalogue record for this book is available from the British Library

ISBN 978-0-9926020-0-0

www.littleschoolpublishing.co.uk

Chapters

Synopsis

The story told in 'Too Many Goodbyes' is that of an eight year old schoolboy, called Geoffrey Sleeman, from south London, who in 1939 was evacuated to the safety of the West Sussex countryside because of the impending outbreak of World War II.

He, along with an elder brother and sister, were evacuated with the brother's school just before the outbreak of the war. This was allowed so as not to split families up.

It tells not only of his confusion and bewilderment but that of every child involved in the mass movement of children. Very few if any understood exactly what was happening or why.

Following the confusion of the tearful goodbyes and the train journey the three siblings plus two other boys were eventually billeted with a very well-to-do household. The house owners were a Mr and Mrs Corbett-Ashby who had a live-in staff comprising a cook, housemaid, a general handyman, and a lady who did mending, sewing, repairs and helping in the kitchen. There was a very large garden and grounds for crop growing and pasture. For this there was a full time gardener who lived in his shack within the grounds.

It was a completely different lifestyle from their modest flat in Battersea, south London, where their parents, two older sisters and a much younger brother remained, trying to carry on life as normally as possible.

The responsibility of looking after these five evacuee children fell upon the cook and housemaid, who were sisters. It was a strange, new situation and this story tells of how everybody had to quickly adjust and try to cope with it as best as they could.

There was not enough room in the village school for the London evacuees so the headmaster and teachers had to set about finding accommodation where classes could be held, and also some equipment to start up their own separate school. This was not easy and took some weeks to achieve – and even then there was very little equipment to be seen.

The village to which they were sent was not exactly overjoyed at having its peaceful rural life disrupted, least of all by this mob of rough and ready London kids, and very often it showed.

There are stories of exciting times like when the Queen (later the Queen Mother) visited the makeshift school and by doing so got the four boys into trouble.

Stories also of the pranks they got up to and of the schoolboy adventures they had. Not forgetting the troubles they got themselves into including falling foul of Mr Harold Macmillan in the very early days of their evacuation. Macmillan was a friend and neighbour of the Ashby's.

Some of the stories are amusing, some are sad, but all are true and much of this was taking place while the Battle of Britain was being fought overhead.

Also it tells of the heartache and hardships of those wartime years. During the London Blitz the siblings' parents had them back to London but only for a day trip. The idea being to show them what was happening to London and why they had been sent away to the country for safety. They saw the Elephant and Castle area at one of its worst times. This had a profound effect.

After being away for nearly three years it was now time to return. Their parents and family had now moved into a fine, big house in another area of London so it was decided it was time to bring them home.

This was just like being evacuated again, more tearful goodbyes, new house, new surroundings and people to get to know - and a new school. Worst of it all was having to get to know his own family again and adapt to their way of living.

The conclusion goes briefly into Geoffs' adult life because on three occasions he meets up with people who he had last seen when a very young schoolboy evacuee. This brings back memories of those wartime schoolboy days.

Prologue

The purpose of this writing is to give my account as to what it was like to be evacuated from London to the safety of the countryside in 1939.

These are my recollections as an 8½ year old boy, as best as I can remember them.

Of course, this was a huge disruption to everybody's home life, and education; it was no different for my sister, brother and myself than everybody else.

But in my own case, the education disruption started a year earlier in 1938. Therefore, I feel it is important enough to start these recollections there, in 1938.

I hope you will bear with me and enjoy reading my story.

Geoff Sleeman
July 2013

1. Trouble Brewing - 1938

In the summer of 1938, I was living with my mother, father, three sisters and two brothers in a small flat in Queenstown Road, Battersea, south-west London.

If my maths are correct that makes eight of us. It was a tight squeeze and, looking back on it, I sometimes wonder how it was managed.

What helped a lot was that my very dear grandmother (Gran) lived in a slightly larger flat only three doors away. My siblings ranged from Daphne, the eldest at 13 years, Phyllis next, 12 years, Jim, 11 years (Jim was really called Derek Edward George), then came Kitty next at 10 years, then me, Geoffrey, 7 years, and last, the baby of the family, Martin, 2 years.

To ease the living conditions, my three sisters slept at Gran's flat every night and at bedtime every night would go trotting along to Gran's, only to come trotting back again next morning in time for breakfast and getting ready for school at Tennyson Street Girls School. I attended Tennyson Infants School as it was then called; Jim being older was at Heathbrook School or, as some people called it, St Rule Street, nearby.

The three girls didn't mind sleeping at Gran's place; in fact they rather liked it, as Gran was much more relaxed in her approach to most things. Our mother had very firm views on behaviour and manners, to the point of being quite strict.

Our dad was like Gran, much more relaxed and fun, but because of his job we didn't get to see enough of him. He worked for a fishmongery chain of shops and it was his job to go to the Old Billingsgate Market and do all the buying for the shops. This had to be done six days a week and meant leaving home very early in the morning so as to get the fish back to the shops by shop opening time. What dad didn't know about fish wasn't worth knowing. Most evenings it was well after teatime before he got home; except Wednesdays which was early closing, or half day. I used to look forward to Sundays and Wednesdays. In later years dad would sometimes let me go with him to the old market; it was fun for me and an experience I will never forget.

During the summer of 1938, I had German Measles, Whooping Cough and Measles all in quick succession. No sooner was I back to school than I was away again, and each time meant an absence of three to four weeks. The general opinion was, 'don't worry, he'll soon catch up'.

Christmas and New Year came and went and everything seemed to be ticking along nicely. That is until I became ill again. This time it was Scarlet Fever! This would be around mid-January 1939. Scarlet Fever was an acutely contagious disease, which meant I had to be admitted into isolation hospital at once. There was at that time a fever hospital in Clapham, South London, and that is where I was sent. My parents were told that the minimum period of time that I would be in there was six weeks, but it could be longer. It was.

My recollections regarding the first few weeks are very vague, probably because I was so poorly. The first thing I remember clearly was Boat Race day, when I was allowed to get up and get dressed in hospital clothes, for a few hours in the afternoons. During those weeks my parents would receive a written progress report from the hospital every Thursday. Sometime during February one of the reports told them that there had been a setback and the six weeks period would have to be extended until they saw fit to discharge me.

As it was a fever and isolation hospital, no visiting was allowed and my only contact with home was a weekly parcel with also a letter in it; but for the first few weeks I think I was too ill to worry or care about it very much.

Slowly, things began to improve. I began taking an interest in my surroundings and what was going on around me and, as I say, by Boat Race day (which was on 1st April 1939 – Cambridge University beat Oxford University that year).

The Sleeman children, at Wickens in 1941
(back L to R Phyllis, Jim and Daphne; seated L to R Kitty, Martin and Geoffrey)
Photo: Author's collection

I was out of bed for a few hours and improving. About this time a German boy of about my age was admitted into the ward. He didn't seem as poorly as most of the children admitted, but I suppose they knew what they were doing. This German boy is the only name I can remember from the hospital. It was Max and he couldn't speak a word of English. This caused a few problems for the nursing staff because none of the staff or the men patients on the ward could speak German.

A nurse from another ward was transferred to our ward for one shift only. Her task was to explain as best she could to Max what was happening and what was likely to happen and why. Her other more difficult job was to see if she could work out some means by which the staff and the rest of us could communicate with him. I cannot remember what she did, but it worked reasonably well.

Us kids were all at one end of the ward, the men at the far end. We were asked to try and talk to Max and, if possible, include him in any of the games we played, like snakes and ladders, ludo, snap and draughts. This we did quite successfully, but the trouble was he won too often. The thing we liked doing most with him was to get one of the weekly magazines that got sent in, like Picture Post, point to things in the pictures and say the English word, then get him to say the German word. We had some good laughs. Two that we joined together that I still recall were Adolf Hitler and Mickey Mouse; even then I thought it a strange combination.

We all got on really well with Max and I for one liked him.

Whilst in hospital, I was not aware of the passage of time. Most of the time I would not have been able to tell you what day of the week it was, or the date and which month we were in. Every day seemed the same, a rather dull hospital routine of medication, meals, and rest, filling in between with the games and comics.

At last doctors and nurses started talking about me being discharged. My parents received a letter giving them my discharge date. Discharges were always done on Thursdays. They were told that my clothes should be left at the Porter's lodge by a certain time.

When my clothes arrived they were not allowed into the ward because of infection. I was taken from the ward (my very first time outside the ward in all those weeks). I was bathed, dressed in my own clothes; I was ready to leave. They did not allow me to say any goodbyes to anybody and I was not allowed to take anything whatsoever out with me, not even the bags in which my clothes had been delivered – they would be burnt.

All this time my father and brother, Jim, were waiting at the Porter's Lodge. They were not allowed inside the grounds. The Matron walked me through the grounds to the Porter's Lodge, holding my hand, and handed me over to dad. It was a bit like handing somebody over at "Checkpoint Charlie".

This all happened on a beautiful, bright sunny day and it was quite warm. My guess now would be first half of June 1939, that is as near as I can get it.

It was wonderful to see dad and Jim again – I don't know who grinned the most.

They did me proud that day. I went home in real style – I went home in the firm's fish van! It was lovely to be home and see everybody and, of course, Gran was there waiting as well. Dear old Gran was always there.

After all the tears, hugs and kisses, and the "my, haven't you growns" finished, it was decided that my first port of call should be the barbers because in all my time in hospital I had not had my hair cut and it was very long. So within about an hour of getting home I was sitting in Mr Bangeebango's shop getting my hair cut, and I got my money's worth that day.

During the next couple of weeks I was mainly left just to settle in the home life again. What I was not aware of was, whilst in hospital, I had had my eighth birthday; it had been very much a non-event. So Gran took it upon herself to arrange some little treats for me like days out and going to the circus. My mum gave a small party for a few of my friends; my first ever party of my own.

Of course this couldn't go on forever and soon there was talk of starting school again, not a good idea. With me now being eight, I was finished with Tennyson Infants School and would have to make a fresh start at Heathbrook Junior Boys School. Jim was with the seniors. This would probably be the latter part of June 1939.

Once started at school, I was in the class of a Mrs Bass and, whilst I didn't find it easy, it wasn't too bad - I coped. It wasn't long before even I could sense that something was happening. From time to time we would hear the air raid warning sirens being tested. I didn't know what they were, nobody told me. Gas masks were issued with their cardboard boxes, "Silly things, what do we want these for?" I thought. Soon I started to hear the word 'evacuation'. I had no idea what it meant, again nobody told me, but I was soon to find out.

The reason for including this information is to show that when evacuation came, it was not the first time I had been parted from my parents and home. In fact, with evacuation at least I had Jim and Kit with me for moral support; in hospital, I was on my own.

The second reason was that my education had already taken quite a hammering, even without what was to follow because of the evacuation.

2. Evacuation

When I awoke on 1st September 1939, little did I realise what a momentous day it was to prove to be, not only for my sister, brother and I but for thousands and thousands of children and their families in towns and cities right across the country. Many lives would never be the same again.

In my own case, when I awoke it was just going to be an ordinary day. Because of this, there seemed to be no need to pay particular attention as to what was happening around me. Nobody had told me I was going away, whether Kit and Jim knew I never asked, but I should think they did know.

It is very likely that I was given my best clothes and told to get washed and dressed, "might be a school day outing, oh good" I thought.

Gran came in and I was told she would be taking us around to the school – I thought "That's a bit odd; I always normally take myself to school".

I remember absolutely nothing of the goodbyes. Mum would of course have been there with little brother, Martin. Surely dad would have been at work. Sisters Daphne and Phyllis had now started going to work, so it's possible they were not there either. I just don't remember!

As we left the Queenstown Road flat, Gran picked up a small case. I now understand that Government instructions clearly said that we should only take with us:

Gran Sleeman – who was always there for us.
Photo: Author's collection

- A change of clothing
- Toothbrush
- Comb
- Handkerchief
- Food for the journey

I thought, "What do I want a case for? It's not a holiday, it's a school trip, I think".

To get to Jim's and my school, we had to pass Tennyson Street Girls' School where Kitty went, but to my surprise she kept walking with us. "What's she coming on our trip for? It's not her school!" I wondered.

We came to a sweet shop. Gran told us to wait. She went in and bought us each a bar of fruit and nut chocolate and two packets of nuts and raisins each. "Don't eat them yet, save them for the journey" she said. "Right!" I thought, "It is to be a school trip, but why is Kit here, and why the case?"

When we got to Heathbrook School, we went to Jim's area of the building and were assembled in the playground. All the teachers were from the senior boys section, so Kit and I didn't know any of them. Most of the children were senior boys because this was their school evacuation. There were a few boys from the junior boys who I vaguely knew were like me, brothers to senior boys, and Kitty knew some of the girls who were sisters to senior boys. They didn't want to split brothers and sisters up.

There were London double decker buses lined up outside the school gate. Lots of mothers and fathers were there, many crying, and any excitement that I had been feeling about 'the school trip' ebbed away and apprehension took its place. I didn't like the look of this one little bit.

Next they came around with labels which they tied onto our coats. Each label had our full name, plus 'LCC 695 Heathbrook School' clearly printed on it. "What are they going to do, post us?" I thought.

After a final roll call we were told to board the buses. Gran, like many of the parents, moved forward with us only to be told, "Sorry, children only". This brought a fresh outbreak of crying, but not from Gran. "Don't worry", she said,

"I'll find you". I didn't understand what she meant, "I'll find you"; we weren't lost.

The buses didn't have far to go because they were only taking us to the railway station. Now I cannot recall which station we were bussed to; it could have been Queenstown Road Station which was nearer the school. But it was more likely to be Clapham Junction, a little bit further away, but a much bigger and better station.

Gran had found out somehow which station we were heading for and beat us to it, as did a few of the mums and dads. Now, Gran did start to fuss over us, and the more she said, "Don't worry, it will be alright", the more I worried. She

reminded Kit and Jim about the S.A.E. (Stamped Addressed Envelope) in the case. "Write and let us know where you are as soon as you get there".

EVEN THEY DIDN'T KNOW WHERE WE WERE GOING.
WHAT'S GOING ON?!!

We were told to get aboard the train and the goodbyes started, some of them very tearful. All the usual instructions had been given about, be good, write soon, don't forget to tell them this or that. The train starts to move, taking us to goodness knows where.

To me, the train journey is a complete blur. There may have been some community singing, I'm not sure. I can't see what there was to sing about. Personally, I was bewildered, confused, call it what you will. I don't think I was frightened, but I was glad that my big brother and sister were with me. Both Kit and Jim were very sensible and I had great confidence in them; they would see everything was alright.

The 'goodness knows where' already mentioned turned out to be Haywards Heath in West Sussex, where we had to disembark.

Something now rather strange that I feel I must relate. Standing there on the platform, I still have the feeling and memory of being very high up, and able to look down across a roadway towards a building that I later found out to be Haywards Heath bus station. It may now seem silly to mention this, but all through the years this has seemed to be very, very important to me, and I don't know why.

Strangely enough, the bus station was our next port of call. It had been cleared of buses and set up as a reception area; loads of tables, chairs and people with clipboards. We were each checked off and as this was done each of us was given a paper carrier bag with:

- Two corned beef sandwiches
- A piece of fruit cake
- An apple
- A quite large bar of chocolate

There were also tables set out with fruit drinks from which we could help ourselves, and we were shown where the toilets were (most important).

We were told to sit down with our eats and drinks, not to wander away. We would soon be told what to do next. Of course, there were lots of teachers with us to keep an eye on us; they spent most of their time trying to cheer us up, it was proving to be a very hard job.

When everybody was ready, the next move was onto some charabanc type buses, to travel ten or twelve miles to a village called Horsted Keynes, where we were taken to the community centre. Again, it was more tables and chairs and lots more clipboards with W.I. ladies attached.

Let me say from the start that everybody was being very nice, understanding, patient and sympathetic. We were told we would all be called for in turn. In dribs and drabs, children were called forward and taken to waiting cars.

The three of us awaited our turn. I don't think much was said. At last "The three Sleeman children, Leonard Haws, William Behoe". I didn't know them, and there was one other boy whose name was called out. I didn't know him either, he was a senior boy and I can't recall his name.

A very friendly lady told the six of us that it was her job to take us to our 'new homes', so if we went with her after a short car ride we would soon be there. She did make a point of telling Jim, Kit and I that we would be staying together; that helped a great deal.

Us six kids, plus driver, had to squeeze into this lady's very small car and this short ride seemed a bit long to me. The car pulled off the road that we were driving along onto a sort of track leading into some woods, and the further we went the thicker the woods got, and the darker it got. It was a bit creepy and I didn't like it very much.

We came to a clearing and there was a bungalow, at least I think it was a bungalow. This was where the sixth lad was going to be billeted. It was where Mr & Mrs Bennett lived with their two grown up sons and daughter. Mr Bennett turned out to be a gamekeeper for Mr Harold Macmillan.

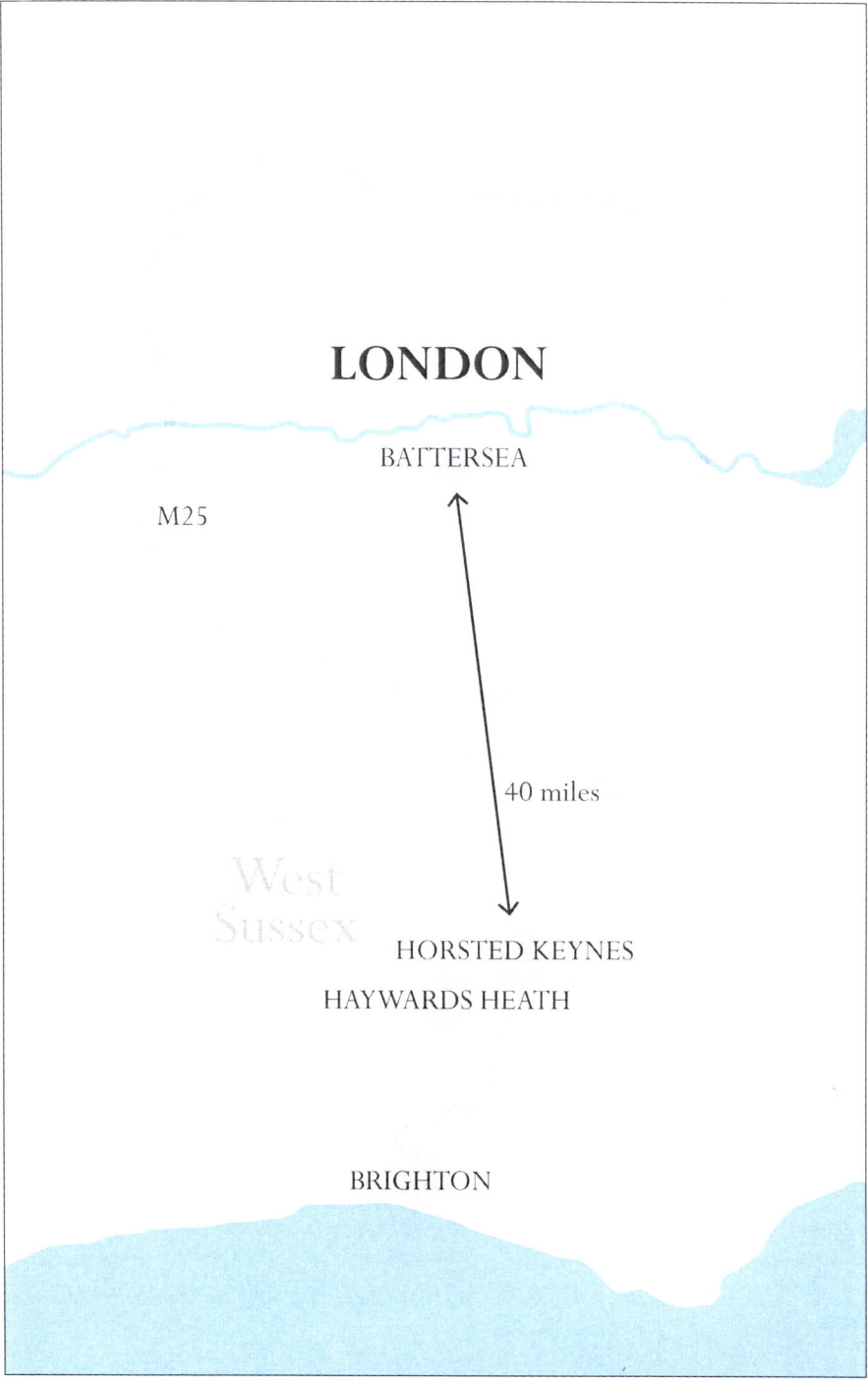

After the lad had been introduced to the Bennetts', both Mr & Mrs poked their heads into the car to say hello and give us a cheerful word. We later found all the Bennett family to be very friendly, helpful people.

One small point worth mentioning. As far as I'm aware, I never saw that sixth lad again. How creepy is that?

We said our goodbyes and moved on; just a short distance along the road once we got out of the woods and we had arrived at last at our destination, our billet, which was:

Wickens
Birch Grove
Nr Horsted Keynes
Haywards Heath
Sussex
(There were no postcodes in those days)

Our lady escort and driver took us to the front door, which was opened by a uniformed maid. After a few words of conversation between them we were all invited in. That was the one and only time that any of us kids ever entered through the front door and in entering we had walked into the world of "Upstairs Downstairs".

3. Getting To Know You

It would be a lie to say that I remember anything else about 'Evacuation Day' because I don't!

As the front door closed behind us I seemed to have gone into complete shutdown regarding memory. Maybe I was just tired; maybe I had just had enough, who can say? Now I can only assume that we were taken to the servants' part of the house and introduced to Nelly, George and Aunty, more about them later. Also, I assume we were given something to eat and drink, shown where we would be sleeping and where the toilet was. No doubt we were asked questions about our homes and backgrounds and after a while a suggestion that as it had been a long, strange day, we might like to go to bed. All this is all logical guesswork, because all I have is a complete blank.

Next morning upon waking I found myself, along with Jim, Len and Billy in a very nice big bedroom, each in a separate bed. This wasn't so bad.

Jim, Len and Billy had all been in the same class in London, so they of course knew each other, without being particularly good mates. Until about 4 o'clock yesterday afternoon I had never seen Len or Billy and now here we are roommates.

For a while we all chatted amongst ourselves wondering should we get up or not. We had no clock or watch so didn't know what time it was. After a while we heard footsteps, followed by a tap on the door. The maid, whose name was Hetty, poked her head around the door, asked were we all right and did we all

Geoff's only photo that was taken at Wickens. It shows at the back left, fellow evacuee Leonard Haws next to Hetty Dilly the housemaid, and George Dilly the house handyman. Geoff is in the front next to 'Aunty' Dilly, the housekeeper. Hetty's sister Nelly (not pictured) was the cook and all four Dilly's were on the staff who lived at Wickens.
Photo: Author's collection

sleep well? We all said, "yes" and "is it alright to get up now?"

She said "Yes, get washed and dressed and come down for breakfast as soon as you can. Kitty is already downstairs."

We took it in turns to get washed, but once dressed we all waited for each other and all went down together into this very strange, very new world.

Reunited with Kit again, we found out that she was sharing a room with Hetty. Kit said she'd rather share than be on her own, not that it made much difference because she had no say in the matter one way or the other.

Kitty was like me, going to have to get to know Len and Billy, because she had never seen either of them before yesterday.

I now think it's time to give a rough idea what us kids were like.

Billy was about the same age as Len and Jim, twelve-ish, had a little bit of a superior attitude but not too bad. He was pretty brainy, well spoken, good mannered and I would say quite well brought up.

Len, same age, a bit more rough and ready, not thick, but not as bright as Billy. Len, when he left London, was in 'The Boys' Brigade' and was a drummer, very keen on sport, particularly football. He had been on two camps with the Boys' Brigade and was much more 'streetwise' than any of the rest of us. He was a natural great comedian and gave us many laughs. He wasn't very polished, but polite enough to get by. It would have been very difficult not to like Len.

My big brother was a very quiet but sensible sort of chap, academically not as clever as Billy or Kitty, but very good with bright ideas and clever with his hands, and good at model making. He had been in the Battersea Sea Cadets for a couple of years and had been away with them for one camp, and was very keen on it. He was a bit short on humour and a bit quick on temper. He, like me, had a slight stutter, so again like me tended not to push himself to the forefront.

Big sister Kitty was a nice, bright, intelligent, smart, good-looking girl. Looking at that lot, it's hard to believe that she was my sister. She was confident and outspoken; she didn't stutter. Sometimes I wished she did. God, she could talk!

Now then, it's my turn.

Nothing I can say about myself would really do me justice. If I had a fault at all, which is very hard to believe, it would be that I stuttered quite badly. Stuttering is a family trait; my father stuttered slightly, also sisters Daphne and Phyllis, my elder sisters, Jim, and myself. It worked out to be the two oldest boys and the two oldest girls. Of all of us I was the worst by far – it was a real problem. It was, of course, embarrassing and I tended to hang back and let the others do the talking for me, which made people think I was shy, which I suppose in a way I was.

I don't remember stuttering at infant school, or in hospital. It seemed to creep in after hospital. Maybe the shock of that haircut! The problem was it was getting worse.

That's enough about me. As you can see, I don't like to sing my own praises. However, I must add that I would like to think that Kitty, Jim and I were considered to be polite and well mannered by everybody.

Back to the main plot. At that breakfast, on the first morning we found out what the arrangements were to be at meal times.

The adults, Hetty, Nelly, Aunty and George would have their meals in the kitchen, whilst us kids would eat together at the big table in the staff sitting room. This format worked very well; we could talk about whatever we liked. They, in turn, could talk about us. We were always well fed and well looked after.

After breakfast, Hetty (the maid) said that once their basic jobs were done for the morning we would be shown over the whole house and told where we could and could not go. Then, after lunch, (what we used to call dinner time) she would show us around the grounds.

It was explained to us that the house 'Wickens' belonged to a Mrs Margaret Corbett Ashby and her husband, Mr Brian Ashby. We were told at that time that Mrs Ashby was a Member of Parliament. It was only recently that I found out that this was not quite true, and I believe only said so as to impress us, as to how good we were expected to be.

At the time of our arrival, Mr & Mrs Corbett Ashby were abroad in Europe and, with the international situation as it was, they were very worried about them getting back to England before war started and the Ashby's were maybe interned, or worse. Looking back, I suppose they were worried about their jobs and where they would live, should the worst happen.

The tour of the house was an adventure in itself.

The staff side was pretty basic. Kitchen and scullery, and a fair size, quite comfortable, if a bit of a dark sitting room, with bathroom and toilet leading off the main hall. Seeing the bathroom / toilet, I thought of the London flat and the tin bath hanging from the wall in the back yard being brought in every Friday evening and filled with hot water from the kitchen copper. This was a different world.

The downstairs rooms were a small breakfast room, which was also called the small dining room, which had a service hatch through from the kitchen, and an adjoining door which led into the large dining room. Both these rooms had the most lovely furniture and glass cabinets.

Then there was a small study that Mrs Corbett Ashby used, with a desk and bookcases.

Finally, the lounge. What can I say about the lounge? It never ceased to overawe me all the time I was there. It seemed to me to be as big as a football pitch, and full of armchairs, sofas, more glass cabinets, drinks cabinets, a grand piano and French window that opened up onto a terrace that also ran along the front of the large dining room. This room would not have looked out of place in an Ivor Novello production.

The main entrance hall was vast. You could have got our entire London flat into it and still had room to spare.

The first thing that anybody who was lucky enough to be allowed in through the forbidden front door would have seen would have been two great big rowing oars. These were the oars used, one by Mr Ashby and the other by the Ashby's son, Mr Michael, both of whom rowed in 'The Boat Race', both in winning Cambridge crews. These oars were hanging on the hall wall opposite the front door with all the crews' names printed in gold leaf on the blade.

One or two antique looking chairs and a matching table, a grandfather clock, plus a lovely ornately carved chest, a small room for hats, coats, shoes and boots in the corner.

There was, of course, a very impressive staircase sweeping down in a nice arc from the first and only upper floor.

The upper floor is much easier to describe (he said, hopefully). A main passageway and two others branching off to the left and right. So many bedrooms that over the years I have lost count, but remember Hetty, Kit, Nelly, Aunty, George, Mr & Mrs Ashby, Mr Michael plus us 'gang of four', and spare guest rooms, it seemed to go on forever.

But I've saved the bad news till nearly last, upstairs there were two bathrooms, plus the one downstairs; three bathrooms. I thought, "What does any house want three bathrooms for? I don't think I'm going to like it here very much"; and, "It's not natural to be so clean, and I'm sure it's not healthy".

Now I'm going to tell you what they hadn't got, but we had in London.

With all this grandeur and opulence, this fine house hadn't got electricity, and this house didn't have a gas supply, and I don't think it was because of non-payment of bills. It just wasn't there to have. Lighting was by paraffin oil lamps, cooking and hot water by a large Aga, room heating from open coal fires.

Looking back on it now, that was, I think our biggest shock; us kids just couldn't understand it.

The area of London from which we came could not have been described as affluent by any means, but all our homes had both gas and electricity. Now here we were in this big, posh house without a gas or electricity supply. It beggared belief.

Having no gas was not a big problem. Even today in the village where I live there is no gas supply. You adapt, and learn to live without it. But no electricity is a different ball game altogether. How other houses in the area coped I've no idea, I was "too busy" to notice.

Now Mrs Ashby and her son, Mr Michael, were both progressive, forward thinking, energetic people. Looking back at that situation I am now very surprised that they didn't install a generator.

During my time there, I heard the situation described as "quaint" and "quite charming", by guests. These were not the words we used when trying to read, or write a short letter home by the dim light given by an oil lamp.

The heating of rooms was by open fires, but they only ever used coal. Even though we were surrounded by woodland, I never once saw a log burnt.

It all seemed to us very Victorian and took some getting used to.

But I digress, back to the "Grand Tour".

The cook was called Nelly, the housemaid Hetty and they were sisters with the surname of Dilly. Both, I would guess to be in their mid-thirties. Old George was their father, also a Dilly. It didn't seem right to call a man in his late sixties or early seventies by his Christian name, a bit disrespectful, but that's the way George wanted it; I think he was just trying to put us at our ease and be friendly. He was a lovely old chap and I became quite fond of him – a bit like another Granddad.

Aunty was also a Dilly, George's sister. They didn't get on very well together. That made her Nelly and Hetty's aunt, thus the name 'Aunty'. More about her later.

There was also the gardener, Mr Billings, who lived in his own place (for want of a better word) in the grounds. At this point, we hadn't met him yet, so he can wait a bit until later as well.

4. Garden and Grounds

After lunch / dinner, Hetty took us on the promised tour of the garden and grounds. All this cannot have been easy on Hetty and Nelly. They were both unmarried and, as far as I know, had had no experience of looking after children. Now through no fault of their own, they had the extra work of five quite large kids, not only the work but the responsibility and they were taking it well, trying hard to be helpful and friendly.

The garden tour started of course from the back door, out through the side entrance into the drive. This drive was about 100 to 150 yards long, with the house, garage and side entrance on one side, but on the other side a great long bank of tall growing rhododendrons. The very first thing Hetty told us we must NEVER do is to pick off the rhododendron flower buds, "Just leave the things alone". It seemed a strange thing to say at the time, and it still does! I never did pick any though. These tall rhododendrons screened the house off from the road that is 'Birch Grove'. There was a much quicker way into the garden but by going out via the driveway, Hetty had been able to make her point regarding the rhododendrons; it seemed to be very important to her.

The garden was very large, and had just about everything that you would expect to find in a large English garden. Whoever Mr Billings was, his garden did him credit. There was of course the obligatory large lawn, which sloped gently down toward a small orchard. Also there were flower borders, a quite large goldfish pond with water lilies, grass pathways with pergolas and climbing roses, shrubberies, and some lovely big trees.

That isn't all. Two quite large outdoor aviaries with quite exotic foreign birds flying freely around. These aviaries had moats around the base, also full of goldfish. I suppose the moats were there to keep the wildlife away from the birds, it was most impressive. There was also a largish enclosure with a golden pheasant.

The small orchard had apple, pear and plum trees and these were the border to the Ashby field, which sloped much more steeply and about two acres of it had been ploughed and planted with potatoes. This wasn't all ploughed though; it joined onto about another three to four acres that was just left to natural growth of grass, heather and bracken.

We were told we could do almost what we liked in the field, "But be careful in the garden".

Over to one side there was an area for growing soft fruits and veg. It was in this area that we met Mr Bill Billings. He was just what you would expect. He was around sixty-five in years, white haired, with a bushy moustache. He always wore a flat cap.

Mr Billings was friendly, pleasant and humorous, "As long as you behave yourselves, we'll get on fine", he said, then he jokingly added, "I shall be keeping a close eye on you", but I don't think he was joking.

The only thing I haven't told about the 'Grand Tour' is the tennis court, which looked pretty new. Hetty thought it would be all right if we used it so long as we were careful, but she would check.

All through the tour, Hetty had chatted in a very friendly way, not laying down the law with too many rules and don't do's. She explained where the Ashby's land finished and the Macmillan's estate and Mrs Corbett's (Mrs Ashby's sister or sister-in-law) land started.

We were beginning to get to know Hetty and vice-versa.

During the tour, we passed where Mr Billings lived. Even to us it was a bit of a shock. It was little better than a very big shed, and I've seen better sheds. It was made completely of wooden, overlapping slats. At the back it was at ground level. By the time you reached the front the ground had dropped away so sharply that to keep it level it had to have stilts about three feet high, and if you wanted to, you could crawl underneath. He used that space for storing things.

To get to his 'front and only door' there was a very rickety flight of wooden steps. In this 'hut' he lived, looked after himself, slept, and did his own cooking. The only time he needed any help was Sunday lunchtime when he cooked his Sunday roast. He couldn't manage the roast joint and Nelly the cook would do it in the Aga, and one of us kids would be asked to "run it along" before it got cold. Thinking back to that shack, I'm glad I wasn't billeted on Mr Billings.

The tour that Hetty gave was very pleasant and done at a very leisurely pace. We could stop now and then to ask questions and have sweets from a bag that Hetty had brought with her. She emphasised that Mrs Corbett Ashby was a Member of Parliament (not true). She also explained that Mrs Corbett Ashby travelled abroad quite a lot, giving talks in places like Berlin, Stockholm and Geneva. She was President to many organisations dealing in women's rights.

I hadn't got a clue what she was talking about. Hetty was using phrases like 'International Conference', 'British Delegate' and 'Disarmament Conference'.

Then she went on to explain that that was the reason why the Ashby's weren't there; they were having trouble getting back from abroad; that's why everybody was so worried - that I could understand.

She went on to explain that Mr Ashby was a barrister. Hang on, I'm confused again. I always thought that a barrister was something you held on to going up and down a staircase. Sounds like a silly job to me, nowhere near as important as being a fishmonger like my dad. But if that's what he wants to be, fair enough, I'll still talk to him when I meet him. Fortunately, I'm no snob!

Of course I didn't say this to Hetty. I didn't want to fall out with her; she was the one with the bag of sweets.

About the final thing she mentioned on our walk was about the Ashby's son, who we would call Mr Michael (Mr M). He was in London training to be a doctor. Hetty told us, "He comes here when he can at weekends. Don't worry about him, he's alright".

The general summing up of the afternoon was, yes, there will be problems but we will sort them out as we go along, and make up any rules as we go along also. Mr & Mrs Ashby might have some rules of their own but we'll worry about that, if and when they get home.

With the morning tour of the house and a shock of the bathrooms, plus the tour of the garden and grounds in the afternoon, it had been quite a busy day and a lot to take in. I think we were all glad to get back to the house for teatime. Teatime brought the first "make it up as we go along" rule. It was explained that some items were already in short supply, sugar being one of them. Rationing had not yet started but was expected quite soon.

Seeing as how Nelly did all her own jam making, sugar would be needed, so we had a choice. If we wanted jam on our bread and butter, it was no sugar in our tea. It didn't take long; we all opted for jam and non-sugar tea. We soon got used to it.

One thing I haven't mentioned, because it didn't seem to fit in right. Right down at the bottom of the potato field was an odd little corner very near the boundary of Ashby's and the Macmillan's land. In this corner was a really nice natural pond. It was fed by a little stream that ran out of one of Macmillan's lakes under the fencing into the pond. It then drained out back again under the fence and back into the lake at another point.

It was a pretty little corner, quite out of place beside the potato field. It had goldfish, frogs, toads and lizards, and beside it was a bench to sit on. This would have been much better in the garden area. The reason I mention it at all is because over the next few weeks it became a favourite meeting up place for us kids if we wanted to have a moan. We called it "Moan Corner". We had another spot by the tennis court which we named "Rabbit Turd Corner", but we won't go into that.

The opinion that I formed of Hetty during our walkabout, childish though it was, never changed in the years that I was at Wickens. Friendly, and fair, good sense of humour, and took a joke well. But if you stepped out of line she would soon let you know. However, she did used to get flustered and embarrassed very easily, and go bright red.

My summing up on Hetty was that she'd got it just about right, as Nelly had as well, but more about her later.

5. Red Alert

It was surprising how quickly we fitted into a routine. Getting to know Nelly was not proving difficult; she was just as friendly as her sister and just as easy to talk to. She also enjoyed a laugh, but Nelly was made of sterner stuff than Hetty, and I don't mean that in a nasty way. It took a lot to faze Nelly and nobody was going to push her around!

My sister, Kit, seemed to get along with both of them, most of the time, which was a good thing. Us boys had each other for company. When we went to bed at night we could talk amongst ourselves, which we did. Kit didn't have that, and it must have been a bit lonely for her, tucked up in bed every night with just a book to read. She wasn't a 'tomboy' so when 'The Gang of Four' went out exploring Kit very often stayed behind to help Nelly. It didn't seem to bother her. Later on she found other girls in the nearby area to give her some company, of about her own age.

After about three days one of the teachers who had travelled down with us turned up one morning on a bicycle. He explained to Hetty, Nelly and us kids that he was going around trying to pinpoint where all the Heathbrook School pupils were. It had been easy to keep track of those billeted in and near the village (Horsted Keynes) but they had rather lost track of those of us billeted in the more remote outlying areas.

He went on to explain that there could be no school for the time being. The reason was the village could not take on this large number of pupils; it would have made class numbers too large.

So, somewhere had to be found for the London children to be educated quite separately. This was proving difficult, but as soon as something was sorted out he would come along again and let us know where to go and when. I thought to myself, "Don't rush, there's no hurry".

So, whilst waiting for all this to happen, this visiting teacher, whose name I never knew, told us all to behave ourselves, try to be helpful, keep out of trouble, and don't let the school down.

As soon as we had arrived on Evacuation Day, I understand that Kit, Len and Billy had been encouraged to write letters home to the parents to let them know that we had arrived safely and to give them an address to which they could send on more of our clothes.

How Nelly and Hetty managed while we awaited these clothes to arrive I don't know, but manage they did; well done to them. How long it took for these parcels to get there, I've no idea – at eight years old it wasn't my problem.

Because we had had to travel so light, upon arriving at Wickens we had nothing to amuse ourselves with, not even a ball of any sort. Either Mr Billings or George had rooted out a couple of old tennis racquets and balls from the garage, or one of the sheds, which was a good start. Also, when Mr Billings found me wandering around on my own one morning, I don't know where the other three had gone, he made a rather splendid bow and arrow for me, to help pass the time – things were looking up.

On the same day as the teacher's visit, I was playing on my own with a tennis racquet and ball in the driveway, banging the ball against the garage door. Even if I say so myself, I was quite good at this and did it a lot.

It was evening, and Kitty came rushing out to tell me something in quite an excited manner:

"Guess what?" she said.

"What?"

"We're at war".

"What, you and me?"

"No, silly. Us and Germany".

"Who's us?"

"England of course".

"Oh, what does 'at war' mean then?"

"Well, you know Hitler?"

"No, but I've heard of him and seen his picture in the newspapers".

"Well, he's going to put his soldiers into aeroplanes, they will fly over here and jump out with parachutes, and fight our soldiers with guns, bombs and tanks".

"Oh great! That will be worth watching", I thought.

We talked it over for a short time then she went skipping back indoors again to see if there was any more exciting news.

The topic of conversation at that time was all about the difficult time that this country was going through, and how "we'd all got to pull together".

So I'd better help.

I put the ball and racquet to one side, went and got my trusty bow and arrows and put myself on duty by the front gate.

"Let them come, I'm ready for 'em".

I stood there for twenty minutes maybe, even half an hour. Nothing happened.

When you are on sentry duty like that you have plenty of time to think. Kitty was inclined to exaggerate at times and have flights of fancy. Maybe I had overreacted. It was time for a break anyway. Let's have another go at the tennis - this I did.

For the next twenty minutes or so, I produced tennis strokes the like of which had never been seen before, or since.

Still no aeroplanes, "Well, I can't hang around here waiting for them forever; it's time to go in and go to bed".

I put my tennis gear away and hid my weapons in the armoury; might need them tomorrow. Went in and got ready for bed.

The news that Kitty came out with regarding the declaration of war came from Hetty's wireless, as they were then called (radio). It was the only one in the house. The Ashby's didn't have one because there was no electricity. Hetty's wireless had to be run on an accumulator, which I suppose Hetty had to pay for herself, so it was used very sparingly. Once the Ashby's arrived back home they wanted to hear the latest news quite often, using Hetty's wireless and taking over the staff's sitting room. It caused quite a lot of staff mutterings and, as time went on, got worse.

What with no gas, no electricity and no wireless maybe we should have had a 'whip round' for them.

It was about this time that Mr & Mrs Ashby returned home from the European trip, much to the relief of the staff, and I suppose the Ashby's. At least the staff's jobs and homes were safe. There was a lot going on at that time that I didn't understand because I was too young. Even if I had understood, it would have been none of my business.

For instance, I never worked out whether George and Aunty were on the Ashby's payroll, or whether they were helping out for their bed and board. Mind your own business Geoffrey.

We didn't get to meet the Ashby's straight away; they'd been through quite enough without us. After all, we weren't exactly the cream off the top of the cake, were we? We were saved as a little treat for later on.

When we did get to meet Mr & Mrs Ashby it was done very nicely and informally. Mrs Ashby just breezed in one morning while we were having our breakfast, told us not to get up and to carry on with our meal. This was of course the staff sitting room where us five kids ate our meals.

She sat down in one of the armchairs, and asked each of us our name and age. We all had to speak for ourselves, there was no ducking out. Mr Ashby came in a few minutes later, just said "hello", then stood, watched and listened.

It was Mrs Ashby who did the talking; it was just like being before a school headmistress, because that's just what she looked like, and sounded like.

It was the usual guff. We were going to be there until it was safe to return home. Everybody was working hard and trying to do their best for us. We, in turn, must try to keep out of trouble and help where we could. They would be seeing us around the garden and grounds and get to know us better as we went along. She had received very good reports on us all from Hetty and Nelly so far. Well done, try to keep it up.

That was about it. Mr Ashby had said one word, "hello".

Mrs Ashby had a presence about her; an authority about her that almost demanded respect. She left you in no doubt who was in charge and it wasn't Mr Ashby. Nevertheless, most times she was pleasant, friendly and helpful.

I have no wish to be rude regarding Mr Ashby, but he was so quiet he almost wasn't there.

He was quite tall and slim and, with his quietness, I could see why he had elected to be a 'banister'! Not for one moment do I think Mr Ashby was being rude or disinterested. He was, I think, just a very quiet, almost shy man.

6. Jim's Birthday and My Cake

The 13th September 1939 was a Wednesday; not only was it a Wednesday, but it was my brother, Jim's, thirteenth birthday. My sister, Kit, and I had walked into the village and got birthday cards for him, whether or not Len and Billy did I can't recall; probably not, due to lack of money.

Nelly had said she would bake him a cake for his birthday. "What sort would you like?" Jim, being Jim, said he didn't really mind, so Nelly let me choose and I said, "chocolate cake". So that's what we would have for our teatime.

Not too much fuss was made over Jim's birthday; after all, we had been there less than a fortnight. I expect he got cards and postal orders from home but apart from that it was an ordinary day. It was, I remember, a dull, dreary, overcast day, no rain, just dull.

The Ashby's or Billings, I don't know who, had decided it was time to start lifting the potato crop from the field. This had to be done by hand with garden digging forks and it was all hands to the pumps.

The line up was Mr & Mrs Ashby, Mr Billings, George, Len, Billy, Jim, and even Hetty in the afternoons once the morning house jobs were done. I don't think Kitty was included. Nelly was excused because of her cooking duties and somebody had to make the tea didn't they?

The garage just inside the main gate was going to be used as a spud store. The Ashby's didn't drive as far as I know, so didn't have a car, and the garage had been

1940
SUNNY SNAPS
7886

Pop, mum and Martin in London 1940 – the year the Blitz began.
Photo: Author's Collection

cleared out ready for use.

Some of the gang dug the spuds up, the rest picked them up, sorting them into two sizes as they went. One size of household useables, second size, too small, no use so going for pig food.

My job in all this was to be around to run messages up to the house, get more sacks from the garage, as needed, and help get the sacks when filled up to the garage.

At about 3 o'clock I'd gone to the garage for more sacks. The garage looked out onto the roadway of Birch Grove and, as I came out of the garage doors, a smallish car slowed down, then stopped. There was a "toot-toot" on the hooter and somebody waved – I didn't know who it was, but being a friendly little chap I waved back.

The car backed up a few yards and pulled into the driveway. I was puzzled; who was this? The car doors opened and out stepped my Mum and Dad.

I was speechless. Dad clapped his hands and I just flew towards them. Dad met me halfway and, although I was eight, swooped me up in an embrace and carried me over to Mum and the three of us just stood there in the driveway with our arms around each other.

Words were not necessary.

Who spoke first and what was said I don't remember. Until that moment I hadn't realised just how much I had missed them. Then the questions started. "How are you? Are you alright? Where's Kitty and Jim?"

"Yes, we're alright. Kit's in the kitchen with Nelly the cook. Jim's helping in the potato field – come on I'll show you".

I took them to the back door, rushed in and told Kit and Nelly the news. They didn't believe me. Mum called out – they believed me then! Nelly invited them in and offered them a cup of tea. They said they would love a cuppa but could it wait until after they had seen Jim (the birthday boy)?

Nelly said all the right things, that she understood and so on, and if Kit and I took them down to the field to find Jim, Nelly would have the kettle boiling by the time we came back. Also, would Kit or I let the Ashby's know tea was being made in case they wanted a break.

We walked, or in my case skipped, Mum and Dad down through the garden not knowing what to show them first. Kit's talking went into overdrive. I did my best to keep up, stutter permitting.

When we got to the potato field, I ran on ahead shouting, leaping, throwing my arms about. I think the work gang thought I was having a fit! I wanted to be the one to give Jim the good news.

But I didn't get the chance to tell him. He soon cottoned on as to who it was. He just chucked down his picking basket and ran over as fast as he could run, to receive the same sort of hugs that Kit and I had got. As we all talked, Mrs Ashby stopped picking spuds and came across. She had guessed what was going on.

Down through the years, I have always remembered that moment because Mrs Ashby looked distinctly disgruntled, whether this was because the production line had slowed down to almost a halt, or whether it was because Mum and Dad had arrived to find us having to work, or maybe Mrs Ashby's back was aching at the end of the afternoon; I will never know, but she was not in the best of humours.

After we'd made the introductions and Mum and Dad and Mrs Ashby had chatted for a few moments, we told her about the tea being made. At that point Mrs Ashby did seem to soften a bit and suggested that everybody went up to the house, and this included Mr Billings, for a cup of tea with Mr and Mrs Sleeman.

So we all trooped up to the house, Dad explaining on the way that this had to be a very short flying visit. They only wanted to put their minds at rest, that we were alright and being well looked after.

At the house Mr & Mrs Ashby didn't go into their own rooms but stayed outside the back door in the yard. Tea was brought out for everybody. Nelly thought this would be a good time to cut 'the cake'. Everyone drank tea, ate cake and chatted. It was a very small, very impromptu party – great! This gave my parents a chance to meet everybody, if only briefly.

Soon, Mrs Ashby made excuses to leave as the work that had been started had to be finished off and tidied up before it got dark. But my family were welcome to visit any time and maybe next time there would be more time to talk.

Before going back to work, Mrs Ashby told Nelly that Mum and Dad, along with Kit, Jim and I should be given the use of the small dining room so we could talk, and my parents should have more refreshment if they wanted it.

My mother asked if Len and Billy could join us because all us five kids were in the same boat and she didn't want Billy and Len to feel left out, and both Mum and Dad would like to get to know them better; this was agreed.

I don't know what we talked about. I suppose we heard about Martin, and Daphne and Phyllis's jobs, not that much would have changed in just a fortnight. They were surprised about the no gas or electricity. It reminded my mother of growing up as a child in Devon. Also, I suppose it's possible that they had brought us down some more clothes, but I don't remember.

Dad explained to us all that his boss (Mr Cole) had asked how things were with us and how the evacuation had gone. The Cole family had known all us Sleeman children all our lives. Once a week Jim would wash Mr Coles' car to earn pocket money. My father said that there wasn't much to tell, the news contained in Kitty's one or two letters was to say the least a bit sparse and he and my mother were both worried as to who exactly was looking after us, and didn't quite know what to do about it.

"Look Bill", said Mr Cole. "Today is early closing day, you start clearing up here, forget everything else. I'm going to take my car and get it filled up with petrol. When I get back, I'll give you a hand to tidy up. You get away as quick as you can and when you go take my car, and you and Doris (my Mum) go and find these kids and make sure that they are all right. Sussex isn't that far away".

My Dad didn't need telling twice, and when clearing up was done Mr Cole sent him on his way. Mr Cole dived his hand into the shop till, pulled out some money (I don't remember how much) and told Dad, "Give this to the children with all our love and tell them we hope to see them back home again very soon". A good boss, and a nice man.

Once Mum was told the plan, she asked Gran to look after three year old Martin, and let Daphne and Phyllis know what was going on when they got home from work. Getting ready I shouldn't think took too long and soon they were winging their way to Sussex. The money that Mr Cole sent, however much it was, was split five ways so Len and Billy had a share. After all, we had seen our Mum and Dad, they hadn't. There wasn't much to spend it on anyway.

About this time, Nelly came in to ask if they would like any more tea. Mum and Dad said they would have to be going because there was the car to be got back to Mr Cole, Martin to collect, sort out and get to bed, and Dad may have even been on fire watch duty. However, Nelly did make one final cuppa, after having a little chat with them. When she brought the tea in, as she went out she took Len and Billy with her, leaving the last few minutes to the family.

The goodbyes were not easy, but they promised that now they knew where we were they would be down to see us very soon. They left to a load of waving and, I suspect, tears. Nevertheless, it had been a lovely surprise and a lovely birthday for Jim, but there wasn't much of that lovely chocolate cake left.

I'm sure that my parents drove home in a much more contented frame of mind, having met our foster parents, because that's what it was like, being fostered. The birthday cake helped a lot, I'm sure. If they made Jim a birthday cake they can't be all bad can they? The last thing I want to do is to give the impression that we were always made to work, because that is not the case.

Just now and then if something was considered important we would be pressed in to help. Most of the time, 95% of the time, if we wanted to help we could, if we didn't we were left to do our own thing. Most of the helping was running errands, no big sweat.

7. Hurt Feelings and "The 'at"

There were some mornings when Len, Billy and Jim just seemed to disappear, maybe asked to do something that I was considered too small or too young to help with. It is just inconceivable that they wanted to go somewhere without ME! It doesn't bear thinking about!

In the very first days as I hadn't had a chance to make any friends, I was on my own and at a loose end. The remedy to this was, I started to help George with his morning jobs. I liked being with George – he was a bit of a grandfather figure and we got on well.

Now I've already explained that no electricity meant lighting by paraffin oil lamps and these oil lamps were George's responsibility. This big house with its many rooms needed an awful lot of lamps. Looking after these lamps took up a lot of time in the winter because of the long dark evenings, but of course much less time in spring and summer with the lighter evenings.

Outside the backdoor in the sort of courtyard there was a shed used for the lamps to be kept in, also anything else to do with the lamps. A big barrel of paraffin was kept in there. It had a tap on it, also spare funnel glasses and wicks. This all had a lovely name, "The Lamp Shed".

Some of the bigger rooms like that massive Ivor Novello lounge would need at least four lamps and everybody's bedroom at least one. What with these three flaming bathrooms, the staircase, hall, and kitchen – it was never ending. So we worked out a system. Hetty would collect them from the bedrooms, and leave them near the staff door leading into the hall. My job was to collect them and take them out to the lamp shed. There, George would be doing his stuff, topping up the lamps, cleaning the glasses and trimming the wicks. Sometimes they would need to be taken back upstairs, sometimes it could wait until the evening, it depended as to what was going on.

Even I could see that this was a help; it was saving both Hetty and George time, and their legs. While George was doing this I would sit on a box and we would talk, I don't know what about, just talk. After about a week or ten days of helping, one day George put his hand into his pocket and pulled out some money, I don't know how much – a sixpence maybe, a shilling? It matters not.

"Here you are", he said. "Here's your wages". I replied, "No thank you George". "What, are you mad? I'm offering you money". "I know you are, and thank you, but I can't take it", and I'm beginning to stutter quite badly. "Why not?" "I've always been told I mustn't take money from people".

By now, George was angry with me and I didn't really know why. He stormed indoors and I wandered away, bewildered as to what I had done wrong.

We kept out of each other's way for the rest of the day. During our meals I tried to explain what had happened to the other four, but I don't think I made a very good job of it.

After tea, Nelly took me to one side. She said she thought she could see what had happened. She suspected that I had been told not to take money from strangers and that I had got it wrong. Hetty was right, that is what I had been told. Hetty explained to me that by now we were not strangers to each other and that it would be quite all right for me to take wages from George if he offered it to me. It would help a lot if I would say I'm sorry to him. Yes! I would say I'm sorry 'cos I was; I wouldn't have deliberately hurt his feelings for the worlds.

Next morning, George was in the lamp shed and I slid in. He didn't say a word. I made my apology and said that I'd made a big mistake – still no word from George. He dived his hand into his pocket and out came the money again.

"Are you going to take this then?" He asked, holding out the coin. I grabbed the money. "Yes George, and thank you very much". "Right, looks like we're back in business again, doesn't it? That's what you'll get every Friday, as long as you help".

I was on the payroll, but more importantly, I was back in his good books. We were mates again. I never heard another word about it.

I can see him still in his green apron that he used to wear, and his battered old brown trilby hat. He was a lovely old guy, who did his best to make things work out for us five London kids.

But that's enough about George, because I haven't told you about Aunty yet, have I? That's because "it aint going to be easy" – she was an odd one.

What can I write about Aunty that won't get me sued? Fingers crossed, here goes.

Aunty was a large lady, quite tall, and rather rotund. This was because she wasn't very active – didn't move around a lot (if at all). Mostly, she sat in a high armchair in the staff sitting room, doing sewing repairs, darning, knitting, sometimes preparing vegetables, like potatoes, beans or peas. To be fair, she always seemed to be busy doing something. Always she dressed in very dark clothes – black, or very dark brown. Her hair was always in a very tight bun at the back and she had very small, thin-framed glasses.

She spoke very rarely and when she did it was in a very soft voice. In nearly three years I never heard her raise her voice. There was something about her, real creepy. There was about her a coldness, a remoteness that was just somehow odd. She watched everybody and everything; she didn't miss a trick.

It was very rare indeed to see her outside the house. Her exercise was coming down from her room in the morning to her chair, and from the chair to the meal table, and back again. She seldom smiled and I never heard her laugh.

Her strangest habit was, if anybody or anything didn't please her, she would go upstairs and get her hat, a real Victorian looking 'monster', and put "this thing" on. It was like an early warning system – if "the 'at" was on watch out, somebody's in for it.

Fortunately, it wasn't very often us five kids. She didn't interfere in our problems very much, but I was never very comfortable when she was about. For some reason, Aunty always reminded me of an Egyptian sphinx, just sitting there, watching. Just try to imagine that, a sphinx sitting, watching with its best hat on.

8. Big Mac v Ben Hur

One sunny afternoon soon after we arrived at Wickens, Len, Bill, Jim and I were walking towards Chelwood Gate. Whether we had been sent on an errand or not up to Mr & Mrs Dovey's shop, I'm not sure. Maybe we were just mooching about killing time. There was a lot of time to kill as nowhere had yet been found for us to go to school and Nelly and Hetty liked to get us out from under their feet.

The road we were on linked Horsted Keynes to Chelwood Gate and was known as Birch Grove. At a point about halfway between Wickens and Dovey's shop the grass verge was very wide, something like 10-15 yards. Mostly it was rough grass but here and there, there were the odd sapling trees and some quite large clusters of bushes.

As we wandered along, talking the silly rubbish kids do, one of us noticed that there was something behind one of the bush clusters. We had nothing else to do so, we thought, "Let's go and investigate".

What we found was a sort of shelter; if it had been bigger it would have been a Dutch barn, no sides, just a curved roof with a support in each corner to hold the roof in place. I don't know if there's such a thing as a Dutch shelter? Well, there is now!

Under the shelter was a two-wheeled pony trap. Both the pony trap and the shelter were in rather a dilapidated condition; even so, this was quite a find. We looked it over. Then one of us had the bright idea of, "Let's see if we can wheel it out". We worked out that if Len and I took the shafts in front, and if Bill and Jim took a wheel each using the spokes, just like they do in cowboy films when the chuck wagon gets stuck in the mud, it wouldn't take long to get 'lift off' and roll it out from under the shelter. I suppose we moved it by about twenty feet.

"Now if only we had a horse or pony, this could be fun". Whilst we stood there discussing the best way to get a horse or pony, my brother, Jim, had climbed into the driver's position and was giving a very bad impersonation of Ben Hur; we all laughed and bounced the shafts up and down.

A big car came along the road going towards Chelwood Gate. We took no notice, but we did when it came to a very sudden stop and out got Mr Harold Macmillan. We could see from his expression that he hadn't stopped to pass

Sir Harold MacMillan and Dame Margery Corbett Ashby (seated) in 1977.
Both of them had input into Geoff's learning in those early days of evacuation.
Photo: Courtesy of Danehill Parish Historical Society

the time of day. He stood leaning on the roof of his car, bellowing at the top of his voice, "Come here, come here!" The three of us dropped the shafts and ran. I don't quite know what happened to Ben Hur; whether he got thrown into a pile on the floor of the trap, or if he got thrown over the front board down in between the shafts, I just don't know. Whichever it was it didn't leave him in the right position for the sprint start that was now required. By the time he'd got himself untangled and sorted out, Mr Macmillan was standing over him. Jim decided to surrender.

In the meantime, us 'runaways' were hiding some yards down the road in one of the clumps of bushes. Seeing Jim was 'captured', we knew that the game was up. He wouldn't just give his name, rank and number, he'd 'crack' under interrogation. So we slowly, and reluctantly, went back to join him.

Nothing was said until us three arrived.

"What do you boys think you are doing?", barked Macmillan.

"Looking at that cart" we replied. The exchange continued:

"Haven't you got anything better to do?"

"No sir."

"What do you mean, 'no sir'?" He fumed.

"We haven't got anything better to do, we are bored."

"Why aren't you at school?"

"They haven't found anywhere to use for lessons yet, sir."

"Are you evacuees?"

"Yes sir."

He looked at Bill. "Where are you staying?"

"Mrs Corbett Ashby's, sir."

He looked at Len. "And you?"

"Mrs Corbett Ashby's, sir."

Jim's turn. "The same, sir. All at Mrs Corbett Ashby's."

"What, four of you? My God!"

Jim ventured, "It's five really, sir. Our sister is with us as well."

Mr Macmillan's mood was not improving. I don't think he was relishing the prospect of having us as neighbours for the foreseeable future. He then said, "Well, you've pulled that out so you can now push it back. Then come over to me at the car."

That sounded reasonable enough, so we did it. He had gone back to the car and was talking to his wife, Lady Dorothy, who was sitting quietly in the car waiting. He was probably giving her the bad news regarding the new neighbours.

We went back to his car, thinking that was almost the end of the matter. Boy, were we wrong!

He told us we should be ashamed of ourselves. "We were a disgrace to our parents, disgrace to our school, disgrace to London", and a disgrace to half a dozen things that I've long since forgotten what they were. He went on, "We were thoroughly 'un-British' and that it was people like us four doing mindless, thoughtless acts like ours that was helping the German war effort!"

Well, he lost me there! How, by moving his dilapidated trap a few feet out of his dilapidated Dutch shelter, we were going to influence the outcome of the war one way or the other was beyond me. But then he's supposed to be the clever one around here, not me.

Still he hadn't finished. He went on and on, standing there beside the road he had a right little tantrum getting himself in a hell of a state. Finally, he told us that he would be watching us very closely and any more incidents like this and we would be in "serious trouble". Well, I thought we were already.

With that, he drove off, but as the car pulled away Lady Dorothy smiled to us and waved. Whether or not we waved back I cannot say, because we were in shock. Len was the first to come to his senses and, with his great gift of the English language, managed to utter, "What the bloody hell was all that about?" The rest of us were in no fit state to answer.

Common sense tells me that if we had been sent on an errand we would have completed it, but I don't remember. Errand or not, we had to return to Wickens, and of course on route the topic of conversation was what had happened with Mr Macmillan. How he'd completely got things out of proportion and how unfair he had been. Bill, Len and Jim all put their points of view, but as I was a very junior member of the quartet by four years, nobody was interested in my opinion, which was a shame because I could have saved them a lot of time, talk and effort with just two words, "He's crackers!"

We took great offence at being called 'un-British'. The war had not been on for very long but already many things were in short supply, petrol being very high on that list. There's 'himself' driving around in a car big enough to get the entire British Army in – well, most of it anyway.

'The three elders' decided that we should not say anything about our 'little chat' with Mr Macmillan. We'd got into a bit of trouble and had been severely told off; fair enough, but there's no point in looking for trouble. Good idea, makes sense.

We needn't have bothered. As soon as we walked in we knew something was up, and what was up was that Mr Macmillan, as soon as he got home, had telephoned Mrs Corbett Ashby to complain a) about our behaviour, and b) that we had been cheeky or rude, I don't know which word he used. There was no need at all for this, and he went even lower in our estimation, if that was possible. The first part was, to use child's language, 'sneaky', and the second part was just not true!

Anyway, we were back in trouble again and Mrs Corbett Ashby wanted to see all four of us in her study, at once!

We were paraded in front of Mrs Corbett Ashby like naughty kids in front of the headmistress. Mostly, Billy was our spokesman. The trap was beside the roadway. We were not trespassing on anyone's land. We had not done any damage and we would have put it back. We treated Mr Macmillan with great respect and no way were any of us rude.

We got a fair hearing from Mrs Corbett Ashby and she seemed to accept most of it, but said we'd let her and everybody at Wickens down badly, so would we please in future try to be more thoughtful and careful. She realised it was difficult for us being away from our homes and family, but everybody was trying to help. We must do our bit by behaving properly. These are difficult times for everybody, and so on, and so on.

We came out of her study much relieved. It begun to look as though we would not be shot at dawn after all!

That's the end of that, we thought, but we were wrong again.

We went into the kitchen to get a drink, because it had been quite an afternoon, and there waiting for us were Nelly, Hetty, George and Aunty, all glaring at us, all with their eyebrows raised enquiringly. It was a bit like the Spanish Inquisition. The bad news was Aunty had her hat on; we hadn't been there very long, but long enough to work out that when Aunty put her hat on something had displeased her and somebody was in trouble and going to 'cop it'. Like when a judge used to don the black cap before sentencing a prisoner to death, only in our case it was much worse!

Anyway, 'the 'at' was on and we had a pretty good idea who was in trouble this time. Us!

Somebody said "Well, what have you lot been up to?" Step forward spokesman Billy. Here we go again, more explanations. This time a bit further, explaining that Mr Macmillan just seemed in a bad mood and had lost his temper.

Nelly, bless her heart, tried to explain that Mr Macmillan had a lot on his mind right now. He's very high in the Government and he's one of the main men who are working with the Prime Minister to get this country out of the mess it's in due to the war.

Up until now, Billy had done a pretty good job as our spokesperson; it would have been better to shut up, but he got a bit carried away and said, "I hope God is on our side because with people like him sorting out our mess, this country is going to need some help from somewhere."

That did not go down well with the inquisition. There were looks of horror, disbelief, indignation and amazement written all over their faces. After a short pause they recovered the gift of speech. Words started to come at us from all directions at once. Words like ungrateful, unkind, uncalled for and blasphemous. At eight years old, I didn't even know what 'blasphemous' meant, but I rather liked the sound of it, it sounded real bad. I'm not sure the others knew what it meant either. The inquisition also added that it might be a good idea if we all learned some respect for our elders and betters. Betters?

When they ran out of words, we were told to clear out and stay out until we were called for, and "No!" we couldn't have a drink; we didn't deserve one. I would point out that all through this Len, Jim and I hadn't uttered a word, but it was "All for one and one for all" (or something like that), so we all trooped out, found an outside tap, had a drink and sat down to discuss the problems that grown-ups were giving us.

Us lads were not having a good day. Like everything else, it blew over in a few days. There were more important things to worry about.

However, the four of us did devise a plan that, should the leopard change his spots and one day offer us a lift, no matter what the weather was like, we would very politely decline the offer. Unfortunately, he never did make such an offer, so we were unable to put our plan into action. Foiled again.

One final comment on Mr Macmillan. This is the man that in later years went on to become Minister of Housing, Defence, Foreign Secretary, Chancellor of the Exchequer and Prime Minister. When these job vacancies occurred nobody thought to contact me for a reference for him. This is just as well really, because if my comments regarding Mr Macmillan had been taken into account, he may well not have got those positions. Thus, the political history of this country would almost certainly have been different.

Lady Dorothy was a completely different ball game. She was charming. She would, unlike her husband, always stop and offer us a lift to or from school. She always seemed genuinely pleased to see us. Everything about this lady was genuine. Not only did you get a lift to school but she would ask where the school was today. In the village school, as sometimes it was, or at the Nissen hut at Dane Hill; wherever it was she would detour and take us right to the gate. Mrs Montiefiore (of whom, more later) didn't quite know what to make of this, us arriving with Lady Dorothy.

During these motor rides, Lady Dorothy would be full of conversation. Had we heard from our parents lately, were our families safe and well, how often did we get to see them, and how was the makeshift schooling going?

None of this came across as prying or nosey; it came across as genuine interest and concern. She was always the same if we met her out walking, always a chat and a nice word. She was lovely. What's more, she gave a lovely Christmas party for all us evacuees at the Macmillan's house. If a Christmas party at the Macmillan's house conjures up pictures of Uncle Harold Macmillan in a Santa's outfit, you can forget it; he was nowhere to be seen, I'm pleased to say. There was, of course, a Santa but it wasn't the real one, but somebody from the estate.

All us kids liked Lady Dorothy and had genuine respect for her.

Before closing on the Macmillan's, I would like to put the record straight on one thing. The remarks I have made regarding Mr Macmillan have nothing to do with the politics; they are purely about the man as seen through the eyes of a boy aged 8½ years, which I was at the time.

I lived there for about 2½ years and saw Mr Macmillan and Lady Dorothy quite frequently. Neither of them ever seemed to be any different from the two people I have already described. At 8½ years old, of course, I was not political. I didn't understand what it was all about. I'm not sure I do even now – I have no interest in politics.

As I've said, Lady Dorothy was greatly respected; he was not. As I see it, respect is not a God given right. If anybody goes around demanding it they will almost certainly not get it. What they will get is a cheap, false imitation. Real respect has to be earned, very often the hard way.

I freely admit I didn't like Harold Macmillan and I never heard anybody of any age say he was a nice man and that they liked him. There was nothing there to like. He was an arrogant snob and a bully.

This might be a good point to reiterate something that I wrote at the very beginning but it won't hurt to repeat. All my remarks regarding incidents and people are as seen through the eyes of a boy of eight, nine and ten years old, which covers the time span of my evacuation. In the case of Mr Macmillan, subsequent events, plus things I have been told and read in printed articles have done nothing to make me alter that opinion. However, I could still be wrong.

9. Three Little Pigs (and more)

Awaiting the news of some sort of schooling starting meant we had a lot of time to kill. Sister Kit seemed to be getting by doing her own thing, which left us lads wandering around exploring everywhere. Trying to keep out of trouble was proving pretty hard work but we were doing our best.

On this particular afternoon, we had roamed a bit farther afield than usual into a very wooded area somewhere near Twyford. To be quite honest, we didn't really know where we were. Nothing new in that!

As we wandered through these woods, talking the sort of silly rubbish kids talk, we came suddenly to quite a large area where all the trees had been felled, every one.

They were pine trees and all the wood had been cleared away, not a trunk or branch to be seen. We could see all the freshly sawn tree stumps sticking out of the ground to the height of 12-15 inches. We didn't know quite what to make of this. Nor could we work out what the little huts were, lots of them placed in and around and sometimes over the tree stumps.

These huts were not very tall, like a load of rooftops, but no walls to lift them off the ground. At the time they reminded me of Red Indian wigwams for some reason. They looked as if they had been painted with creosote.

It was pretty obvious that we shouldn't be there, but there appeared to be nobody about so we thought that, rather than backtrack, we would just walk quickly through and out the other side, touching nothing on the way. There was nothing about, apart from a bit of a pong.

We got to the other side of the clearing and came across two strands of wire, not very high – a sort of low fence. Now thus far we hadn't come through any gates, nor had we climbed over any type of fence – it was all a bit odd.

It was Billy, always the clever one, who worked out that these strands of wire were electrified.

"No problem, we can step over that", said Billy, which he, Jim and Len did with no trouble at all. "Come on Geoff".

"No way! Your legs are longer than mine."

"Come on, we'll lift you over."

"You won't! You might not lift me cleanly, or worse still, drop me onto the wire."

Billy said, "Look, there's a bucket over there. If you go and get that and up-end it near the wire, you can then stand on it and jump over, can't you?"

"No."

"Why not?"

"I might lose my balance before I jump."

They were all getting pretty fed up with me and I can't say I blame them, but I've always been scared of electricity; I still am.

Anyway, Billy decided to climb back into the enclosure to help me. Once he was in we went to get the bucket. As soon as Billy touched that bucket, all hell broke loose. Pigs appeared out of those huts, dozens of them. There were suddenly pigs everywhere, making the most frightful noise.

At infant school, I had been taught that "little piggies on the farm go grunt, grunt, grunt". Nobody had told that to this lot. They were screaming and screeching their silly ugly heads off, not a grunt to be heard! I was really frightened.

The pigs took one look at Billy and I with the bucket and I suppose they thought it was food time. Well there was no food in the bucket, so that only left us two!

They started trotting towards us, but this trot was fast turning into a piggy stampede. We were only a couple of town lads not used to dealing with ferocious beasts like these. It was quite clear to me that we were going to be trampled to death under their horrible little trotters, or worse still be eaten alive!

I could see my promising young career finishing up as nothing more than pounds and pounds of pork sausages. Such a waste!

My brain said, "Run!" My legs were happy to obey and, from somewhere they found extra reserves of energy. Billy and I raced for the wire together. Upon reaching it there was no time for carefully climbing over or standing on buckets, not with that screaming mob gaining on us with every stride. It was just shut your eyes, pray, jump and hope that somebody up there loves you.

We both landed safely on the other side and sat there recovering. The way we cleared that wire should have done credit to a couple of top class Olympic hurdlers.

Now, I'm not like my sister, Kitty, given to gross exaggeration, but looking back on it now I'm sure some of those pigs were as big as hippopotamuses, and large ones at that.

All through this incident we had seen no one, but that didn't matter. We didn't need anybody to tell us that this place was off limits. We never wanted to see it again, and gave it a wide berth in the future.

10. Starting Off Schooling Again

It is difficult to be exact about the timing, but somewhere around the end of September 1939 the teacher with the bike rode out to see us again, this time to inform us that somewhere had at last been found for us to have some schooling, and this would be starting on the following Monday at 9.00 am.

Us four boys were to go to a house belonging to a Mrs Montiefiore at Dane Hill just outside the village. This Mrs Montiefiore had a very nice Nissen hut at the bottom of her garden, instead of fairies, and she had agreed to let the school have the use of it for the time being.

There was a small group of girls attached to our school; they, like Kitty, were the younger sisters of the senior boys. These girls were given an address of a house in the village where they would have daily classes. A lunch / dinner would be available for all.

So, that was it! We were going back to school again, or that's what we thought.

That first morning was a bit of a shambles. We had already found out on the Friday before where Dane Hill and Mrs Montiefiore's house was and how long it would take us each day. It was a hell of a long walk, that's for sure.

Anyway, on the first morning we all had to wait at the front gate, then be escorted down through the garden to the school hut. Inside the school hut there were tables and chairs and nothing else.

I would not blame you if you don't believe me, but there was no blackboard, no chalk, no textbooks, no exercise books, no paper, pens, ink, rulers – nothing!

The first thing they attempted to do was call the register, or roll. This was from the list of all of us that got on the train about a month ago. It was surprising how the numbers had gone down; it seemed some parents had already taken their children back to London for one reason or another.

In some cases they were not sure whether some children had gone back to London or not, were they still here, and had not been informed about this marvellous new school? They didn't know what they were missing, or maybe they did!

By the time they'd got roll call sorted out it was time for dinner. This meant another long walk into the village and down a very long church lane, which was also a very steep hill; then through the churchyard to the village school and playground in which stood the dinner hut.

We were not allowed to eat at the same time as the local children. I think the hut couldn't take that many on one sitting, so London children were always the second sitting. More news about the meals later on.

After the meal it was the long walk back to the school hut most afternoons, but not always.

If, as sometimes happened, for some unknown reason the village school was not using a classroom, our teachers could use it. This of course was an improvement; at least there was the use of the blackboard. There was also a piano on which our head teacher, Mr Jones (Old Jonah), used to thump out "Greensleeves", his favourite piece of music.

Very soon the teachers began to beg, borrow or steal paper for us to write on. A lot of it was scrap paper and came in all sorts of shapes, sizes and colours, that didn't matter, as long as it was clean plain paper it was fine. We were asked to take pencils and rulers to school with us if we could. If we weren't very careful, we'd be learning something soon.

Geoff's evacuee school photos taken whilst at Horsted Keynes.

In the top photo, taken in Mrs Montefiores' garden, far left back row is Mr Jones with Billy Behoe on his left. Geoff is standing in front of Billy, with his brother Jim on his right. Geoff can remember the names of the teachers and some of their nicknames, e.g. Mr Jones (Old Jonah), Mr Thew, Mr Whitehouse, Mr Curry (Old Hot Stuff), Mr Gough, and Mr Burbidge (Old Burb). Mr Jones retired and then Mr Bellamy (Old Ding Dong) took over as Headmaster.

In the bottom photo, taken at the village school, on the back row the teacher on the left is Mr Whitehouse. On the far right is Mr Thew, with Jim at his right shoulder. Geoff is seated in the middle row, third from the right.

There were three different places for our schooling to be held:

1. The school hut (Nissen hut).
2. The village school (occasionally).
3. The community centre, occasionally to start with but gradually more and more, and towards the end of my stay it was in full time use.

The boys' group was divided into two classes - juniors and seniors. In the school hut it was one group to each end.

To start with at the hut it was not like school, more like a club, or playgroup. There wasn't much to do and I remember playing hoopla with one of the teachers (Mr Burbridge) keeping the score.

During the mornings, the senior boys would go into a playfield that we had use of and play football or cricket, whilst the juniors amused themselves in the hut. In the afternoons we changed over. We went on nature rambles and gathered acorns to help feed the farmers' pigs (pigs again!).

Old Jonah had been, I think, a very keen cricketer so we had talks on bowling a good length and keeping the ball up, on wicket keeping and running between the wickets, how to field and how not to field.

A lot of time was being wasted walking to and from the hut at Dane Hill and to the dinner hut, not that it mattered very much – we weren't doing anything important. I don't think Mrs Montiefiore was very happy about us using the school hut and was always watching us in and out, and if she wasn't about then one of the gardeners would always be on hand working in the area, keeping an eye on things. Can't say I blame her for that; I think I'd have done the same thing myself.

We were told that Mrs Montiefiore had given permission for part of the field that we used for playing and sport to be used as a school allotment. Any produce that may come later would go to the school dinner hut kitchen to help towards the school dinners. This was to be a senior boys project only. The work was considered too hard for us juniors. Quite right. Old Jonah delegated this allotment project to one of the teachers, a Mr Thew, who seemed very keen on the idea. This was just as well because none of us could imagine Old Jonah digging.

The area was pegged out in the corner of the field. One big problem though - no tools! An appeal was put out around the village, and I think that because the appeal came from something to do with Mrs Montiefiore's place, the response was quite good. Soon there were enough tools to start preparing the ground. This was done with a small group of about six or eight boys working for an hour or hour and a half, when the next shift would take over and so on through the school day.

Whilst all this was going on, Old Jonah had managed to get hold of quite a lot of books from somewhere, and started a school library; but being new to the countryside, there were too many other distractions going on and it never really caught on. Nevertheless, it was through these books that I was first introduced to Robin Hood.

This sort of slipshod schooling surely could not carry on for too long without somebody making a few comments. This proved to be right and, although I didn't know anything about it at the time, things were going on behind the scenes to try to do something to improve Kitty's and my education.

How Kit was getting on with her daily classes, I don't know. I've no doubt, knowing how Kit could talk, that she told us, but I just don't remember. I don't even remember how she got on with her dinner times either. The girls certainly didn't come to the dinner hut.

This business of not schooling with the local children, and not eating at the same time, was beginning to cause not bad feeling, but resentment. As we waited in the playground for our turn to have our dinner, the local children would be on one side of the playground and us on the other side, and we didn't think it was the children's fault.

At no time was anything arranged in which we could participate together; no sports matches, no sports day, just keeping us apart; it was like segregation.

Our school name of Heathbrook was becoming extinct; we were "The London

Children".

The only intermixing was if any London children were billeted onto a family who had children of their own – then, of course, they had to mix. I'm just glad I wasn't one of them.

When it came to the letter writing home, it was "good old Kitty" that did the bulk of the writing home with Jim and I just putting in a few words here and there. Whether or not Kit let Mum and Dad know what was happening at school, I've no idea.

What I suspect happened is that Mrs Ashby, with her connections with the local women's organisations, like W.I., was getting some feedback, rumours, gossip, call it what you like, and I don't think Mrs Ashby was very impressed. It is likely that she wrote to my parents and invited them to come down for a visit and talk the matter over, and that is what happened.

The outcome of this meeting and chat was that Kitty and I would be taken out of our London (L.C.C.) schools and put into a public school, which was also evacuated from London that was much nearer to Wickens and was up and running reasonably well.

The suggestion didn't cover Jim, Billy or Len as they all had less than a year's more schooling, and it looks like they were given up as a lost cause, I just don't know. The trouble is when you are eight or nine years old, grown-ups don't consult you on such matters. Very thoughtless!

Very generously, Mrs Ashby offered to help my parents out by offering to pay the school fees for one of us; this my parents gratefully accepted.

All this was due to happen as soon as could be arranged. It didn't take long.

As far as I can remember, this school came from the Peckham area of London but I can't be sure. However, as it was now located at Twyford, it became known as Twyford School, yet another school losing its name and identity. We were to find out all too soon that it's temporary accommodation was in what looked to me like a chapel stuck up on a very high bank miles from anywhere.

11. Hair Do's

Getting to the school hut at Dane Hill was a long walk; I would think between one to two miles, it's hard to remember distance. There was a school car laid on for the children in the outlying areas. Unfortunately, Wickens failed to qualify for its use by about 500 yards, so we had to walk.

We might sometimes get a lift in it if there was room in the car, depending on who the driver was and what sort of mood he was in. It was all very hit and miss and most days we finished up walking.

We were now into November 1939 and the pheasant-shooting season was on. This was something very new to us, but we all soon cottoned on as to what it was all about. The "three elders" found out that they could earn themselves pocket money each Saturday by going as beaters for these shoots. It was considered that I was too young to go; this irked me a great deal.

The lands in the area of Wickens were not given to what I considered normal farming. There were very few (if any) herds of cows, no corn, wheat or barley. There was a lot of woodland, many large orchards and much land used for growing soft fruits.

The reason for this was that there was a jam making factory in the area. This belonged to Martin's Jams, a well-known brand during the war, and these fruit fields and orchards belonged to Mr Martin.

With so much wooded land around, shooting was not a problem and most

Saturdays the "three elders" trotted off, leaving me with my bow and arrows. They got paid a few bob (shillings), got some lunch, kept them out of mischief and out of Nelly and Hetty's way.

Kitty, as usual, would be off doing her own thing. She seemed to be making friends all over the place. One of the people Kit had got to know was Mrs Jay, who lived in Birch Grove Cottage just 500 yards further along Birch Grove from Wickens. This cottage was the qualifying point for car rides to school.

This cottage was owned by Mr Martin, the "jam king", and Mrs Jay was his rather glamorous housekeeper. She had a son, Arthur, who was about a year younger than I. Kitty thought it would be somebody for me to play with. Good idea.

It was nice to have somebody to knock around with of about my own age, and even nicer that I was just a little bit older than him. We got on quite well together. Arthur was a bit spoiled and pampered by his mother but not too bad. He went to school in Haywards Heath.

It seemed it was quite alright for me to take Arthur into the Wickens grounds to play football or whatever we wanted to do, so long as we didn't do any damage and behaved ourselves. So, sometimes we played at Wickens, sometimes at Arthur's home; sometimes, in fact quite often, we just roamed around amusing ourselves as we went.

There didn't seem to be a Mr Jay, and it was something that we never talked about. At eight and a half years old I couldn't have cared less anyway.

This Mr Martin who owned the cottage never seemed to be around very much. In fact, as far as I'm aware, I never saw him. Most times when I called for Arthur, I would be invited in and Mrs Jay, who was a very nice, friendly lady, full of fun, would chat away until us two boys made up our minds what we were going to do.

On the rare occasions that Mr Martin was in residence for a few days or maybe a week, I could call for Arthur, but there was no hanging around the cottage; we'd have to go and play elsewhere.

One Saturday when the "three elders" weren't beating because there was no shoot taking place, either Nelly or Hetty announced that it was time that all us lads had a haircut. I don't know what George and Mr Billings did for haircuts; I suppose they went either to East Grinstead or Haywards Heath, and both these were considered to be too far for us to go, bearing in mind that it now got dark quite early. The date was Saturday 4th November 1939, and I remember that because at breakfast that morning we had been talking about Guy Fawkes Night and what a shame we couldn't have one this year because of the war.

Back to haircuts. We were told that they had made enquiries and there was a barber's shop in Chelwood Gate who cut boys' hair. We were given money; who supplied that I do not know, and we were packed off. We had had lunch / dinner so it was afternoon.

We had never had any reason to go to Chelwood Gate before. It was a pretty long walk, past the pony trap, past Mr & Mrs Dovey's shop, past Mr Macmillan's house. We always had to walk everywhere; there was no bus service to Birch Grove at all.

We found a pub. I think it was called The Red Lion. We wandered around a bit and found a few shops. There seemed to be more shops here than in Horsted Keynes but we couldn't find a hairdresser or barbers shop. One of the "elders" asked somebody and we were pointed to one of the shops in what looked like the High Street.

The shop pointed out to us looked like a very high-class establishment. The owner had had it done out in the style of a cycle repair shop. We nervously went in, each of us trying to be last.

A charming man asked, "What do you lot want?"

"Haircut."

"Which one of you?"

"All of us."

"Oh Christ, sit down."

We looked around at the décor; it really was very well done. There were bicycle wheels on the wall, bike chains hanging from the beams, the odd inner tube and bicycle tyre – really very good.

There was another quaint rather novel idea. This was where we had been told to sit down and wait our turn. There was a row of rather natty wooden boxes turned upside down. The reason for the décor was it was a cycle repair shop and he was just cutting hair as a sideline.

We didn't have to worry though; he had all the right equipment. A chair for the 'victim', hand clippers, comb, scissors, a bit of sheeting to put around your neck and, oh yes, first aid plasters.

As to who had the honour of going first, I don't know. There was nothing there to read so you were forced to watch; at first it was easy but as one followed another the pile of hair grew taller, like a barricade of human hair, and if you were still interested you had to peep over the top.

This barber / mechanic would put the piece of sheeting really tightly around your neck to stop hair going down your neck; then every so often he would nick you with the hair clippers. If you jumped it meant he hadn't pulled the sheet too tight and that you were still conscious.

Being a cycle repair shop, I now hate to think what he put on our hair as he finished with each of us. On completion he was duly paid. We staggered out into the open air again; light headed through loss of hair, weak from blood loss, and with splinters in our bums. Upon leaving that hairdressing salon, I thought if only he knocks those sitting boxes apart and makes a frame for a sofa he could stuff it with our hair. I'm sure there's enough of it. It would be splinter-less and more comfortable.

With our hair now cut, now came the long trek back to Wickens.

We never called it "home", always Wickens. Home was London.

Now we hadn't exactly hurried on our way to Chelwood Gate and four haircuts take quite a while, even the way he did it. So by now the light was beginning to go. We walked and talked about past firework nights back in London and how it wasn't going to be the same this year. Nobody was allowed to have bonfires at night and there'd be no fireworks at all. As we talked and walked, it grew darker and darker.

We had forgotten to take a torch with us, even if we'd been allowed to, so it was just a case of follow the road, if you can see it.

The trouble was that after a while all sorts of little green eyes were watching us from the hedgerows on either side. We didn't know what they were. My thoughts went once again to the man-eating pigs, you know, those really big ones. I can assure you that the trip back took much less time than the trip out.

On arriving at Wickens, there were no shrieks of laughter as we walked in, only a few comments along the lines of "that's a bit better".

So the haircuts can't have been that bad; just seemed like it. "Come back Mr Bangeebango, all is forgiven!"

There were some comments made about how long we had been and I think it was Len who said there were a few in front of us. So that's the end of another little adventure, not what you would call a hair raising one either.

The date of these haircuts was 4th November 1939.

12. V.I.P. No Dinner

It was a good job we had had our haircuts because on Wednesday 8th November 1939 we all trooped off to school at the hut as usual. Upon arrival, we found Old Jonah and the few teachers that we had left in a state of great excitement. As soon as we arrived we were called into the hut, not left outside to amuse ourselves like normal.

We were told that our school was going to be honoured with a visit from a very important person, but we weren't told who. Our brief was to tidy the place up – well, that didn't take very long because we hadn't got that much stuff to start with.

The second brief was, "Now, tidy yourselves up". Ah! Now that's a lot more difficult. Socks were pulled up, shirts tucked in, shoes were spat on and made to look as if they had once been clean. There was a rush for the outside tap and hair was plastered down with water. If any boy was sissy enough to be carrying a comb, he suddenly became everybody's best mate, so they could use his comb. Nobody thought to wash; things weren't that serious, or that important.

The normal practise for the morning was to do physical exercises. These we used to do to music from an old gramophone supplied by Mr Thew. One piece of music used that I remember was a song called "Little Sir Echo".

It was decided that these exercises would be the party piece for the juniors to do for the "important visitor".

Left to right, Archie and Jim dig for victory on the school allotments during the Queen's visit.
Photo: Author's collection

About half of the senior boys were taken down to the school allotment and set to clearing and digging the ground. All the three elders were in this group. The remainder of the senior boys were set some work at their tables, making it look like they really were learning something.

The stage was set, the actors all in position, now we just waited.

We didn't have to wait too long. Old Jonah stood by the door. Suddenly he called out, "All stand". We stood. There was a brief conversation by the door; we couldn't see to whom he was speaking. Jonah stepped to one side and into our hut walked Her Majesty the Queen!

There followed a whole host of other people as well, none of whom we knew, except the local vicar. We weren't bothered about them; all eyes were on Her Majesty.

Our three or four remaining teachers were presented, except Mr Thew, who was still on the allotment; his turn was yet to come.

After the teachers, the Queen showed some interest in what those working at the tables were doing. Then the Queen turned to our end; it was our party piece time. The Queen had spoken to a couple of the senior boys; I didn't want any of that with my stutter, so as we took our places for our demonstration, I was careful to get at the back.

We had a set routine for these exercises, so once the music started it all kicked in and, as I remember, it went pretty well. Her Majesty spoke to some of the boys in the front row, said, "Well done" to us all and that was that.

The next move was down to the allotment site and much the same happened there, I was told later, because we had to stay in the hut. The Queen took a quick look around, asked one or two questions, and spoke to a couple of boys – tour over.

Whilst Her Majesty was at the allotment, us in the hut had been told to put our coats on and assemble in the roadway up at Mrs Montiefiore's gate; this we did. At the gateway there was quite a crowd. This was because Her Majesty had not only visited our school, but also other groups of London children in the area who had been evacuated. This included groups like W.I. who had worked hard to carry it out. The word had got around the village and everybody wanted to see.

Somebody from the Montiefiore's household had produced a Union Jack and put it by the front gate. Not only was the royal car there, but also all the cars belonging to the entourage. It wasn't long before the royal party came up through to the garden, everyone doffing caps and hats, bowing and curtsying. As I didn't have a cap, and had never been shown how to curtsy, I did nothing, except smile. As I wasn't thrown into the Tower of London, it looks like I got away with it.

There was some hand clapping too, I remember.

The Queen paused at the car and thanked various people including Old Jonah. She turned and waved to the crowd that had gathered. Old Jonah called for three cheers for Her Majesty the Queen, "Hip hip!" The cheers were lusty and as they died away the Queen gave one final wave, got into the car and the car pulled very gently away to more cheers. The other cars followed.

There was now a buzz of conversation and excitement, but very slowly the people began to move away, to go back home or back to work. The show was over.

After a few moments, Old Jonah called the boys together. "If any of you has anything in the hut to collect, go and get it because after such an exciting morning I can't expect you to do anything else today. So it's half day holiday – see you all tomorrow."

So Jim, Len, Billy and I started the long walk back to Wickens without our usual school dinner.

By the time we had walked back to Wickens, we must have arrived somewhere around two o'clock. The adults had had their lunch and were having their after lunch cup of tea in the sitting room. Probably George would have been having a snooze, and Hetty and Nelly reading the Women's Weekly or some such thing, when us four burst in.

They were suspicious right from the very start that we had been up to no good. "What are you all doing back here at this hour?"

"Our school had an important visitor today and when it was over Mr Jones said we could have the rest of the day as a holiday, and we've had no dinner."

"Well, you will have to have an early tea. Who was this important visitor?"

"All have a guess – bet you don't get it."

"School Inspector?"

"No."

"The Vicar?"

"Wrong again."

"The nit nurse?"

"You don't get half day off for the nit nurse."

"Look, we are getting fed up with this, who was it?"

"The Queen!"

The looks they gave each other were a sight to behold. "Stop this at once and tell us what you've been up to!"

"We have been up to nothing. We went to school and the Queen came to visit us at the hut at Dane Hill, and she went down to look at our allotment, it's true!"

"It's all lies, isn't it?"

"No!"

"Do you think that our Queen has nothing better to do than visit you lot? Don't be so silly."

Now Nelly took over. "You say you've had no dinner. Well you'll get no tea either unless you admit that you are all telling lies. Say you are sorry and tell us what's going on. Well?!"

Not a word from any of us four.

"Right, that's it! Go to your room and stay there until one of you comes down and does as I say. Off you go!"

So off we went to our room. There we laid on our beds and grumbled, and discussed what the hell's up with these people; they always seem to be flying off the handle. We were all a bit hungry, but nevertheless we all agreed that nobody was going downstairs to say sorry for something we hadn't done. Us Londoners had our pride.

As it was November, it got dark quite early and we had no oil lamp. Even if we had we had no means of lighting it. So we laid there in the dark, grumbling, and thinking what a dump this place was; we may even have fallen asleep.

When Kitty arrived at Wickens at her usual time, her little group had not been included in the royal visit, and Kit knew nothing about it. This, of course, made matters worse for us. Dear little Kitty had tea all on her own. She may have missed the H.R.H. visit but at least she was getting her meals.

We still had no clock in our room; even if we had, I doubt whether we could have seen it, so we didn't know what time it was.

At a time that I would guess to be about eight o'clock, we heard footsteps in the passageway. Our door slowly opened and we saw a light, which was quickly followed by George's head with his finger to his lips for silence. In a hushed voice he told us to pull the blackout curtains, which we had left open to try to get some moonlight. Once the curtains were drawn, he brought the oil lamp in and set it down. He then went outside and came in with a tray.

On the tray were four glasses with drinks of fruit cordial and a plate with some biscuits and four pieces of cake. Still in his hushed voice, he said, "They don't know I've brought this up to you so be careful with the crumbs. Eat over the tray, don't give me away. I'll try to get back for the tray later." We thanked him and he slipped out.

About an hour later, he came back for the tray and told us we were still in trouble downstairs. "Get undressed and into bed and turn the lamp out. Goodnight."

In the morning we got dressed and went downstairs altogether. We were very apprehensive as to what sort of greeting we would get. We were greeted quite normally, the happenings of the previous day not mentioned at all, and off we went to school. That incident was never mentioned again, ever – not once.

Thinking back on it over the years, I just don't see how George could have gone into the kitchen, prepared four drinks, cut four slices of cake, and biscuits, got a tray and a lamp and got upstairs without Nelly, Hetty and Aunty seeing what was going on. Nothing escaped Aunty's eyes.

They had, I think, found out that we were not lying but didn't want to lose face, having made such a fuss, and the drinks and cakes smuggling helped to ease their consciences. Nobody ever said that we were right and that they were sorry. There are only two occasions that I can remember on which I would consider them unreasonable - one, the Macmillan pony trap affair and, two, the Queen's visit. It seemed we would have to be more choosy about the company we kept in the future!

Like many other things, it soon all blew over and was almost forgotten, but not completely by me.

13. The Village

As yet, I have not written anything about the village of Horsted Keynes.

The village had just about everything that the ideal English village should have: village green, blacksmith's forge, The Crown Pub on one side of the road and I think it was The Green Man on the other side. There was a village hall or community centre, a village store and a post office.

The blacksmith's forge was on the corner of Church Lane, which was both long and quite steep, only to climb up again to the churchyard gate. The village school was behind the church and had to be entered via the churchyard into their playground.

As you went down Church Lane, there were some groups of cottages on the left-hand side. On the right-hand side was a very steep embankment and this, if I remember rightly, ran the whole length of Church Lane.

Running along this embankment there was a track that was no more than 15"-18" wide. We called it "The Goat Run". This track dipped up and down and became even narrower in some places. There were places where it had eroded away and you had to jump across. It was fun but a bit scary. It was a lot easier for the senior boys than the junior ones, obviously because they had longer legs, in most cases. There were a few falls but I don't remember anyone really being hurt, nothing that a bit of spit and a rub with a dirty hanky wouldn't put right.

We were all warned by the teachers not to do "The Goat Run", but nobody seemed to take any notice. It was considered to be a test of one's bravery and it was! 'Elf' and safety would have had a fit.

The dinner hut was behind the church in the school playground. As I think I've already said, sometimes we would have the use of a classroom in the village school, sometimes at the community centre, but to start with mostly at the Nissen hut at Dane Hill. It was difficult sometimes in the mornings to work out where we were supposed to be going to school. This was because sometimes not all four of us agreed. It didn't matter if we were late, there was nothing to do anyway.

Another little shop in the village was Mrs Fry's tuck shop, which stocked all sorts of interesting things, and sweets when available. The lady in charge, Mrs Fry, was always friendly, helpful and understanding to our financial problems. It was one of the few places in the village that us boys didn't mind going into. Most of the rest were not hostile, but decidedly frosty towards us, so we tried to keep clear.

The blacksmith's forge was another place where we were always welcome. Seeing a horse shod was a new experience for a lot of us. As a kid, I always had "a thing" about horses, so to be able to stand there and watch was just great. As he went along the blacksmith would explain what he was doing and why. Smells are very nostalgic and whenever I smell that smell of a hot horseshoe being applied to a horse's hoof, my mind goes back to that forge, lovely memories.

The only other place I liked going to in the village was to a Mrs Silvester. This lady ran a sort of first aid clinic for us kids from her kitchen. She was an extremely nice lady who I would think either was or had been a nurse or even a matron. There was no doubt that she knew what she was doing and had all the right equipment. If any of us children had any cut, bumps, sores, bruises, anything at all, you had to "go and see Mrs Silvester".

That was not a problem because I never came away from there without some sweets, or an apple, pear, peach or some plums or cherries.

Even at that early age, I had a "soft spot" for ladies that gave me things, so Mrs Silvester was high on my list. There was a problem though. I began to find it very hard to find enough things wrong with me so's I could keep going back. It was a very hard life.

Unfortunately, I cannot recall the name of the village vicar, but I do remember him as a very pleasant and friendly man. Sometimes I would be asked to take messages and letters to the vicarage by Mrs Ashby, and whenever this happened he would invite me in to have a little chat.

He was particularly interested in people's Christian names and told me that my name of Geoffrey was from a famous knight of old and was always associated with great bravery. He was such a nice man, so I let it go; I didn't want to disillusion him.

The only other name I remember from the village is Mrs Montiefiore. You see, Mrs Montiefiore never had the pleasure of meeting me, nor I her.

The blacksmiths shop, a place to watch and listen.
Photo: Author's collection

True, she was letting us use her Nissen hut for schooling, but I was never convinced that she was too happy about it. She always seemed to be on the lookout for something to complain about. There was an air of authority about her. The sort of lady who would walk into a meeting and expect to be made Chairperson even if there was no committee. Even Old Jonah didn't like crossing swords with her. She seemed to carry a great deal of influence around the place. Maybe I'm being unfair but that's the way I saw it at the time.

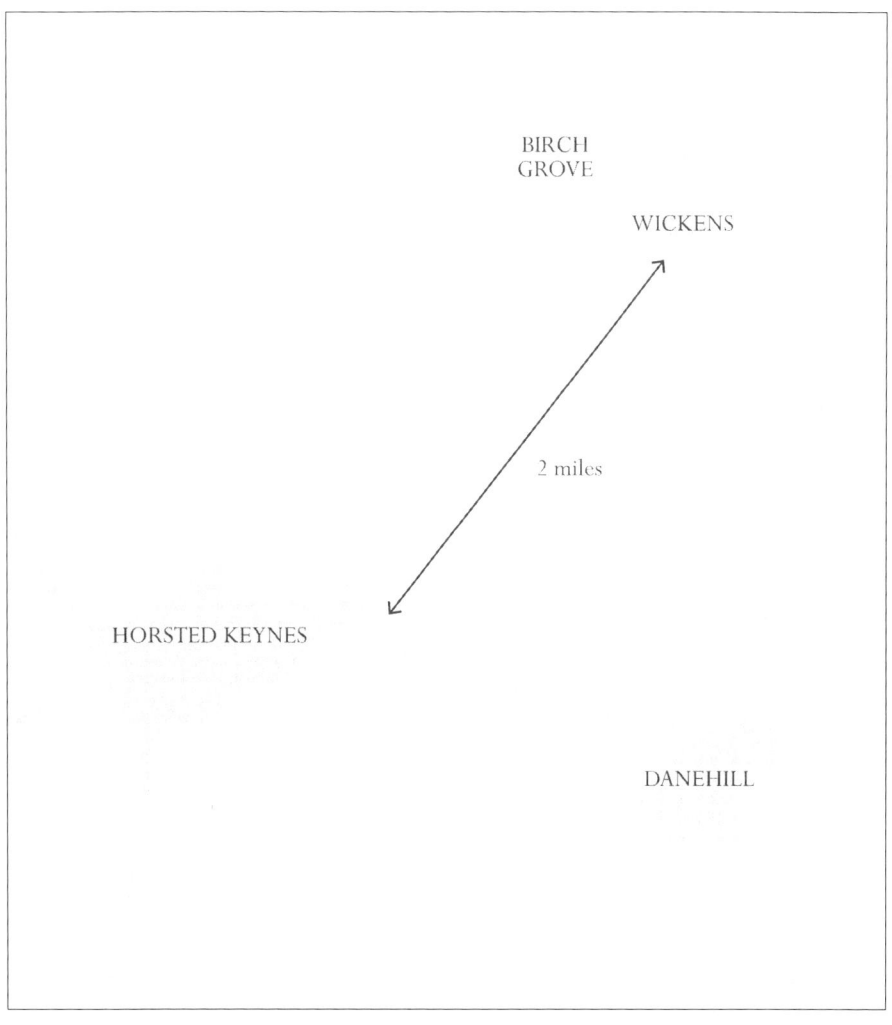

Apart from Mrs Fry, the blacksmith, Mrs Silvester, and the vicar, most of the people were as I've already said, "frosty" towards us. The people outside the village were totally different. On the way back to Wickens from school each day, people in their gardens would wave to us, and if in the front gardens, come across and talk and be really friendly. Everybody in Birch Grove (except Mr Macmillan), people like the Bennetts', the Jays and many others could not have been more friendly and pleasant. They obviously hadn't got the message from the village.

Fortunately, we didn't need to go to the village very often and that suited us fine.

As well as their frostiness, there was also what I call the "blame game". As soon as anything went wrong in the village or surrounding area, any little misdemeanours, something going missing, or broken, damage being done, the accusing finger was always pointed at us. We were like Fagin's gang as far as they were concerned. Sometimes it would have been our lot, I'm quite sure of that. But not all the time.

What little contact we had with the local children we found out that even they also thought it was unfair; that's to their credit. It really was most unfair and even writing about it now still makes me angry. I'm going to try not to mention it again, but it would be seen as though we were not the only ones to have experienced this frosty feeling. I have read of several other cases where evacuees experienced the same thing in other parts of the country.

14. Public School

It was not long after Her Majesty the Queen came to visit me that Kitty and I started at the public school, Twyford School to be exact.

On our first morning we set off not knowing quite what to expect. If I had known, I'm sure I would have walked a lot slower.

We waited with the other children outside, waiting to be called in. We vaguely knew some of the children who were local and whose parents had moved them to Twyford School, a) because they were hoping for a better education and, b) it was nearer to their homes, as these were not village children. The village was much further away. I remember Mr and Mrs Dovey's two boys being there.

Once inside, we could see that Twyford had all the equipment that Heathbrook lacked; blackboards, books, pens – even ink. I didn't like the look of this at all!

The head teacher's name was Mr Kendal. It seemed that the week started with an assembly, no problem with that. Then followed French!

French! French! What do we want to learn French for? We're English, and with my stuttering, I have enough trouble speaking that. I could see that I was in trouble. We opened the French textbooks and I hadn't got a clue. It might as well have been printed in Chinese.

Two or three children were made to stand up and read passages in French, then he called my name, and I stood up.

Complete silence reigned, not a sound. Kendal tried to get me started; nothing happened. He asked me what was wrong and, because of my stutter, the words wouldn't come out and the harder I tried the worse it got. Then he started, "No point in trying to speak French if you can't even speak English. What's the matter with you boy? Speak up."

At that moment I knew this school wasn't going to work for me. He carried on in the same vain for a while, with me standing there acutely embarrassed and humiliated. I hated that man.

Eventually, after a lot of sniggering from the other children and he'd had his fun, I was told to "sit down and go back to sleep".

This was to be the pattern on almost a daily basis. I was his figure of fun. My stuttering started to get worse; I was not a happy bunny.

Perhaps I should explain the set up at Twyford. With Kitty attending, you will have gathered that it was a mixed school. The school was not very large, about 30 to 40 pupils all told. Like Heathbrook, it was divided into two groups, senior and junior. There were only about eight senior pupils and Kitty was one of them. As I've said before, Kit was quite bright and well able to hold her own with the other seven.

The only respite that there was from Kendal was from time to time another teacher, who's name I do not recall. This was a lady teacher who would sometimes take the junior class while Kendal concentrated on the seniors, lucky them. This lady was much more understanding to my problem, but she didn't come often enough for my liking.

The other children were not too bad, but during my few months at Twyford, I never really made what you would call a "best friend". They were all just children I knew.

Never before had I had a problem about going to school; it wasn't my favourite pastime but you had to go so might as well make the best of it. Now it was very different. I hated the school and I hated Kendal. The weekends could not come quick enough and when they did I hated the thought of Monday morning coming.

There were two boys in the senior group that I particularly remember – one named Basil, one called Raleigh. That surely must have been his surname; nobody would have a Christian name of Raleigh. Anyway, that's what everyone called him. These two were the apple of Kendal's eye, his prize pupils.

The timing of Kitty's and my starting was some time in the autumn. Whether it was halfway through a term or not, I don't know, and I don't really care very much.

Normally I pride myself on my memory of my time during evacuation, but my memories of my time at Twyford are mostly very vague. I think this is because I was so very unhappy.

There were times when Kendal would leave the school in charge of Basil. That was all right by me because Basil seemed quite capable of running things. He was by far the tallest boy in the school; he was intelligent and fair. When left in charge, he didn't chuck his weight about; also, he had a bit of a crush on Kitty – this helped quite a bit.

Because of the vagueness of this period, I can't go into a lot of detail. Twice a week, we had football, which Basil took. Apart from that, there's not much to report.

The stuttering was very bad now and somebody must have been trying to do something about it, because one Saturday morning somebody from the Education Authority came to Wickens to assess me. She said that I must at one time have been left-handed, and then made to write right-handed, and I would soon grow out of it.

Fat lot of use that was, even if it was right. But apart from the stuttering, I was getting very jumpy and having bad dreams and, I'm afraid to say, wetting the bed. Later, I was told by Kitty that I had become very withdrawn and I'm not surprised to hear that. Because of the stuttering, I would only speak if someone spoke to me – the words just would not come out. It was both embarrassing and frustrating.

Also embarrassing was, of course, the bed-wetting. I felt really bad about that.

This was something that I'd not done even in hospital.

Looking back on it, Nelly and Hetty were really good about it. Obviously, they were a bit annoyed because it meant extra work, but they didn't rant and rave. Hetty had a quiet word and said "no drinks after tea time and make sure to go to the toilet last thing before getting into bed". Also, I was given a torch, not to play about with but in case I needed to get up during the night. It was to be kept under my pillow at all times. The 'no drinks after tea' was not a punishment, just a sensible precaution, and that's the way I took it. I didn't want this to keep happening any more than they did.

The adults must surely have talked about this amongst themselves. Whether Mrs Ashby knew what was happening, I know not, but I suspect they were thinking along the lines that earlier in the year I had been in hospital for a long period, then evacuated, then my school was changed. It must surely have some effect. "Let him settle into his new school and make a few friends and he'll be all right". That's easier said than done.

Outside school hours, I tried to blank Kendal and the school out completely and, when it was school time, take each day as it came, and bite the bullet.

15. Winter Evenings and Christmas

Sometime during November, tame rabbits were introduced into Wickens, not many at first, probably about eight to start with, in all sorts of colours. We were all delighted with this and spent a lot of our spare time fussing over them. Little did we realise that these "dear little things" would finish up in the pot.

The idea was to make Wickens as self-sufficient as possible and this was just the start. As time went on with these eight rabbits doing what rabbits do best this very quickly became forty or fifty, maybe even more. To start with, looking after them didn't pose too big a problem, but as time went on it did, as you will read later.

Right from the very beginning we had been expected to go to church every Sunday morning at Horsted Keynes church. This, as I've said before, was a very long walk, to a dull service, then a long walk back. The object of the exercise, I think, was to get us out of the way for a while.

Then somebody heard of a Sunday school that was held on Sunday mornings at Chelwood Gate, so we started going there instead. Much to my surprise, I enjoyed it. The lady who ran it also lived in Birch Grove. She had a very interesting way of putting religion across. She could take an incident from the Bible and tell it in a way that really gripped you, not the usual stuffy biblical language. She was good and I didn't mind going there; also, sometimes we got a lift home.

Time was ticking by, things with Twyford and Kendal carried on as before. Kitty was quite happy to play Juliet with Basil as her Romeo. By now we knew our way around pretty well. We knew what was expected of us at Wickens. We'd made up our minds as to who we did or didn't like; in other words, we had got into a routine.

With the darker evenings there was no time for fooling around outside after school and, of course, there was strict blackout enforcement.

Keeping ourselves amused in the evenings after teatime was not easy. The wireless was used very sparingly, mainly for the BBC's evening news. If the Ashby's were in residence, then Nelly would have to prepare evening dinner for them and Hetty would have to wait on table; sometimes afterwards we would help with the washing up.

All of this would have to be done by the dull light given off by the oil lamps, as would anything else we would be trying to do like writing a letter home, reading, or playing any sort of game.

It turned out that Mr Billings had what looked like a homemade bar billiards table and the balls were golf balls; there were four cues. He was quite happy to loan us kids this table for a while to help keep us amused. He and George lugged this table along from his shack and set it up in the sitting room. It helped pass a few hours, but couldn't stay there indefinitely because it took up too much room, but it was a very nice thought.

When the billiard table disappeared, Mr Billings came along with a bar skittles, and that was much more acceptable for everybody. There were other amusements that he brought in from time to time, rationing them out so that over quite a long period we had something to do.

The only comics that we saw would be if Mum and Dad brought some down with them when they came visiting, which wasn't too often. Even then, the comics had to be kept out of sight. Mrs Ashby didn't approve of comics – they were not very educational - nor was picking potatoes!

The days and weeks passed and soon we are into December 1939 with its cold and frosty weather. We are finding out that country cold was colder than London cold.

People's thoughts and talk turned to thoughts of Christmas. Us kids wondered what it is going to be like and didn't know what to expect. But it was the same for everybody, everywhere. These days, nobody knew what to expect next.

Our parents sent a letter about two weeks before Christmas, saying that they would be sending a very big parcel to us by train. It would be too big to send by post. They would let us know details very soon. Great excitement, as we waited eagerly for the letter with the news to arrive.

When it duly arrived, it said that this very big parcel would have to be collected from Horsted Keynes railway station on Wednesday. It was very big and quite heavy and would need some lifting and carrying. If some sort of truck or barrow could be used it would help greatly.

The railway station was some way away from the village in the opposite direction to Wickens; it was going to be quite a walk.

It was decided that "the Elders" should ask to leave the school early on that Wednesday afternoon and do the collecting. This they did, and they had managed to borrow somebody's bicycle. With this bike they sat this large, long box on the handlebars and saddle and with one either side pushed the bike along. With three of them they were able to take it in turns to have a rest and not have to push.

It really was a very long push and a valiant effort on their part. They arrived at Wickens long after normal teatime, very tired, but successful and, I've no doubt, hungry.

We had already been told that the box could be opened, as there were presents inside all wrapped. We all helped with the unpacking amid great excitement.

I'm pleased to say that there were presents for everybody. Len and Billy got presents like Kit, Jim and I. Also token presents for Hetty, Nelly, George, Mr Billings and even Aunty (but not a new hat). All presents not to be opened until Christmas morning.

It began to look as though it might be something like Christmas after all — we shall just have to wait and see.

Between us, Kit, Jim and I bought a few Christmas cards and sent them. The weather was seasonably cold and frosty. It did snow but whether that was before Christmas or not I don't recall.

We had invitations to at least three Christmas parties; Lady Dorothy Macmillan's was a really good party. All the evacuee children got a present from under the big Christmas tree. I got a penknife – what more could a little boy ask for?

The second party was from somebody at Twyford School. I wasn't too sure about this one. The invitation was only for Kit and I, because the "three elders" didn't attend that school. Lucky old them. Off Kit and I went and, to be fair, it was a pretty good party, not in the same class as Lady Dorothy's but a very good effort. Guess what I got from under their Christmas tree? Another penknife!

The third so-called party was Kendal's Twyford School party. Now I really didn't want to go to that. It was bad enough having to go there five days a week and see HIM, without Saturday afternoon as well! The adults said I had to go, it would be very rude not to. So I went, determined to hate every minute of it, and I succeeded. It was more like a wake. Whether or not there was a Christmas tree or presents, I don't recall. I just wanted to get out of there as quickly as possible, but I suppose even I should give him credit for trying.

It is a shame I do not recall the name of the Sunday school teacher, because she had found out about a couple of Christmas events at places reasonably nearby, which she offered to take us to if we would like to go.

These events were held on Saturday afternoons, so I suppose "the elders" were out somewhere beating for a "shoot" and only Kitty and I went on these trips. We were picked up by the Sunday school teacher in her car, and I don't know where we went to for the first event, but it was a long trip.

The event proved to be a carol concert or service with about four choirs singing. It was a bit over my head, but at least it was something to do with Christmas, which in our family was always a really special time.

On the second trip, which was at a church in East Grinstead, it was a nativity play, not with children but adults. There was a lot of singing and these people really could sing. The whole thing – singing, costumes, the way it was staged and presented was most impressive; so much so that I have never forgotten it. Glad I went.

Christmas Day came at last and everybody did their very best to make it enjoyable. It just wasn't like being at home, but there were thousands of people in the same boat and we all had to make the best of it.

Us five kids had all clubbed together to buy some small presents for all the adults; just a small something to show some appreciation of what they were doing for us. The idea came from Mum and Dad and they sent some postal orders down to help out with the cash.

We, in turn, got presents from them, mostly practical things like scarves and woollen gloves. There was also, very thoughtfully included, a compendium of board games to help pass the long, dark winter evenings.

From home, I don't remember what the others got, but I got a model aeroplane to fly in the playfield, and some other bits and bobs. Also, my parents had put in a package for all us boys to share. It turned out to be a football. We were all pretty pleased with it, but Len was over the moon – he loved football, so he got the job of pumping it up.

Looking back on it, it wasn't a bad Christmas; I've known a lot worse since then.

The New Year was a non-event. We just did what we could outside in the cold weather, tried out the new football and waited (not very eagerly in my case) to return to school and wonder what 1940 had in store for everyone.

16. Refugees

After Christmas, there was snow and with every season we were discovering how different each of the seasons was proving to be in the country as opposed to London. Snow in London was great fun for a while, but the novelty of it soon wore off.

Snow in the country seemed much more exciting, as there was so much more to do. Going into the fields and surrounding woods, seeing so many animal tracks and to be able to follow them. Some of the tracks we knew, some we didn't, so we tried to get books to find out.

Motorcars had chains on their wheels; I'd never seen that before. Also, you had to be much more careful on the roadways because you couldn't hear the cars coming so well.

One weekend Mr Michael had come home for the weekend as he quite often did and had brought a male student colleague with him. The weather was extremely cold and Mr Michael telephoned Mr Macmillan and asked, if his lakes were frozen over enough would it be permissible to skate on them and, because the Ashby's and Macmillan's were friendly, permission was granted.

Much to our delight, Mr Michael said we could go as well if Nelly and Hetty didn't mind. He never minded having us kids around, particularly Len, who was a natural comic and was always making people laugh with his remarks and antics.

The two men went ahead and tested the ice and, with a large piece of wood, cleared the snow away. The men put on their skating boots and were soon zooming around at top speed.

Meanwhile, Len knew of some old clip-on skates in one of the sheds. He went and dug them out, two pair. So Jim, Len and Billy took it in turns. The skates were too large for me. Not that that worried me; I'd already slipped over twice and banged my head on the ice. In spite of the bumps, it was a fun morning. Kitty had elected to stay indoors in the warm. Further trips to the ice were strictly forbidden after that, on grounds of safety.

The situation at Twyford School was much the same. I wasn't at all happy there but didn't see what I could do about it, so just made the best of a bad job. The friendship between Kitty and Basil was still going strong. I only saw my playmate, Arthur Jay, at weekends because the evenings were dark by the time we got back from school.

When I could, I still helped George and got my weekly wage, whatever it was. The rabbit population was growing quite fast and there was talk of getting some chickens in the spring.

All this time, us five evacuees were under the illusion that Mrs Ashby was a Liberal Member of Parliament, because that's what we had been told, whether Mrs Ashby knew this there's no way of knowing. For over seventy years I went on believing this. It was only very recently I found out differently.

The reason I raise this point now is that about this time there seemed to be a lot of rather strange houseguests arriving. They seemed to stay for one, two or three nights and then suddenly be gone. Some of them we met, some we didn't.

Those that we met were very quiet. They would just smile and nod. It appeared that most of them could not speak English and those who could spoke it very badly.

When we asked about them, Hetty explained that they were in fact refugees and quite important people in their own countries and, because of Mrs Ashby's position, she and people like her were being asked to give those people temporary accommodation until something could be sorted out for them.

There were two families that stayed a little longer than the rest. We knew the first family as Mr and Mrs Aaron and they had a little daughter named Inger who must have been about six years old. Two things that I remember about Inger was that she had lovely long platinum blonde hair; in fact, she was a very pretty little girl. The second thing was that she hated to wear anything on her feet and most of the time would run around with bare feet. This would be quite regardless of what sort of surface she was walking on.

All three spoke English quite well, but Inger's English was almost fluent. I have a faint memory of Inger telling me that they came from Sweden. They seemed to be around for one, maybe two weeks, and we would bump into them from time to time, then suddenly one day they were gone! That's the way all these people left, suddenly. Sometimes, Hetty and Nelly didn't know when they went out whether or not they were due to come back that evening or not. In most cases they didn't return.

During this time our parents came to visit as often as they could, I should think it was about every six to eight weeks. During one visit they told us that our grandfather (Gran's husband) was in hospital but didn't go into any details as to how serious it was.

Granddad was a lovely man but we didn't get to see quite so much of him as we did Gran because he was at work. He was a proof-reader for Odham Press. He was always jolly and good fun and, most important, very generous with 'sweety' money.

Although Kitty, Jim and I were getting regular visits from our parents, Billy and Len had had none at all from their parents. In fact, there seemed to be a bit of a mystery regarding Billy's family. He never seemed to talk about his father and he didn't talk about his mother all that much, but when he did you got the impression that maybe she was not very strong. Mainly, Billy didn't talk about living in London, but how he had spent a lot of time living either in or around Hastings. He was always banging on about Hastings and the different colour sands you can find there, and what a lovely place it was.

Eventually, his mother moved back to Hastings and, when Billy left school and Wickens later in 1940, that's where he went to, never once having had a visit from his mum.

The subject of Len's conversation, apart from the Boys' Brigade, was his mum and his elder brother who was in the Army. His brother was Len's hero. His father didn't get much of a mention and when I met him later on I could see why. But more about that later on.

The refugees continued to come and go at regular intervals even when Mr and Mrs Ashby were not in residence. This didn't please Hetty and Nelly very much; letting complete strange foreigners have the run of the house and be waited on hand and foot went very much against the grain, but there wasn't much they could do about it.

Time was ticking by and slowly, just like every other year, the spring evenings were beginning to get lighter and, with the lighter evenings, trouble from another source at Twyford School.

When I previously wrote about Twyford School I mentioned two boys who were the apple of Kendal's eye. One was the mighty Basil, the other by the name of Raleigh.

Now, Raleigh was a creep of the first order, a real "Yes sir, please sir, you're so right sir" type of creep. He also knew he could do no wrong as far as Kendal was concerned.

Having watched Kendal go through his almost daily humiliation routine with me, Raleigh had decided to get in on the act.

So, when schooling finished for the day, Raleigh, by using his bicycle, would get ahead of me. Kitty stayed at school for music lessons of some sort. There was a narrow track way I had to use to get to Wickens and Raleigh would block this with his bike and only let me pass if I would say, "Please sir, will you let me through?" and I wouldn't. When I spoke to him I was stuttering badly and he took the Mickey. Also, he said when I spoke to him I must call him not Raleigh, but Sir – again I wouldn't do it.

He didn't attempt to hit me but was pushing his front wheel onto my toes and pressed it against me, sneering and mimicking my stutter. He was a much bigger build than I was; I just had to await my chance and make a dash for it, which I managed to do for three or four evenings.

One evening, he kept me there so long doing his act that Kitty came along. She'd caught me up. Kit saw what was happening and told Raleigh what she thought of him. Then he started on her and that was his big mistake.

How we got away from him that evening I don't remember but we did. We ran hard and kept to the trees that slowed his bike up and eventually he gave up. We had to stop and rest because we were both out of breath, then Kit started asking questions as to how long this had been going on for. "Don't worry", she told me, "I'll see something is done". She was as good as her word — help had arrived at last.

Arriving at Wickens, Kitty herself was quite upset by what had happened and I think everybody could see that. Kit was a tough little nut and it took a lot to ruffle her feathers. It was not Nel or Het's place to really do anything; they, after all, were only employees, but nevertheless I'm sure they took note.

That night, Kitty wrote to Mum and Dad and let them know what had happened, not only to herself but to me, with Kendal on a daily basis. We sat back and waited.

The next day at school, Kit told Basil the whole Raleigh saga. During break time Basil came to see me and told me he knew what had happened, but not to worry, he (Basil) would sort Raleigh out. During break times I was to stick close to Basil and he would see Kit and I got no more trouble after school, but of course Basil couldn't do anything about Kendal.

The grounds surrounding the chapel, or whatever the building was that Twyford was using as a school, were quite open. There was enough space for quite a large playing area, enough in fact for football to be played on recreational afternoons.

However, there were some really big and fine trees around the perimeter and I can't be sure but I think some of them were Beech. On one of these trees Basil was carving Kitty's and his own initials, and doing it really deeply, so it took several days to do… aint love grand.

As he did this, a whole group stood around watching and talking and generally messing about. The tree on which he was carving had branches very low down on the trunk and, in some places, almost touching the ground.

At some point somebody, I don't know who, took hold of one of these low hanging branches and pulled it back quite hard under the tree, towards the trunk, then he let go. The branch sprung back into its original position with great force, taking with it bits of grass and twigs that had been lying on the ground. The force and noise took everybody by surprise because it was so unexpected.

This started a whole line of conversation as to how much force was involved and whether it would be possible to throw something by that method, and how far would it go. It was decided to do some tests.

Somebody said, "There's a log over there. If we used that and a stronger branch with a fork in it so we can lay the log across the fork, then let the branch go". That seemed like a good idea to everybody so that's how it was done.

The launch was a great success, so we had one or two more test firings, each time propelling the log a little further, by pulling the branch further back. How the branch didn't snap, I don't know.

This went on during break times over the next couple of days and it was beginning to lose its interest. Then somebody, and I promise you it wasn't me, said, "Why don't we try with somebody, instead of the log?" This was met with great approval. The next question was who.

Then somebody (and I promise you it was me) said "Raleigh". Now Basil was running this experiment and he in his infinite wisdom saw the justice in my suggestion, so Raleigh was given the honour of the first flight.

It took a lot to convince Raleigh that he had volunteered for this mission; he didn't want to do it, nobody did. It was a good idea so long as somebody else did it.

The branch was hauled back and Raleigh took his place in the fork of the branch, with the prongs of the fork tucked neatly under each armpit. Real nice and snug.

On the word, "Fire!" there was a scream and he was gone. Poor old Raleigh, he was whipped off his feet and thrown through the air several yards. It was quite disappointing really – I'd hoped he'd be thrown a lot further. Raleigh wasn't hurt, he could still move, just about. Some said it had all happened too quickly and they didn't see what happened. So it was decided to have a re-run and Raleigh was told that as he'd done such a good job he could do the re-run as well.

While all this was happening it began to dawn on me that I wasn't the only one who disliked Raleigh - everyone seemed to and we all seemed to be enjoying seeing him suffer. In fact, a voice from this lynch mob suggested that if we could pull back one of the slightly higher branches we might get greater elevation and greater distance. That seemed like yet another good idea and it was decided to give it a try.

It wasn't a unanimous decision though. Someone voted against it – I think it might have been Raleigh. The slightly higher branch was pulled down and back. It was hard work, but by now everybody was involved and helping.

Our 'spaceman' was helped into position, the command was given, there was a whoosh of leaves and twigs brushing along the grass and there he was – gone again.

Why did he have to scream like that every time? Personally, I found it most upsetting, but that was one of Raleigh's troubles; he was very thoughtless regarding other people's feelings!

The launch though had been a great success and now I can't recall whether we had time for another one or two chances to hurl him into "the wide blue yonder" before break time ended. By the time that arrived Raleigh had had enough, and as we went back into class he was sobbing. I actually felt sorry for him.

But I remember that within our line of fire I could see a not too large clump of gorse bushes that I had my eye on. It occurred to me that it might be a nice idea if Raleigh visited them, by air of course. Have I mentioned to you before, I didn't like Raleigh very much.

There is some doubt in my mind as to whether or not we quite reached my target. Never mind, you can't win them all. Maybe this was my bridge a bit too far.

The small group of seniors in the school, there were about eight of them, used to sit around a very large table at one end of the room, and this table was on a sort of podium.

Once back in class after the break everybody went to their places and got on with what they were supposed to be doing.

The teacher, Kendal, noticed that Raleigh was looking a bit distressed because tears were streaming down his face. He asked, "What is wrong with you Raleigh lad? Why are you crying?"

"I'm not crying sir, but the sun is shining straight into my eyes and making them water."

"Well you silly boy, move your chair round a bit."

Move his chair round a bit? That's a laugh. Raleigh could hardly move himself round a bit, let alone his chair!

The next day at break time many wanted to carry on with our space programme. Raleigh wasn't too keen; in fact, he begged to be left alone.

"I know what this is all about, and I'm really, really sorry", he said between sobs. Big Basil, or Bas, as he was known, had decided enough was enough and that it was time to stop before somebody got badly hurt.

Never have I seen such a look of joy and relief on anybody's face as there was on Raleigh's. He cried with relief and went around shaking hands with everybody. The incident was over and, as far as I'm aware, Raleigh never caused any more trouble to anyone. He was a changed bloke.

Nevertheless, I believe that Kit and I were not the only ones to have suffered from his intimidating tactics and he had found out that "what you sow you reap".

This incident with Raleigh is one that I am not particularly proud of. Bullying is wrong and, in this case, I think went a bit too far. Nevertheless, some good did seem to come out of it, but I have to say that break times for the next few days did seem a bit dull.

In April 1961, the Russians announced to the world that Yuri Gagarin was the first man launched into space. Don't tell the Russians, but Raleigh was!

17. Back to Heathbrook

The saga of Raleigh was over but that didn't help with the problems of Kendal. As far as I was aware, there had been no response to Kit's letter. Even if there was, I'd be the last person to know.

In fact, things were not quite so bad as they were at Twyford; the situation had eased slightly. It seemed as if Kendal was getting tired of his constant Mickey-taking and was now just having the occasional dig now and then.

A small group of us had been removed from French lessons, much to my delight, and that of the French. The French were having enough trouble with Hitler, without me mangling their language up. Can't see why they have to talk like that – you can't understand them. Why can't they speak English like normal human beings?

The work being set for our little group was much more within my capabilities and, knowing that Basil was around to help where he could, things were not too bad. That didn't mean I liked it, but I could live with it if I had to.

This also eased the situation at Wickens. The precautions taken by Nelly and Hetty regarding my night-time problems seemed to be working. All in all, things were improving.

It wasn't too long before a letter arrived from home telling us that Mum and Dad would be coming to visit. Whenever news like that arrived, it was something to look forward to, this time even more so.

The Sunday visit day came at last and Kit, Jim and I walked into the village to meet the bus, the same as we always did. When they arrived there were all the usual greetings and we started the walk back to Wickens.

My Dad always liked to do that walk and see the countryside. He was a countryman at heart. He came from Somerset.

During this walk there was no talk at all about school. This perplexed me somewhat and worried me quite a bit. Was nothing going to be done about it?

Arriving at Wickens, again all the usual greetings and cups of tea and talk about how London was doing. On these visits Dad would always bring with him some of Het and Nel's favourite fish and some kippers for George. This of course put him in their good books.

My Mother would always bring enough sandwiches so we could eat together as a family without using up their valuable household rations. It seemed to work because they were always made welcome. During these visits every effort was made to include Len and Billy as much as possible because, as yet, neither had had a visit from their folks, whereas we had had three or four.

Very soon after lunch my parents said we were going to have to amuse ourselves for a while because they were going to talk with Mrs Ashby. My spirits rose – it looked as if something was happening after all.

Following that meeting, Mum and Dad had another cuppa with Nelly and Hetty, said their goodbyes and we started to walk back to the village again, and it was only about two o'clock.

On the way, they told us that very soon Kit and I would be taken out of Twyford School; that I would hopefully be rejoining Heathbrook School, along with Jim, Len and Billy. My happiness knew no bounds. I was overjoyed! They explained that we were on our way to the village expressly to see Old Jonah, but they called him Mr Jones.

Apparently, Old Jonah made himself available every Sunday afternoon on the village green so any visiting parents could have a word with him if they wished.

Maybe Jim had been asked to pre-arrange this, I don't know.

At the village, Jonah was there on the green talking to other boys' parents; we waited our turn. When it came, Dad explained the problem and said it had been a big mistake, and they thought I would be happier back at Heathbrook – would that be all right with Jonah?

Old Jonah put his arm around my shoulders and gave me a little squeeze and said, "Of course Geoffrey can come back to us, this is where he belongs". He was carrying a big thick walking stick at the time and he waved that in front of me as he said, "And I promise I won't use this on him". Handshakes all round, it was settled – my own personal nightmare was nearly over.

As for Kitty, she wasn't going back to that caper of somebody's house in the village, even if that was still in operation. She would be attending a quite large grammar school in Haywards Heath. This school was highly thought of in the area and several children from the village went there. There was a school bus from the village green and back every day, for which Kit would get a free pass.

Now Kitty had passed an examination whilst at Tennyson Street School in London, which could have got her into grammar school. Whether or not this had anything to do with it I've no way of knowing. Or did Mrs Ashby have some influence and pulled a few strings? It doesn't really matter - she was in.

Rather than walk back to Wickens, Mum and Dad caught the next bus to Haywards Heath station. By now, time was getting on anyway. It had been a rather short visit, but a good one as far as I was concerned.

As far as I can remember, we had to stay at Twyford until we broke up for Easter, which was about a couple of weeks. You would have thought that after all that had happened I would have remembered my last week, or my last day, but I don't! Old Kendal didn't beg me to stay, as far as I know. It's just a complete blank.

That wasn't quite the last we saw of Bas. He kept calling in to Wickens to see Kit, but it gradually faded out, like it often does.

The prospect of going to school was beginning to look a little more inviting again.

Quite soon after Mum and Dad's visit, Len had a letter from his mother asking if it would be all right for her and Len's father to come and visit him one Sunday soon. Of course the answer was yes, with a capital Y. Len was quite excited and we were all pleased for him. He was very popular with everybody – he was a really nice bloke.

The date was fixed and, when the day arrived, it was thought it best that Len went to meet them on his own. This was to give them plenty of time to talk family matters on that long walk back to Wickens.

Upon their arrival, Mr Hawes made it quite plain that he didn't approve of walking of any kind – long walks or shorts walks were out.

Now, Mrs Hawes seemed like a nice lady and was trying so hard to make a good impression, which was understandable. But the poor lady was completely in awe of the surroundings that she was in, just like us kids had been, and she was struggling. Whereas Mr Hawes wasn't struggling. He wasn't even trying to make a good impression. He would have been overawed by any surroundings that weren't a four-ale bar.

It was not going well, and it got even worse when Mr Hawes started to break wind, often and loudly. Then, to make matters worse, he would laugh hilariously at what he'd just done. Breaking wind was not what us kids called it, but never mind.

Poor Mrs Hawes didn't know what to do with herself, and a walk around the gardens was suggested; still he kept on doing it and laughing. Everybody was embarrassed and didn't quite know what to do or say.

In Nelly's case she went around wearing a very indignant look, Hetty became very flustered and bright pink, George disappeared and Aunty went to her room.

We waited with bated breath; if Aunty reappeared wearing her "at" he was in trouble. She'd let him know all about "wind in the willows". But she stayed in her room – at least that crisis was over.

The hours dragged on until about three o'clock when Mrs Hawes said that they really ought to be making a move because they had things to do when they got home. Some very strained goodbyes were said, but no mention of "you must come again". Again, it was Len's mum who suggested that all us kids could walk down and see them on the bus; that way, Len would have some company on the walk back. So, off we toddled.

All the way to the village, Mr Hawes moaned and whinged. "Didn't anybody around here have a car to give people lifts in?" "Why wasn't there a bus service?" "What a dump to live in - not a pub in sight", and so on. All this to an accompaniment of his favourite sound.

Poor Mrs Hawes, on the other hand, tried very hard to be cheerful and pleasant. She remarked, "He's not always like this – he's just nervous". Nobody made any comment.

By the time we reached the village green Mr Hawes had just about had it. He'd even stopped complaining and he was really puffing and blowing. But there was more blowing than puffing, not surprisingly.

We saw them on the bus and waved until it was out of sight, and turned and started the long trek back to Wickens. At last he was gone, gone with the wind. Poor old Len – he didn't know what to say to us, nor us to him. The day that he had been so looking forward to had been ruined by his father's tactics; he didn't deserve that. We all felt so sorry for him.

Like us, Len was wondering what was being said about the visit by Nelly, Hetty and co while we were out. Also, what was their reaction going to be, particularly towards Len, because there was no doubt whatsoever about their displeasure about Mr Hawes' behaviour.

Fortunately, there were no repercussions at all; they appeared not to hold it against Len, which was fair; nothing was ever said - the incident was closed.

But Mr and Mrs Hawes never came again – I wonder why?

18. The Ashby's

Seeing as how all us kids were living in Mr & Mrs Ashby's house, I think it's only fair to write something about them, don't you?

But that is a bit easier said than done. Quite a lot of the time they were in London, not even at Wickens every weekend. So there were long spells when we just didn't see them.

Apart from Wickens, which was their country house, they also had a London home in the Lower Richmond Road, in the Putney area of London. How big this house was I've no idea, but they had a maid named May, who was younger than Hetty and Nelly, a lot more scatter-brained, and very deaf. More about her later.

Whereas Mr Ashby was always addressed as just that, "Mr Ashby", Mrs Ashby liked to be addressed as "Mrs Corbett Ashby", Corbett being her maiden name. She was a very energetic lady, always on the go, always doing something. A person who was fair but didn't suffer fools gladly, and I always thought a bit on the short-tempered side.

When at Wickens her main hobby seemed to be gardening, and if she thought I was at a loose end it would be, "Come along Geoffrey, you can come and help me". She loved to plant long rows of dahlias along the grass walkways or paths. Mrs Corbett Ashby would plant, stake and tie; it was my job to trim the grass edges with edging shears and pick up trimmings, then working behind Mrs Corbett Ashby, level off the soil and with a hand fork leaving a nice gully rounded at the base. She always told me I was very good at that. She always

Dame Margery Corbett Ashby in 1973, in the garden of Wickens, near Horsted
Keynes, where Geoff, Kitty and Jim lived when they were evacuated in 1939.
Photo: Courtesy of Danehill Parish Historical Society

had some boiled sweets in her pocket, which we shared. It was a good working partnership.

It was, I think, Mrs Corbett Ashby who planted the seed of gardening in me (please excuse the pun) that later led me to take up gardening as a career. Dahlias were the very first plant that I learned to identify by the leaf.

Apart from her gardening, Mrs Corbett Ashby was involved with no end of women's organisations, like W.I. and many others beyond my understanding. Often I would be asked to take a letter or message to an address in the area, which I was happy to do.

As I worked with her we talked about all sorts of things, like what would I like to do when I left school, and it was no good giving silly answers because I wouldn't have given her many marks for sense of humour. We found out that we shared the same birthday. In fact we chatted as best I was able to; she was a very down to earth sort of lady and I rather enjoyed helping her.

The gardener, Mr Billings, had a dog named Smoker to guard his shack when he wasn't around. Mrs Ashby seemed to be the only person to ever take it out for exercise; in fact, Mrs Ashby and Mr Billings were the only two who had any control over the dog at all. Smoker was a nasty beast and I for one kept well out of his way.

The myth that Mrs Corbett Ashby was a Member of Parliament came from the fact that she stood unsuccessfully as a Liberal parliamentary candidate on seven occasions. So Hetty and Nelly perpetuated the myth in the hope that it would impress us enough to make us behave ourselves. Some hope.

Now, Mr Ashby is a much harder task to describe. Quite tall, slim and very quiet in his manner. In nearly three years that I was there, I can only remember one conversation with him.

One evening I was asked to take something along to Mr Billings in his shack. It was a dark but really bright moonlit night, so I had no trouble seeing where I was going; I knew the way well enough anyway.

Having given whatever it was that I had to deliver to Mr Billings and had a short chat, I decided that as it was such a nice night I'd walk back the long way through the gardens, and not use the back path which was the way I had come.

So down through the vegetable garden, down to the orchard to the big beech tree at the bottom of the main lawn, up towards the house heading for the corner where the kitchen was.

Now, Mr Ashby was a very keen amateur astrologer and whenever weather conditions were right and it was a nice clear sky, he would set up his very large telescope on the veranda outside the large dining room. There he would stay for ages just gazing up at the stars.

He was doing just that as I crossed the lawn coming back from the errand; he must have seen or heard me crossing the lawn and called out, "Who is there?" I stepped forward and identified myself.

"What are you doing out wandering around on your own after dark Geoffrey?"

"Hetty asked me to take something along to Mr Billings, sir, and as it's such a nice night, I thought I'd walk back through the garden instead of the back path."

"Good idea, because it is a very nice evening." He went on, "Do you ever look up at the stars Geoffrey?"

"Er, yes sir."

"I do it a lot; it's my hobby."

"Yes sir."

"Do you know Geoffrey, there are other worlds up there."

"Er, no sir."

It seemed like a good idea to put on my intelligent look, but I hoped this wouldn't take too long, as I find looking intelligent very taxing.

He carried on. "Yes, there are lots of planets up there, which are really other worlds."

"I see."

"Would you like to take a look through the telescope?"

"What?" I just didn't know what to say, so he asked again.

"Yes please sir." He went and got a chair or something I could stand on.

"Don't put your hands on the telescope, or you will spoil the setting."

"Right sir." He steadied me as I looked through the scope, even then I nearly fell off the chair. What I was seeing was like something out of 'Star Wars'. There seemed to be at least three golden coloured orbs up there in space, and I got the feeling that they were moving, or spinning.

He helped me down from the chair and I must have looked pretty surprised.

"Well, what do you think of that?"

"Blimey!"

"Well, yes, pretty surprising isn't it." I could only nod my head.

"What you've just seen are some of the satellites that are going around the planet", and he told me the names, but it was all over my head at that age.

"Yes sir, that's very interesting. Thank you very much, but I think I'd better be getting in – they will be wondering where I've got to."

"Yes, all right Geoffrey, I quite understand, but before you go, if ever you see me out here again using my telescope you are quite welcome to come out and I'll let you take a look at whatever I'm looking at, do you understand?"

"Yes sir, I understand. It's really very kind of you. I shall look forward to it.

Goodnight sir and thank you."

"Goodnight Geoffrey, don't bother to walk all the way round, you can go in through to the dining room."

"I don't think they would like that sir. I'll stick to the back door." He smiled. "Please yourself – goodnight."

"Goodnight sir, and thanks again."

That really was the most unusual encounter to have had, especially with Mr Ashby. As I walked around to the back door I thought about what I had just seen. Yes, it was interesting, but also a bit frightening. Other worlds up there – what does he want to go poking his nose into them for? Good grief, aren't we having enough trouble down here with the one we've got?

Reaching the back door, I went in. Kit and the elders were in the sitting room. I went through into the kitchen; both Hetty and Nelly were there, getting the Ashby's evening dinner ready. One of them said, "You've been a long time. Been talking to Mr Billings?"

"No, I've been looking through Mr Ashby's telescope."

Nelly froze, stood stock still; Hetty went very pale.

"Oh my God, don't say you've been messing about with that. He'll kill you! Tell me you are joking."

"No, I looked through it, it was very interesting."

"Young man, you could be in serious trouble when Mr Ashby finds out."

"No, Mr Ashby was there. We had a talk about the stars and things and he got a chair and helped me up to look through the telescope – it was good."

There were big sighs of relief all around. Hetty felt so odd, she had to have a sit down.

"Well, you didn't tell us that, did you."

"You didn't ask me."

"So, come on, what did you see?"

"Search me, but it was all a bit scary really. You know, we've no idea what's going on up there; there are other worlds."

By now, Hetty was fast recovering and she retorted, quite sharply for her. "I don't want to know, thank you very much. There's enough trouble down here already without looking up there for more."

Intelligent woman that Hetty, 'cos that's my own view exactly.

That night, as all of us boys laid in bed talking with the lamp out and the blackout curtains pulled back, I told the others what I'd seen through the telescope. They all had their say of course, but when the talking stopped I lay there thinking.

Strange man that Mr Ashby. Don't know why he does that funny job of stopping people falling off staircases, 'cos he seems quite intelligent really. Still, that's none of my business. Must give him a lot of time to think about things; that's probably why he does this star-staring caper. Then, just before I went to sleep I thought, I wonder who looks after the staircase when he's not there? Goodnight.

The last Ashby to tell you about is the son, Mr Michael, and we saw even less of him than we did Mr & Mrs Ashby.

A medical student training in London, he came to Wickens when he could for the weekend, sometimes a bit longer. He would often bring a friend with him, sometimes male, sometimes female.

He was quite fun to have around and was very friendly to us kids. Full of energy, like his mother; he was always repairing or building something. He drove an Aston Martin sports car in which he would give us rides if he was going somewhere local. Four of us crammed into this little car, I seem to remember, two in the passenger seat and two in the open boot, with very little to hold on to. The louder we screamed, the faster he drove. It was scary but great fun.

But there were times when he was not too popular with the kitchen staff, and it all centred upon Hetty's wireless.

Wireless sets, as they were then called, used to be run off things called accumulators, which was very much like a car battery, to which the wireless set would have to be connected. Each accumulator would last only a few hours before running down and having to be recharged, so it paid to have at least two accumulators, one being used, one away being recharged. It was not terribly expensive, but it was a nuisance taking it to and fro to the shop to get it recharged about once a week.

All the Ashby's liked to listen to Hetty's wireless to hear the evening BBC news. This meant they would take over the staff sitting room for about twenty minutes. Aunty didn't like that one little bit.

But also Mr Michael liked to listen to a particular comedian called Jack Warner, who was just starting his career as a stand up comedian. In later years, this same Jack Warner went on to become TV's Dixon of Dock Green. His act was full of catchphrases, such as "Mind my bike", "My little gal" and "Blue pencil", the latter being a reference to wartime army postal censorship.

Well, Mr Michael just couldn't hear him often enough, and from the newspapers would find out when he was on, which was quite frequently and always in the evenings.

If the broadcast happened to coincide with the time of the Ashby's evening dinner, then he would excuse himself from the dinner table, leave the room and come into the staff sitting room, much to Mrs Ashby's annoyance. Once he walked into the staff sitting room anyone in there was expected to stand up and remain standing until invited to sit down again. He would take one of the armchairs and everybody was ill at ease until he went out again. It was annoyance all round. It was also using up Hetty's accumulator power for which she had to pay. Why the Ashby's didn't get a wireless of their own and have it in their own room is anybody's guess; it would have avoided a lot of backstairs grumbling.

That was not the end of it either. By leaving the dining table, Mr Michael threw out the whole sequence of Hetty and Nelly serving the meal. Sometimes his meal would have to be kept warm whilst he listened to the wireless and the others would have to wait for dessert whilst he caught up with his meal.

All this made Hetty and Nelly late in clearing away afterwards. His visits were not looked forward to by them; in fact, at times he irked quite a few people, except Kitty.

My sister, Kitty, thought he was wonderful. All I got most of the time was, "Mr Michael is ever so good at this or that. Mr Michael's got a lovely singing voice. Mr Michael is ever so strong. Mr Michael is ever so funny. Mr Michael ......"

"Oh, for goodness sake shut up! I'll be glad when he goes back to London."
In later years, I was to briefly meet Mr Michael again, but I'll write about that when the time comes.

Now, as I've already explained, "The Ashby's" were away from Wickens a lot of the time. This, of course, made life easier for Nelly and Hetty. But when they were in residence they would occasionally have guests in the evening for dinner. Mostly these would not be large dinner parties, either four guests, but sometimes only two.

Among the most frequent guests were "The Macmillan's" (Lady and Mr), with whom "The Ashby's" seemed to have a very good friendship.

On these "dinner party" evenings there was always extra pressure on Nelly and Hetty; so they used to get us kids out of the way by packing us off to bed early, except dear little Kitty who was a useful help to Nelly in the kitchen – Kit enjoyed that.

As us blokes were shushed upstairs to our bedroom we would be asked to keep our talking down as low as possible, so's not to disturb the guests.

There was one time following one such dinner party which "The Macmillan's" had attended. The following morning Hetty told us that Lady Dorothy and Mr Macmillan were "most impressed" they could not believe that there were five evacuees staying in the house because it was so quiet!

Well, I didn't believe that then, and I don't believe it now. It was just their way of saying "thank you, well done".

19. The Great Escape

Once I had restarted back with Heathbrook again, I felt a lot happier about everything. It was spring and, after Twyford School, I would gladly put up with that long walk to school and back; I was back where I belonged.

Although we still chopped and changed from one school site to another, the daily routine was a bit better organised. Not so many country rambles and some real lessons. There was a little more in the way of materials and equipment but not much more.

If the first session of the day was at the Nissen hut, Old Jonah would bring in a wireless set. The BBC was running educational programmes each weekday morning and the morning's work would be set around what we had heard on the wireless. It worked very well.

The number of pupils had dropped away quite sharply whilst I was at Twyford, so had the number of teachers. We now had Old Jonah, Mr Thew, Old Burb, and Mr Gough. Because air raids on London had not really started, many parents had taken their children back to London. Some kids were just plain homesick.

About a fortnight after my restart at Heathbrook, our first session of the week on Monday morning was in a classroom at the village school. The locals were not using it for some reason or the other.

It was one of those mornings when you could tell by the atmosphere around that something was wrong. We were all quickly assembled and three boys, two were brothers and their friend, were made to stand in front of the assembled school. We were soon to find out what this was all about.

It appeared that these three boys, the two friends were senior boys, the third a younger brother, were all billeted on the same family. Now, whether these boys were just fed up with country life, or being ill-treated in some way, there is no way of knowing because they refused to say.

But they had decided that they had had enough and were going home to London. They hitched a lift to Haywards Heath railway station, because they had no money, and got aboard a London bound train.

Upon reaching London and being asked for their tickets, they said that the tickets were in the pocket of a coat that fell out of the train window en route. Not surprisingly, nobody believed them and they were handed over to the police. This had all taken place on a Saturday morning, whether anyone had yet missed them at Horsted Keynes, there was no way of knowing.

The Metropolitan Police contacted the two sets of parents. What happened regarding the train fares, I don't know. Somehow, all the relevant people in Horsted Keynes were contacted and made aware of what was going on, and where the missing boys were. Old Jonah was also informed.

After staying the night in London, the three escapees were then brought back to the village by their parents on the Sunday. There followed meetings with the 'foster parents', the real parents and Old Jonah.

We never managed to find out whether these three boys had their billet changed, because that did happen sometimes, but not often. Anyway, they were back.

On the Monday morning we were schooling in a vacant classroom at the village school. These three lads were stood out in front of the school at assembly and Old Jonah went to town on them. All these well known phrases that we'd all come to know and love so well – anti-British, ungrateful, thoughtless, selfish, stupid – they were all trotted out – letting the school down, breaking the law. He went on to say that "in times like these the police have got more important things to do than run around after silly little boys". This was of course true.

There was all the usual stuff about helping the Germans, and it had ruined his weekend. I wasn't clear as to which was the worst offence. All this lasted about an hour.

Their punishment was that during morning and afternoon break times, they would stay in class wherever it was held and do some set written work; the same applied as soon as they'd finished the midday meal in the hut. No playing around, back to the class. It soon all blew over.

As time went on, there were other attempts by kids to get back home, for one reason or another, but this was the first and had the greatest impact.

Now, I'm going to jump ahead of myself by a few weeks, because these same three boys, along with a few others, got themselves into hot water again. A lot of fuss was made of what I thought at the time was a silly, harmless schoolboy prank. I thought it was amusing at the time, and I still do.

The three 'naughty boys', plus about five friends, and I'm going to call this group "The Tribe", came up with an idea for what they thought was a joke.

Each day after being dismissed from the 'dinner hut', there was quite a long period for play. This allowed Old Jonah time to get back to wherever he was living and have lunch with his wife and daughter.

"The Tribe" must have spent a couple of days preparing for this joke, and on the day that they were ready they slipped away from the playground, as was usual for them. They pulled up a lot of bracken and tucked the stems into their trouser belts, thereby making the bracken look like grass skirts. Those wearing long trousers rolled the legs up. Some took off their shirts and nearly all of them tied something around their foreheads and stuck shorter pieces of bracken to make headdresses. They had already spent a couple of lunchtimes making spears, clubs and bows and arrows. With a bit of moist mud smeared on their faces, they looked the part. You can see why I called them "The Tribe".

Apart from "The Tribe" nobody else knew anything about this, and the rest of us were in the playground doing our own thing. Bearing in mind the golden rule that it's us Londoners on one side of the playground and village children on the other.

The plan was that "The Tribe" would make a mock attack on the village school. To do this they would have to go through the churchyard; there was no other way.

Everybody was minding their own business when suddenly all hell broke loose and "The Tribe" came rampaging through the churchyard and into the school playground. It was so realistic that some of the village girls started to cry and scream and run for cover.

Unfortunately for "The Tribe", the formidable Mrs Montiefiore was in the church arranging flowers, or some such thing. Upon hearing the commotion, she went outside to investigate. She later claimed that she, Mrs Montiefiore, "was nearly knocked off her feet by these savages!" Oh dear!

She gathered up her belongings and headed for her home at Dane Hill. She was going to do something about this outrage. She stomped out of the church and churchyard into Church Lane, and who should she almost bump into but Old Jonah on his way back from his lunch. He was in a good mood – that didn't last for much longer.

His smile and his good afternoon greeting were soon wiped off his face, and he soon found out that it wasn't such a good afternoon after all.

We understood from what we heard from him afterwards that Mrs Montiefiore didn't mince her words. She let him have both barrels at point blank range, and he just had to stand there and take it.

While Mrs Montiefiore and Old Jonah were having their "little chat", most of us London kids were having a good laugh about what had happened. Only "The Tribe" knew of the encounter with Mrs Montiefiore and they kept it to themselves.

The gate between the churchyard and school playground flew open and in strode Old Jonah, and he was hopping mad! He was bright red in colour and so angry he was almost unable to speak. He saw "The Tribe" standing there in their tribal costumes and growled. "Get yourselves tidied up at once, then come and see me!" Off they went.

He then ordered our whole school, juniors and seniors, into the classroom immediately. When "The Tribe" had tidied themselves up they sheepishly appeared and were lined up in front of the assembly.

Never before or since have I seen Old Jonah so angry. The haranguing that he gave for "The Great Escape" was but a warm up for what followed now.

It appears that Mrs Montiefiore told him she was fed up with antics of his London 'savages', "who seem to delight in causing trouble, intimidating the local population, and worst of all, desecrating their lovely churchyard." Poor Old Jonah went on, "It's my job to look after you boys, and I do try to stand up for you all, but in this case I can't because I agree with them, this was well out of order!"

He went on, "You must know that most people here are watching you like hawks, just waiting for somebody to do something silly like this, and you lot go and hand it to them on a plate. I just about despair of the lot of you sometimes!"

He then set the same sort of punishment as before but for a longer period; I don't remember how long it was. The only recreation they were allowed was working on the school allotment at the Nissen hut; this was still going strong, under Mr Thew.

One final point about all this, because I was confused again. It's about the churchyard being desecrated. Now, I thought that desecrated was a sort of finely ground coconut that my mother used when making cakes. I didn't see how you can do that to a churchyard. I'm not surprised some of us get into trouble; we don't know what the adults are talking about half the time! I do wish they would speak English.

20. Let's Go Punting

Whilst all the happenings were going on at our boys school, sister Kitty was settling in at her new school in Haywards Heath. I've no idea what it was called, it was just 'Kit's School'. She was very adaptable and seemed to have taken the move in her stride. She'd got her pass for the special school bus and it wasn't long before she got herself involved in a lot of the school's activities and was coming back to Wickens in the evening saying how much she loved it. Loves school? She must be barmy!

The 10th of May was Gran's birthday and there's no way we could forget that. So we bought a birthday card which Kit, Jim and I all wrote something in and Kitty put in a very short letter saying that we hoped Granddad would be well enough to be out of hospital soon, and sent it off.

Within a few days we had a letter saying that Mum and Dad would be coming down to visit us on Sunday; don't worry about meeting the bus as they would be using Mr Cole's (Dad's boss) car.

Sunday morning arrived, so did the car with Mum and Dad, and also much to our delight Gran was with them. After the hugs and kisses of hello, it was quickly explained to us that our Grandfather had died of cancer. The funeral had only been a couple of days before, and the idea was that seeing us three grandchildren again after all these months might cheer Gran up a bit.

It was a lovely sunny mid May day, warm enough to have a picnic lunch in Mrs Ashby's lovely garden. My Gran grew up in Somerset so was a country girl at heart. We showed her the rabbits, by now there were also some chickens, the golden pheasant, the goldfish pond, the aviaries – we showed her everything.

During our picnic lunch, I told Gran that just outside the main gate at the end of the drive I had found a robin's nest; it was in last year's long grass – it had three eggs in it.

Gran asked if when we'd finished the picnic I would show it to her. She said "I haven't seen a robin's nest since I was a girl". Everybody wanted to come and see, but Gran said, "No, just Geoffrey and I. Too many people will frighten the mother away." That's it; Gran had spoken, so we went on our little walk. The hen was not sitting on the eggs and Gran was able to see those three little pale blue eggs. She seemed to enjoy that. Then she made us wait to make sure that the hen returned to sit on the eggs again.

Many years later, when I was married and had children of my own, I was talking to Gran about my years of evacuation, and she reminded me of our little walk, the robin's nest and those three eggs. Gran had not forgotten either.

It has to be said that Nelly and Hetty were super to Gran that day; made her welcome and rather fussed over her. All in all, considering the circumstances, the day went off quite well. Once again, another big thank you to good boss, Mr Cole.

That visit from Gran was the first time we had seen her since leaving her on Clapham Junction the morning we left London. It really had been lovely to see her again. I do so hope that seeing us three kids for a few hours helped her in some way and took her mind off of the loss of our dear Grandfather, even for just a little while. He was a lovely man. I wish I'd been old enough to know him better.

During the visit, Jim had told Gran that he, Len and Billy were saving whatever money that they managed to earn on fruit picking and any other odd-jobs that they were offered. With this money they were going to get themselves second-hand bikes, so's they could cycle to and fro to school instead of walking. "What about Geoffrey? What's he going to do?" asked Gran. Jim explained that he would get a carrier and put over the back wheel for me to sit on. Gran wasn't very happy about that. "Don't you worry", she told me, "I'll get you a little bike. It won't be new but I'll have it done up and send it down to you, as soon as I can." That was a typical Gran gesture. I would have to wait a bit but it was something to look forward to.

Once the visit from Gran was over, life got back into its normal swing again, as it always did.

It was during May of 1940 that the Government introduced a thing called 'Double British Summer Time'. This was a scheme where the clocks, instead of going forward one hour, were put forward two hours, thereby keeping it daylight until quite late in the evening.

The idea behind this was to give farmers longer to harvest crops that were urgently needed, whilst the crops were dry. Because of the strict blackout, no lighting could be used. The idea was fine for farmers but it made getting to sleep at night in broad daylight very difficult. Governments don't stop to think about things like that, do they?

But, looking on the bright side, it also gave us more time messing about outside in the evenings.

Now, down in the corner of the potato field that we called 'Moan Corner', there was a little gateway leading into Mr Macmillan's land – it was all woodland.

We had never gone through that gateway and one evening we were a bit bored so we thought we would give it a go, so through it we went.

These woods seemed to go on forever, then we came upon a nice little stream with some very small fish in it. Of course, Billy knew what they were – he was a right 'clever Dick'. He said they were Minnows. We spent the rest of the evening laying on our stomachs trying to catch some, and we did too. But as soon as we caught them Len insisted that we throw them back in, which we did – no point in just killing them.

We went back again for the next couple of evenings but the novelty was wearing off, so we pushed on deeper into the woods and we came to one of the Macmillan lakes, and we realised that this was where we had come with Mr Michael, ice skating in the winter. As the weather was warmer now, we had a better look around.

We discovered there was a boathouse. How could we have missed that the first time round? Like the pony trap shelter, it was there just waiting to be explored, so that's just what we did. Inside we found a punt, not in great shape, it has to be said, but at least it floated. Should we try taking it out on the lake, it was discussed, and although we had no idea what the time was, we knew it was getting a bit late. So it was decided to leave our cruise until tomorrow evening, but try to make an earlier start, and not a word to anybody.

The next evening could not come quick enough, but when it did we got away as quickly as we could and got down to 'our boat'.

Right from the start, Billy, who was always full of chat, announced that he would be the captain. That's in spite of the fact that Jim had been in the Sea Cadets for two years. Well, Jim wasn't too bothered about who was captain – he wasn't the pushy sort.

Getting the punt out and afloat was no trouble at all; the trouble was that we couldn't find the punting pole, but we did find some short lengths of planking that could be used as paddles. Soon we pushed off and were afloat.

It was Len and Jim, one paddling on each side (port and starboard); Billy at the back (the stern) using a piece of plank to try to steer. Me, I was the passenger. All was going well; we were making good headway. We were now about 20 to 30 yards from the bank. Yes, this was the life; punting was great fun! Well, it was until we started sinking!

Once the alarm had been raised, it's difficult to find the right words to describe the scene, but panic would be very high on the list. The three elders were trying to reassure me that everything will be alright, and were being very brave.

Now, I don't do brave. I specialise in panic, and I do it very well. So, I thought, seeing as how Billy is the captain, he's the one to go down with his ship, so I'll say cheerio to him first, but not before I've pointed out that in these sort of circumstances it's women and children first and, as there's no women aboard and I'm by far the youngest, it's his job to save me before he goes down. He just told me to shut up. That's not the way the Captain should speak to a passenger, is it? It's not nice!

We just about reached the bank before the boat filled up and we leapt ashore with great relief. Some socks and shoes got a bit wet but we thought we could get away with it.

Then we had to empty the water out of the punt before we could put it back into the boathouse. There was a lot of twaddle talked about repairing the punt; if we could paint the bottom with tar. Where were we going to get tar from? What a daft idea, and why should we repair his punt anyway? Just forget it, and that's what we did. Nobody ever found out about the punting incident, so you won't tell anybody, will you?

21. La La Time

Still this steady stream of people kept coming that we were told were important refugees, not all the time just a few here and there. Always the pattern was the same, stay for one or two days then suddenly they'd be gone. Always very quiet, and keeping very much to themselves, always very polite.

As mentioned before, the Aaron family stayed longer than usual, the only other couple to do so were Doctor and Mrs Ongar.

It would be about the second half of May when we first met the Ongar's. We were all in the garden when Mrs Ashby brought them over to where we were and introduced them to us.

The doctor was a man of about forty to forty-five years old; it's difficult to guess ages when you are only nine, but even at that age I was impressed by his manner of dressing. He was extremely smart. Everything about him was crisp, his manner, everything. If somebody had told me that he was a military man in civilian clothes I would have believed them. He spoke very good English, was pleasant and friendly and came across as a very nice man.

His wife, Mrs Ongar, was, I guess, maybe ten years, maybe more, younger than the doctor. She was quite slim, fair-haired – a very pleasant looking lady; smartly dressed, she had a very friendly personality, but her English was very poor. They chatted to us as best they could for a short while, then Mrs Ashby continued showing them around. Us kids got on with whatever we were doing, and thought no more about it.

The next morning, Kitty and I had been to Mr Billings' shack for some reason and on the way back to the house we bumped into the Ongar's who were taking a morning stroll in the garden. We said, "Good morning". They replied and Kit and I went to move on but the Ongar's seemed as though they wanted to talk, which was most unusual for refugees.

So, we stood and talked to them, or Kitty did. I left all the talking to her. I didn't want to make a fool of myself by stuttering; I wasn't very good in situations like this. Then, Mrs Ongar, noticing that I wasn't saying anything, spoke to me directly, and waited for an answer. I went bright red and tried to answer, but I'm afraid I made a right mess of it.

Seeing and hearing this, Mrs Ongar looked at Kitty enquiringly and Kit explained as best she could (this was not easy because of the language barrier) – the doctor had to step in and help out.

It seemed that Mrs Ongar understood but could not get her tongue around the word 'stutter' and it always seemed to come out 'sut-ter'. She moved over and stood beside me, slipped her arm around my shoulders, gave me a little hug and said, "Poor Geoffrey, I will help you". I was feeling better already and after a few more moments Kit and I went on our way.

The next day was Monday, so it was back to school as usual and I thought no more about the matter. Upon getting back to Wickens, after an uneventful day at the Nissen hut, I was just killing time really. It was no good going to find my playmate, Arthur Jay, who lived just further up Birch Grove, because he goes to school in Haywards Heath and it takes him a lot longer to get home. Then by the time he's changed his clothes and had his tea it's well into the evening before he's allowed out to play. So, as I say, I was killing time.

Along came Mrs Ongar. Now I cannot hope to write her broken English way of speaking, but I'll do my best.

"Geoffrey, I have been looking for you. I would like to talk to you. Is that alright?" I nod. "Can we go and sit down somewhere?"

I nod again – I'm not feeling very chatty because I'm not sure what's coming next.

"Have you been to school today?"

"Yes."

"Was it good?"

"It was all right."

"Geoffrey, I need some help, and I was wondering if you would help me. Would you be prepared to help me?"

All this took a long time to say because there were a lot of mistakes and stumbles on the way.

"Yes, I'll help if I can. What do you want me to do?"

"I would like you to teach me to speak better English. Would you do that for me?"

I thought, 'O Lord!' Here's another one that's crackers, and she seemed like such a nice lady. I just could not believe what I had just heard. I'd never heard anything so daft in my short life. There must be something in the water here that makes people go funny. I'd better watch out.

She must have seen the look of incredulity on my face; this was crazy. "Geoffrey, I know you can do this, you helping me; talking to me will help your sut-ter."

I couldn't see it, "You would be better to ask my sister, Kitty, to help you."

"I don't want Kitty to help me. We will help each other. Wait, look what is this called in English?" And she pointed to a wheelbarrow near where we were sitting.

"Wheelbarrow."

"Veelbarrah."

"No, wh, wh, wheel."

After three or four attempts she got 'wheel' right, then she got 'barrow' right. We joined it together and she got 'wheelbarrow' right. She was so excited.

"You see Geoffrey, you can do it. You teach me wheelbarrow. You can teach me other words, please say you will try."

"OK, we'll give it a try."

"Thank you Geoffrey, you will not be sorry, it will be fun. We start tomorrow."

Deep down, I couldn't help but wonder what I'd let myself in for. She'll soon get fed up with it, and anyway these refugees never stay more than a few days. We talked for quite a bit longer. I had to admit I liked this lady. During our talk I was stuttering quite a lot. Mrs Ongar said, "This is where I help you. You must talk more slowly Geoffrey, slowly, and when you sut-ter, stop, take a deep breath and as you breathe out start talking again, but slowly Geoffrey, slowly."

All next day whilst at school I kept wondering how this was going to work. I wasn't at all happy about it. Maybe by the time I get back from school they will have gone; these refugees have a habit of going very suddenly. But soon after I got back to Wickens and we had had our tea I went into the garden as usual and Mrs Ongar was there, waiting.

"Are you ready, Geoffrey?"

"I suppose so, what do we do?"

"We go for a walk, and we talk, don't worry, it's easy."

This really wasn't going to be easy, because she spoke English quite badly. Every sentence was a struggle for her to speak, and me to understand but, in turn, she could not understand what I was trying to say to her. There was an awful lot of stopping; hand and arm gesticulations and miming went on and somehow it was working – we were getting on OK. The first walks were in the Ashby grounds, and as we walked and talked she would suddenly stop and point to something that caught her eye.

"What is this called?" It might be a garden tool or a beehive, a gateway or gatepost, and it was my job to tell her the name of the object. She would repeat it over and over again until she got it right.

Near enough was not good enough. She was very hard on herself. It had to be exactly right. When she thought it was time we would turn around and go back on the same route. On the way back, I had to test her on the items that she had learned on the outward trip. She didn't get many wrong. But that was the easy bit; the hard part was the conversation between each item. Sometimes we got ourselves in such a tangle with our words and miming, we could only stand there and laugh ourselves silly. She had been right; it was fun!

I could write pages and pages of what happened during those talk walks, but I will not bore you. However, I will write one instance just to give you some idea as to what I'm talking about.

On one of the earlier walks we were going through the usual routine but by now we had ventured outside Ashby's land and were roaming all over the place. If at any time I started to stutter I would get the warning, "Slowly, Geoffrey, slowly."

On this occasion, she suddenly stopped walking and said, "Geoffrey, can you la-la?" What's she on about now? What's la-la? I shrugged and put on my blank look. We stood there in the road united only in our bewilderment as to what the hell we were supposed to be talking to each other about. It was stalemate.

Then she had an idea. "La-la", she said, and started to softly sing a song in her own language, then stopped and said, "Music words."

"Do you mean singing?"

"Yes Geoffrey, can you sing?"

"A bit."

"Sing for me, just a short bit."

"Why?"

"It is important, please sing."

I was very self-conscious about this but sang a few lines from a school song that I'd remembered.

"You should sing more often Geoffrey, you sing good; it will help you a lot."

"How?"

"Nobody ever sut-ters when they sing."

I thought about it, and she was right. I'd never worked that out for myself.

She went on to explain that it's to do with the way you breathe when you sing. This woman was no fool. Of course if you don't breathe you won't stutter either, but I don't think that's quite what she meant.

Another thing she told me was don't try to fight a stutter; if you get stuck just stop, relax, breathe deeply and start again. The harder you try to push those words out the worse it gets, and she once again was right.

All the time the Ongar's were there she never missed a day of these so-called lessons. There was one very big shed, large enough to be a workshop; if it rained we went in there, and went through the whole range of tools, the roof, floor, beams, screws, nails, the whole lot, and on the way there were plenty of laughs.

What the doctor was doing during these times I've no idea. He was still staying at Wickens because he was there for dinner with the Ashby's in the evenings. That's if the Ashby's were there themselves. Whether he went out early every morning, or whether he was in the house writing, there's no way of knowing.

These daily lessons went on every day all the time she was at Wickens. Everybody teased me and pulled my leg a great deal. This was because if Mrs Ongar could not find me in or around the garden at any time, she would come around to the back door and say, "I cannot find Geoffrey anywhere. Is he in there?" Then Hetty would come and find me, saying "Your lady friend wants to know are you going out to play", and off I would go like a little puppy dog with two tails, both of them wagging.

You see, it was almost unheard of for a houseguest to come to the back door, but they had to get used to it.

The stuttering seemed to be getting less of a problem; whether this was down to the breathing and 'slowly, slowly', one cannot be sure. Personally, I put a lot of it down to the fact that, with her, I felt completely at ease and relaxed. After the first few days, I didn't have to watch my 'P's' and 'Q's'; I felt I was doing something useful – I could be me! But most probably it was a combination of the two. In a nutshell, I was quite happy.

Don't think you've read the last of Mrs Ongar, because you haven't!

22. On a Bicycle Made For Two

Right from the very first on our wanderings around discovering and exploring the local countryside, we had noticed this tendency for people to just dump things in ditches, hedgerows, or the corners of fields or in the woods. This was nowhere near the scale that fly tipping is today and, for the most part, it was just the one odd item. A very large percentage of this junk was bicycle parts, frames, front forks, front and rear wheels.

All these parts started an idea in the head of one of "The Elders"; you can guess what it is.

"Let's build ourselves a bike."

"Yeah, it would be handy, wouldn't it?"

"Do you think we can do it?"

"Of course we can – may have to buy a few bits but there's enough stuff laying around to give us a good start. Who's going to have it though?"

"We'll share it."

"Good idea."

So the idea was born, and as we explored we also hunted, not for big game, or even little game, but for cycle parts. Not that it had everything to do with me!

Whatever sort of contraption they built, it would be too big for me, but I was quite happy to help out if I could.

The first bit of luck they had was they found a frame with the front forks still on, no handlebars, but you can't have everything. This was where brother Jim stepped into the limelight. This was right up his street. He was good at this type of thing; in no time at all he had the front forks off, checked and greased all the ball bearings, and the same with the spindle that takes the pedals. Then a half decent back wheel was found. Again, Jim checked it over and cleaned it up as best he could. Now the search was on for a half decent front wheel of the same size.

But while all this was going on they had started to work out what these 'few bits' were that they were going to have to buy, and it was more than they had bargained for. They'd found a pair of old handlebars, but it still left saddle, mudguards, pedals, brakes, bike chain and many other things that I've forgotten. It looked as if business was about to pick up for the Sweeney Todd of the bike world at Chelwood Gate.

At last a front wheel was found of the right size. Jim duly checked it over and it was fitted into place; it was beginning to look a bit like a bicycle.

It is possible that I am giving the impression that this all happened suddenly, and that would be quite wrong. The idea was conceived very early in our walkabouts and the pieces picked up as and when found, if they fitted the bill. The work that Jim did was done in the big shed / workshop that I've already mentioned. The parts we kept in an old caravan that was parked or dumped near Mr Billings' shack; this we used sometimes and I'll tell you more about it later.

As we came into the spring, with the summer to look forward to, the appeal of having a bicycle to use now and then began to look more attractive so "The Elders" decided to push on a bit and start spending some of their hard earned money.

They thought that there was no chance of finding a saddle that would be fit for use, so that would be the first item on the list to buy. So, one Saturday afternoon they went to Sweeney Todd's in Chelwood Gate to buy one.

My playmate, Arthur Jay and I were building ourselves a sort of hideaway den in the Ashby field, in which we played. We were using sticks and last year's bracken; it was coming along nicely. So when the Elders went shopping, I stayed behind with Arthur and we worked on our den. If I remember rightly, they came back with quite a good second-hand saddle that Sweeney had let them have cheaply. There was a rush to get the saddle fitted; yes, everything was shaping up nicely.

By now, Nelly and Hetty had got wind of what was going on, and they didn't really approve. For no other reason that they thought the Elders were wasting their money. They didn't interfere but said, "It's your money but we do think you are being silly and wasting it." Nobody took any notice.

Although we all spent a lot of our spare time together, at other times we went our separate ways and did our own thing; in my case, knocking around with Arthur, who was more my age. What the others got up to I don't know, 'cos I wasn't there, was I?

One afternoon there seemed to be only Len and I there, hanging around, at a loose end. Then Len said, "Let's go and look at the bike." Well, I'd got no better ideas, so off we went.

When we got to the caravan we got 'the bike' out. It didn't look too bad, but it didn't look all that good either.

"Let's try it out" said Len.

"Don't be daft, it's got no pedals, chain or brakes."

"Well, if you were to push, it wouldn't need chain or pedals, and if I'm careful, we won't need brakes."

"So you sit and ride, while I do the pushing? No way, I'm not daft."

"If I give you sixpence, will you push?"

"No."

"If I give you a shilling?"

"OK, but not too far." We had a deal.

We got this monstrous looking contraption out onto the road, Len climbed aboard and off we went.

Now, remember that apart from the other little luxuries that this 'so called' bicycle didn't have, it also didn't have the luxury of inner tubes and tyres. The one thing it certainly did not need was a bell.

With the clank, clank, clank it was making as it went along, you'd have heard it from a mile away. It was making enough noise to be a tank.

We reached the top of Twyford Hill where Kit and I had gone to that horrible school and, by now, I needed a breather. Len was enjoying himself; I thought I was being under-paid!

Twyford really was a ford, at the bottom of the hill. The ford ran across the roadway, and the traffic, such as it was, would have to splash through it. There was a very nice wooden footbridge for pedestrians and a short stretch of tarmac footpath leading you onto the footbridge, on either side.

When I'd got my breath back, Len suggested, "Look, it's downhill from here on; if you get on the crossbar you can have a ride too."

"Do I still get me shilling?"

"Yes."

Now, I knew this area better than Len, having been to the school here. I don't think he realised just how steep this hill was, with a sharp right-hand turn at the bottom, just before you go through the ford. It was very stupid of me not to tell him, but I wanted a ride. I think I did mention something about no brakes, but Len thought he could slow us down by using his foot. OK, let's go!

It wasn't a comfortable ride; lots of bumps, but it was better than pushing, or so I thought. The beginning was all right but as we began to gain speed I was starting to think that this was not going to be one of our better ideas. Soon, we were shooting down this hill at an alarming rate. I hoped Len had got his eyes open, 'cos I know I hadn't. I took a quick peek; that sharp right-hand corner was approaching very fast. It occurred to me that Len might not even know about the ford crossing the road – no matter, he was soon going to find out!

As we turned the corner, Len saw that he had to make a decision; through the water or over the footbridge. He chose the bridge.

What Len didn't see or know was that, because this was a very minor, little used road, there were a lot of very weedy grass verges on both sides of the road and this verge was hiding quite steep kerbstones along the edges of the tarmac path approach. We were still going at full speed when we hit the kerb; the bike came to a sudden halt – we didn't!

In many ways it was very reminiscent of Raleigh's flights; the only difference being that Raleigh went solo, whereas Len and I had each other for company. Such was this companionship that we both landed at the same place in the hedge.

We set about sorting ourselves out; we were lucky, just a few small grazes and scratches; no need for spit and dirty hanky. There was plenty of water there, waiting to cross the road, no real damage done. Wish I could say the same for the bike – the front wheel was a mess. It was quite clear that Jim was not going to be very impressed with the way we had realigned that wheel.

I was right about Jim. He wasn't very happy. There were times when Jim could be a bit short on temper; he chose this to be one of them. To be honest, he was hopping mad and the trouble was he had every right to be, because he had put much more into this bike thing than the other two.

To his credit, Len just stood and took it, offered no excuses, even offered to try to buy another wheel, second-hand, but for a while Jim was inconsolable; it was war!

In all the time that us five kids were together we had very, very few disputes; of that few, this one was by far the worst. Jim felt that the trust we had in each other had been broken, and I suppose he was right.

When we went in and sat down for our tea that afternoon, there was a stony silence instead of the usual chatter; it was not a very nice atmosphere. It is not therefore surprising that Hetty noticed that something was wrong. She had to keep bobbing to and fro through the room in which us kids eat, as she had to serve the Ashby's their meals, and there was always a lot of banter and backchat as she did this, but not today.

So she stopped, "Come on, what's the matter? Who's upset who?" Nobody answered. Hetty sat down in one of the armchairs. "Well, I'm not moving from here until we've got to the bottom of this, because we are not having this all evening, so somebody better start talking."

It was no good asking Kit; she wasn't there, and it's nothing to do with her anyway. Much the same went for Billy, except he had a small interest in the bike. Jim refused to discuss the matter; he was too annoyed about it. Len didn't want to admit what a silly thing he had done.

Me? No good asking me, I stutter, don't I?!

Bit by bit, Hetty coaxed the story out; by now she'd been joined by Nelly, who could hear that something was amiss. She sat in the other armchair and they both sat, listened and asked questions. Somewhere in the telling, both Len and I forgot to mention one or two things; things like the steep hill, the ford and bridge, and above all else the kerbstones. How could we forget that? Must have been delayed shock. The story somehow came out that, going over some grass verge, Len hit a large boulder that neither of us saw; funny thing, shock. But Len seemed to be more in shock that I was because he also forgot to pay me my shilling!

When the sisters had heard what they thought was the story, they didn't exactly say "We told you so", but something very close to it. They didn't really need to tell Len and I that we were in the wrong and that Jim had every right to be annoyed; we already knew that, but they told us anyway. Then they came out with their suggestion.

"Why don't you stop chucking your money away on that load of old junk, and the three elders save the money that they sometimes get sent from home, their beating and fruit-picking money and each buy themselves a second-hand bike? They are not too expensive and there's plenty of shed room around here for you to keep them in."

"Think about it; you'll be able to cycle to and fro to school and back, plus it will give you much more scope to get out and about in your free time." The elders took some convincing but, in the end, all agreed that it made a lot of sense and all agreed to give it a try.

The row between Jim and Len rattled on for a few more days but petered out and it became a race between the elders as to who could get their bicycle first. A sort of bicycle race.

This was the news that Jim was telling Gran when she visited us in May. Gran said she would help Jim out if she could, as well as saying that she would get me a small bike and send it down – good old Gran!

In case anybody is thinking, "That's all very well, but poor little Kitty has been forgotten"; well, she hasn't. Because Kit had to catch the special school bus from Horsted Keynes every weekday morning, if we were walking she would have to leave quite a bit earlier than us boys. Now Mrs Ashby had an almost brand new bicycle, which she would use if she wanted some local shopping, like Mr Dovey's further up Birch Grove, but mostly the bike was hardly used.

The offer was made to Kitty that when Mrs Ashby was not in residence Kit could use Mrs Ashby's bike to get to and fro for the bus each day. But if there was ever any damage done to the bike, this privilege would be stopped at once. Also, Mrs Ashby had made arrangements with the garage on the village green, from who she hired all the chauffeur driven cars that she and Mr Ashby used, that Kit could leave the bicycle there for safe keeping during the day, ready for the return trip each evening. So, that's Kitty taken care of. She was so careful and the privilege was never withdrawn.

Now all I had to do was wait for my noble steed and, in the meantime, keep walking.

23. Round Up Time

By now we were into late May, early June 1940, and the weather was lovely. Every dawn seemed to bring a lovely, bright, sunny day with clear blue skies, and with this double British Summer Time, the days were longer; they seemed to go on forever. Of course, that's my memory playing tricks on me; common sense tells me that it must have rained sometimes, but with the longer daylight hours it did seem as though Sussex was the county on which the sun never set.

The Wickens tame rabbit population had grown very large, very quickly, and was forever increasing. It would be impossible to give the number of rabbits that there were now, the number could range anywhere between forty and sixty. All these rabbits had hutches for the night-time, but during the day ran loose in large wire compounds or enclosures made of wire netting, and the hutches would be inside the compounds. These compounds were set up in any area where the grass seemed semi-rough; places like the orchard.

Each evening, all the bunnies had to be caught and put into their hutches for the night. In the autumn, winter and spring, this was always done by the time we got back from school and had our tea, and sorted ourselves out.

But with the longer evenings 'round-up time' became later and later. This was much to the annoyance of Mr Billings and 'Old George' who understandably didn't want to be too late finishing their work. They wanted to be finished and get to the pub for a drink before all the soldiers got there first and drank the lot! So they were not too happy about this bunny chasing, so us kids got roped in to help. We loved it, because these netted compounds were quite large and these rabbits could really give you quite a run around; to catch all the rabbits could take quite a long time – precious drinking time ticking away.

Don't get me wrong, they were not a couple of old drunks, they just liked a drink in the evening. The village had the nearest pub and, as I've said many times before, it was a long walk so the sooner they got started the better.

This ritual of rabbit catching became known as 'round up time' and us kids looked forward to it. The big snag in all this was there were about three of these enclosures and from time to time they would have to be moved around into fresh grass.

Nearly always in the enclosure would be a clump of closely growing bushes or shrubs, into which the rabbits would run and hide. No amount of shaking of the bushes would get them out; in fact it only frightened them, so sticks and poles would be fetched and, with a lot of poking and prodding, they could be reached and put into the hutch for the night. This made for a lot of wasted time and frustration on Mr Billings and Old George's part.

One evening during the round up, Mrs Ongar came walking by and enquired what was going on; she asked if she could help and her offer was gladly accepted. It all went as normal until the last bit – the hideaways in the bushes. She very calmly but firmly put a stop to the poking and prodding with sticks. "I will show you", she said.

She told everybody to keep very still and make no noise, then she crouched down and started talking to the rabbits in a very low pitched sing-song voice, almost like crooning. It was a mixture of her own brand of broken English mixed with her own native language. It was fascinating to listen to – I don't know what effect it was having on the rabbits, but I was completely mesmerised; it was almost hypnotic.

It went something like this:

"Come on my darling, it's alright, we are not going to hurt you. Come, come, it's alright, we keep you safe for the night. That's right, come on, nothing to be frightened of is there? You are quite safe with us, there's no danger, it's all alright. That's right, come to me my darling because we are not going to hurt you. That's right, come along, come along."

This, as I say, was done in a musical sing-song crooning voice; a mixture of English and her own language; it was quite fascinating and I could have knelt there and listened to it for hours on end.

There was one word in particular from her own language that she kept repeating over and over again. That word was "malutki" – I'll never forget that word. Repeatedly she would say this "malutki, malutki darling come on then."

All the time her eyes would be fixed on one rabbit, talking to it; she was like a horse whisperer, but for rabbits.

Then, slowly, almost imperceptively, the rabbit would start to edge toward her. Even though you were watching very closely you wouldn't see it, but it moved nevertheless. There would be just the faintest ripple of muscle under the fur and it would move forward a fraction of an inch. She kept talking, the rabbit moved slowly, closer and closer to her until she was able to reach out and gently pick it up. Then she would hold it up in front of her face, look it in the eyes and say, "There you are, I told you we would not hurt you. I'll see you tomorrow." She would then hand the rabbit to one of us kids to put it into its hutch. Then it was 'eyes down' and start all over again, and this went on until all the rabbits were tucked up for the night.

This became a regular routine every evening, with Mrs Ongar coming to help. Except there was one slight difference, and that was that Mrs Ongar would not bother with chasing the rabbits around, but would get straight on with the malutki malutki bit, and guess who was her little helper? Me! By doing it this way, it cut down the time by quite a lot, so for a while everybody was happy.

You will note that I used the term 'for a while'; you see I was about to change all that.

Once the rabbits were housed every evening, we would go indoors and have to start thinking about going to bed because time would be getting on. The trouble was that because of British Summer Time it was still broad daylight and you didn't feel tired. Also, being the youngest, I always was first on the list to get washed and ready for bed.

So, one evening as the 'rabbit whispering' went on and I was being handed the captives to be hutched, I had this idea to prolonging the evening's events by accidentally forgetting to fasten the catch on the hutch door. Then I went back to help Mrs Ongar.

Suddenly, there was a mighty roar; Mrs Ongar and I looked at each other. "I wonder what is the matter?" she asked. I think I knew.

There was Mr Billings on the other side of the bushes. What was up? He's gone bright red, and I could swear that there was steam coming out of his ears; and why is he glaring at me like that with those mad, staring eyes?

"Somebody has left the catch undone and all the bloody rabbits are getting out!" he thundered, still looking at me.

Both Mrs Ongar and I stood up; I felt quite safe. The bushes were too wide for him to be able to grab me around the throat. Boy, you could see that he was absolutely furious and still wouldn't take his eyes off me!

Up spoke Mrs Ongar. "I'm sure that whoever did it didn't do it on purpose. How you say? It was a mistake."

Mr Billings transferred the long, hostile glare in her direction. As Mrs Ongar was a houseguest, he had to be careful what he said, so he said nothing, just kept up the long glare for a few more moments, turned away and, muttering under his breath, slowly walked away.

Did I imagine it, or were there little vapour trails of steam still coming from his ears?

With the immediate crisis over, Mrs Ongar and I returned to what we were doing. She let it go for a while then quietly said, "Geoffrey, I think it might be better if you went indoors." She put her finger to her lips to show it should be done quietly. "I'll see you tomorrow. Goodnight." And I quietly slipped away.

The next day on our usual walk and talk, she suddenly asked, "Did you leave the door to the rabbit house open on purpose last night, Geoffrey?"

I admitted, "Yes I did."

"Why?"

"Once that's finished, I have to go to bed, and I didn't want to do that."

She slipped her arm around my shoulders and gave me a little hug as we walked along, and she chuckled as she said, "That was a very naughty thing to do Geoffrey." I just wish all reprimands could be done so pleasantly.

After that, Mr Billings would allow me to help up till the last few, then it was 'goodnight Geoffrey'.

I was very careful not to upset Mr Billings again, because as he stood at that clump of bushes I don't know what effect it had on the rabbits, but it sure scared the hell out of me.

24. Goodbye Mrs Ongar

This is the part I have not been looking forward to writing, but when I started all this writing, I promised myself that everything that I wrote would be the truth, as far as my memory allows; that includes unpleasant things as well, and I do not enjoy what follows one little bit.

Of all the people that stayed at Wickens, like houseguests, the Ashby's friends and refugees, Doctor and Mrs Ongar had been there the longest, by a long way; that is apart from us evacuees. The Ongars had been staying there now for about a month.

Although they seemed to get on very well with everybody, and that includes the staff, questions were being asked in the kitchen as to how much longer this could go on for.

Then, one morning, with the sun shining as usual, all five of us kids were down in 'Moan Corner' by the goldfish pond at the bottom of the potato field. It was a weekday and I can't remember for the life of me why us kids weren't at school; it must have been some sort of holiday, but what, I don't know.

It was not unusual for us all to be in 'Moan Corner' altogether; it had become a meeting point away from the house and adults, where we could talk without being overheard. Sometimes it was grumbles about this or that, hence the name. The time was about nine o'clock.

The three Elders were just killing time before going fruit picking to earn 'bike money'. I was deemed too young to go fruit picking, so would have to amuse myself. Don't ask me what Kitty was going to do; we never knew where Kit was going or what she was up to – she had friends nearby and kept out of trouble.

Then we noticed Mrs Ongar walking down the path beside the potato field towards us; she was carrying a parcel. As she approached she said, "I have been looking for you all." We all waited, wondering why she wanted to see all of us.

She continued. "My husband has to go away suddenly and I have come to say goodbye."

I didn't want to hear this; this was bad news. I just couldn't believe what I was hearing – I was stunned. We had had such pleasant, happy times walking together over the last month, and now she's saying it's over. I started to cry.

First, Mrs Ongar went to Billy, Len and Jim. She spent a few moments talking to them in a low voice, shook hands with them and they turned and walked away to go to their fruit picking.

Next she went to Kitty, who she'd got to know a little better than the Elders. They talked a while then Mrs Ongar gave Kit a hug, and turned to me. I wasn't ready for this.

We sat down on the bench that was there. Kitty had stepped back, but not gone away.

"Geoffrey, I have enjoyed our walks and talks so much. Thank you for helping me with my English."

By now, I was in a terrible state of crying. I was trying to speak but was getting myself so tongue-tied with crying and stuttering, the words just wouldn't come out. She took hold of my shoulders, saying, "Always remember what I've taught you – slowly, Geoffrey, slowly."

At last I managed to splutter, "Where are you going?" I was hoping it was somewhere nearby.

Her reply was, "I cannot tell you."

"When are you going?"

"Now. The car is here and waiting for me. I've told them to wait. I would not leave without saying goodbye to you. Geoffrey, I want to give you these." And she opened her parcel and took out two large books. One was Peter Pan, the second was The Water Babies. She handed them to me. "Geoffrey, I want you to promise me something. I want you to promise me that you will read from one of these books every day. Not read quietly to yourself, but read out loud by yourself. It will help your sut-ter. Do you promise me that?"

I was in such a state I couldn't speak. I could only nod my head, which caused tears to fly everywhere. Never had I cried like this before.

She put her arms around me and gave me a big, long hug and kissed me on the forehead. "Goodbye Geoffrey." And she was gone. I didn't see her go; I didn't see anything. I was blinded by my tears. The sobs I was giving were actually hurting me.

Big sister Kit came and sat beside me to try to help. I brushed the tears away as best I could, pushed the books into her hands, got up and I ran away as fast as I could. I just wanted to get away from that spot.

My running took me straight across the potato field from corner to corner. That would get me into trouble but somehow I didn't care. Running on through the orchard and the vegetable garden, past the tennis court into the field in which Arthur and I had built our 'den' of old bracken, and when I got there I crawled in; I didn't want to see anybody. I just wanted to be on my own.

Having crawled into our little den, I have no idea whatsoever as to whether I continued to cry, or just lay there; maybe I fell asleep, I don't know, but I think it highly unlikely. What I do know is that I completely lost all track as to the passing of time.

The most likely thing I think I did was to lie there and try to work things out. Why had I reacted like that? Why had I felt the need to run? Years later, I've worked out that I ran because deep down inside I was scared. Let me try to explain.

Don't forget that I was away from my family in isolation hospital for some months, then evacuated soon after. I had my schools chopped and changed around. We were getting so used to saying goodbye to the family it was becoming almost like second nature. All this I thought I'd coped with pretty well, apart from the bullying at Twyford School.

Now I'm shattered about saying goodbye to a lady that I have only known for about a month; I think the reason was I was scared of my own feelings.

There can be no denying that this had been a special friendship, because it was. This was, I'm pretty sure, due to the fact that we were 'in the same boat'. Both away from our homes due to no faults of our own; both with a communication problem – Mrs Ongar with the language barrier, me with my stuttering – it gave us a sort of bond.

Personally, I don't think she needed any help from me with her English, even though she did speak it pretty badly, but she was clever enough to use this so as to get me to speak more freely to her, so that she could help me. It is quite possible that she was a speech therapist, married to a doctor. In later years, I did have to attend speech therapy classes, and much of what I learned there was based on the same principles – never try to fight the stammer or stutter. Just relax, deep breaths and the words will come. Just as she taught me, 'slowly, Geoffrey, slowly'.

She had been very kind to me, in a practical way, and helped me a lot, and I like to think that just maybe I was able to help her a little.

Her kindness was the way she treated me as a person. She would talk to me as though I was an adult; never talked down to me – I was an equal. Sometimes she would even ask my advice on matters. She made me feel needed, and important. I wasn't used to that.

She was kind to me by just being there and I was going to miss her very much.

What brought me back into the real world again was hearing Kitty's voice calling my name. She was looking for me. She found the den and the next thing I saw was her head and shoulders in the little doorway. "There you are. Where have you been all day?"

"Here."

"What, all day?"

"Yes."

"We didn't know where you'd run to. Aren't you hungry?"

"Not particularly; a bit thirsty."

"Come on, let's get back to the house. You can't stay in here forever." She said coaxingly, and I crawled out.

"What time is it?" I asked.

"I'm not sure, but the rest of us have had our tea."

O Lord! I was really in trouble. I had no idea at all that I'd been in our little den all day. I'd missed lunch and tea. "Am I in big trouble?" I asked Kit, as we walked back to the house. "Well, I'm not sure, but I don't think so," was her somewhat surprising answer.

When we got to the back door, I went sheepishly in; they were all there, Hetty, Nell, George and a hatless Aunty. They all actually looked pleased to see me; there was something quite wrong here. It was Nelly who spoke first.

"Where have you been? What have you been doing all day? We've been so worried." She then carried on talking as though she didn't want an answer, so I didn't give her one.

It was left to Kitty to explain about me being in the den all day, and I'd had nothing to eat, and was thirsty. Suddenly everybody was falling over themselves to get me a drink, sitting me in an armchair and standing there, smiling at me. Even Aunty was smiling whilst I had my drink.

Then the drink was finished. Did I want any more? "No thank you."

"Right, you go and have a nice wash and tidy yourself up a bit. By the time you've done that I'll have your meal ready for you. Alright?"

What was up with everybody behaving like this? First running across the potato field, then missing two meals; I thought I'd be in deep trouble, but I wasn't.

After I'd had this so called 'nice wash', I went back and there are no other words for it, I was 'fussed over'. Kitty sat at the table with me. I had my meal; she had a cup of tea and some cake. It was difficult because I just couldn't believe what was happening, and didn't know what to talk about.

When the meal was over I didn't know what to do. I didn't want to help with the rabbits, and just hung around outside. After a while, Nelly came out. "Look, it's been a bad day for you. Would you like to take something to read and go to bed early – have an early night? You don't have to; I'm not sending you to bed, but it's alright if you want to." It seemed like a very good idea, so that's what I did.

When I got to the room that I shared with the Elders, there on my bed were Peter Pan and The Water Babies. I gently moved them to one side. I could not face them tonight. It had been a promise I was never able to keep. I was never ready to read either of those books.

The next morning, things were more or less as normal except that for the next few days I was treated with kid gloves; left very much to do my own thing. I missed the walks and talks but that wasn't anybody's fault, and nothing could be done about it.

As far as I'm aware, nobody ever mentioned the name, Ongar, again; at least not in my presence. That was another kind of kindness; a very thoughtful one. It wasn't too long before I was back to being my usual horrible little self.

25. Party Time

It was June 1940 and still the sun seemed to shine all day every day; things were just ticking along as far as we were concerned; then, us kids started to hear talk from the kitchen about a forthcoming party – that really made our ears prick up – a party, oh good!

This didn't seem to be any sort of big secret – it was being talked about quite openly, but not to us kids. From what we could gather, it was going to be quite a large affair and some help was going to have to be brought in from somewhere. It all sounded pretty exciting. Eventually, curiosity got the better of us and one of us asked what it was all about; I don't remember who asked, but I know it wasn't me.

"Well, Mrs Ashby is giving a garden party at the end of the month", explained Hetty.

"What's a garden party? 'Cos we don't have many of those in Battersea."

"It's an afternoon tea party held in the garden."

"Suppose it rains?"

"Then it's held indoors."

"In which case, it's not a garden party, is it?"

"Don't be awkward."

"I was only asking."

"Well don't!"

"Who's going to be coming to this party then?"

"All the ladies from one of the groups that Mrs Ashby belongs to. Mrs Ashby is the chairwoman."

"What's that?"

"Never you mind."

"How many will be coming?"

"Not sure yet – somewhere between sixty and eighty."

"Blimey!"

Well, at last we knew what was going on. There was a lot of extra work going on in the garden and, whilst we were at school, there must have been many more deliveries than usual, because boxes were being stacked everywhere. We were under strict orders not to touch anything.

At times like this, when there was an extra large function going on, the maid from the London house would come down from London to help. Her name was May and I have mentioned her before; she was a few years younger than Hetty and Nelly and much more lively – also very deaf. She was fun to have around. May was a housemaid not a cook, and was there to help Hetty with serving the guests; this was the first time we had met her.

As the day drew nearer, Nelly asked Kitty if it would be alright to take a day off from school on the day of the party, as Kit would be very useful helping Nelly in the kitchen. Kit said she would ask, but was sure it would be alright, and it was.

That rather put the noses of us lads a bit out of joint; nobody was asking for our help. So it was decided that, without telling anyone, on the day we would explain to Old Jonah that our help was desperately needed because of this garden party, so could we please have the afternoon off.

Much to our surprise, he already knew about this party. We supposed it was possible that his wife and grown up daughter were going, because they now lived in the village and could well be members of this women's group. Old Jonah thought it an excellent idea that we should help out and gave us his blessing. So, after we had had our lunch, we returned to Wickens. By now we had found a short cut which cut off a big corner, but it only worked out if we were at the village school, not for the Nissen hut or the community centre. We used this short cut on this day and were soon back at Wickens.

We were not exactly welcomed with open arms when we arrived and announced that we'd come to help! It was a bit like when we walked in following the Queen's visit, a few jaws dropped.

Some tables and chairs that had been hired, to be set out on the lawn, should have been delivered in the morning but had only just arrived and there was a bit of a panic on. Old George said they can take that stuff round to the garden, so almost at once we were being useful. It saved George and Billings having to do it; Old George just stationed himself on the lawn and said, "Put that one there, and that one over there." Panic over, we'd saved the day, or so we thought.

Once that was done the three Elders were asked if they would keep an eye on the driveway and make sure that it didn't get too congested with cars, by helping with the parking, and once the driveway was full, standing at the front gate and politely explaining to drivers as they drew up that the drive was full so could they please park on the grass verge outside.

They could come back into the garden when it seemed everybody had arrived. All this they did quite well.

Meanwhile, Kit was busy in the kitchen and thoroughly enjoying it. I was a general 'gofer'. By the way, it didn't rain.

Apart from Hetty and May, on these big occasions there was another maid who used to come and help; I can't remember her name but she would be borrowed from another big house in the area, but which house I never knew. So there were now three uniformed maids bobbing about. The place was beginning to look like a pre-war Lyons Corner House.

As these ladies began to arrive, most with fancy hats on, I was told to go and tidy myself up and put on a clean shirt, then I could help with going around with plates. That way I would see what was going on.

It has to be said that I was getting a great buzz out of all this. I'd never seen anything quite like this before.

After the proceedings had been going for about half an hour, Mrs Ashby stepped to centre stage and made a short speech of welcome and, as she concluded, she introduced another lady who was going to entertain the guests for a short while.

Remember, I was only nine years old so I can't be absolutely sure of my facts here, but I am ninety-five per cent certain that the lady entertainer that was introduced was a quite young Joyce Grenfell.

We had been told that, whilst the entertainment was going on, all serving of refreshments should stop as too much moving around might cause distractions. Which meant everybody, including the staff and their 'little helpers' could also enjoy Miss Grenfell's performance.

Somewhere Nelly and Kitty were hiding behind a door, Aunty was watching discretely from an upstairs bedroom window. No doubt she was coveting some of those strange hats that were on display. I wonder where some of those ladies got their Christmas crackers from during wartime!

The start of Miss Grenfell's entertainment was a very moving and very patriotic poem, which was very appropriate at this time of national crisis. I'm not sure, but I think the poem was called "This England". During Miss Grenfell's recitation, I noticed many a dainty handkerchief gently go up and gently dab the corner of many a moist eye. There was great applause when the poem was concluded, then the mood changed — it was laughter time.

There then followed three humorous monologues which lightened the mood a great deal. During one of these monologues the voice of one of the characters involved caused Miss Grenfell to raise her voice to a high pitched screech, saying, "Jim, where's that Jim?" All of us that knew Jim turned to him grinning and sniggering. Poor old Jim, he was so embarrassed he didn't know what to do with himself and wished he was anywhere else than sitting on the garden steps.

All too soon, Miss Grenfell came to the end of her entertainment spot and normal tea service was resumed. During all this Mrs Ashby flitted from table to table, having a word here and a word there. After a while one or two said they had to leave; once that started others soon followed.

The three Elders were asked if they thought they could help drivers out of the driveway safely and I went around collecting dirty cups, saucers and plates and maybe even the odd cake or chocolate biscuit.

Once all the tables were cleared, a halt was called, tea was made and everybody relaxed for a short while. Us kids were told we could help ourselves to whatever was left because we had indeed been most helpful.

With the break over and with a few more empty plates, we pitched in and got the tables and chairs back into the driveway ready for collection. We also helped pack away the crockery that had been hired, which had been washed up while we boys were moving the tables and chairs. By then it was rabbit round-up time. We were then finished, a job well done; and I can't speak for the others but I was tired and nearly ready for bed, but not before one final tuck into the leftovers. A successful garden party; when's the next one?

The next morning back at school, Old Jonah called us four over and said he'd heard that the garden party had been a great success. Also, he'd heard that we were a great help – well done! So we were in his good books.

That evening, whilst we were having our tea, Mrs Ashby came into the sitting room where we were eating, which was most unusual. We all made ready to stand up, but, "No, sit still and carry on with your tea. I've just popped in to thank you all personally for your help yesterday, and it is all the more appreciated because you volunteered; you didn't have to be asked. That shows the right spirit; well done, keep it up."

So let's sum this up. We are in Hetty's and Nelly's good books, and Old Jonah's, plus Mrs Ashby's. We'd better make the most of this while it lasts, 'cos it sure won't last very long.

For the next few weeks, that saying of "Jim, where's that Jim?" became something of a catchphrase in and around the kitchen. Most of us used it if we were looking for Jim. It was quite funny for a time and, although Jim didn't like it, he took it in good part. After a while the joke wore a bit thin and most of us dropped it, but not Hetty and Nelly. They kept it going and it began to annoy Jim a bit. Now at times Jim could be a bit tricky with matters like this temper wise, but I'm pleased to say he kept his cool and in the end even Hetty and Nelly got fed up with it, so trouble was avoided.

With the garden party over, once all clearing up was done and the household was back into normal routine again, whatever that was, May, the London maid, was due to return to London. Us kids were sorry to see her go; we all liked her. That doesn't mean to say that we didn't like Hetty, Nelly and George, because we did, but I'm going to pass on Aunty. It's just that May was a lot more lively and more fun.

When May got back to London she somehow managed to get hold of quite a large quantity of mixed sweets which she parcelled up and posted to us to be shared between us. Now I liked her even more.

Another thing that she did which was both kind and thoughtful was, as soon as she could find the time, May travelled from Putney to our London home in Battersea to let our mother know that she had recently got back from Wickens and that we were safe and in good health. May would stay just long enough to have a cup of tea and a chat; both Mum and Dad really appreciated that.

Whether or not May did the same for Billy's and Len's parents, frankly I would doubt it.

Not much news came from Billy about his mother and, as far as I know, nobody asked too many questions; maybe it was best to leave it alone.

As for Len's parents, particularly his father, I think enough has already been written; maybe some of that had been passed on to May, I don't know. If she did go, again, that was kind of her; it was her decision.

Anyway, one thing is for sure, we were all looking forward to May's next visit, even if there are no sweets.

26. Trilogy

It has been my practice with this writing up till now to try to keep each event or incident in the correct order in which they happened – that is as far as my memory allows. But now for a short while I'm going to break away from that. The reason being that I want to do three different stories because there is, I think, a link between them. In fact, it's going to be a trilogy, with each story spaced months apart, but I will keep them in the sequence that they happened.

Are you sitting comfortably? Then I'll begin.

Once upon a time four young boys were wandering through some woods. They had just been evacuated into the countryside because of the nasty war, and they were exploring the countryside around the house in which they now lived.

In these woods, which were nearly all pine trees, they suddenly came upon a very large clearing; it was large enough for somebody to have built a quite large, fine looking bungalow.

There were no boundaries, like fencing, or hedging, no wires, no netting. There was no garden either, just straight out of the woods onto this flat piece of land, with a few large flower pots and garden tubs dotted around with a few motley looking plants and shrubs in.

There appeared to be nobody about, no cars parked, just deserted. Like they always did when they found something interesting, they explored further, took a look around.

Things looked much the same all the way round, except on one side there was a very nice swimming pool, a bit small, but a swimming pool nevertheless; that was very interesting. There was a garage and both doors wide open. There'd not be room in there for a car because it had a table tennis table set up in there with its little net fixed on, two bats and a ball. Well this was good – a bit like a sports club.

Len and Bill went into the garage and started a knockabout game of table tennis. Jim and I followed in and watched. After about five or ten minutes a lady suddenly appeared. "What are you doing?" She asked quite nicely. "Er, playing table tennis madam."

"I thought I heard somebody about out here. Where are you from?" Billy and Len went into the usual ritual of London evacuees staying with Mrs Corbett Ashby at Wickens. As far as I can remember, this lady made no comment about any of that.

"While you young men are here, would you do something to help me?" There were a lot of nods and a chorus of, "Yes, of course we would."

"Well, you see those four car wheels leaning against the wall over there?" she said, pointing. We all nodded again. "Well, I want to make enough space in that corner of the garage." She pointed again, "And then I'd like the four wheels stacked there on top of each other. They are too heavy for me to do it on my own. Can you lads help?"

Her "poor little me" act worked beautifully and almost at once two of us went to get the wheels while two started to make space in the designated corner. Then madam said, "I made some homemade lemonade yesterday – would you all like some?" A chorus of "Yes please."

"Right, I'll go and get it while you carry on with that." We carried on like good little helpers. It didn't take very long to get the wheels in and stacked, or it wouldn't have if Jim hadn't started being so fussy about all the stuff that had had to be moved out of the way. He could be a right "fuss arse" at times with his neat and tidiness; he really let the side down sometimes. We finished tidying up nearly the whole garage!

But madam was well pleased (and so she should be). She left four glasses of really lovely lemonade on a tray and, saying she had some writing to do, went back indoors, telling us to leave the tray on the table tennis table when we left. Also, when we'd finished playing table tennis and left, would we please push the garage doors shut. We didn't stay too long after that, finished every last drop of the lemonade, pushed the doors closed and wandered off to find somebody else to annoy.

Now, when I look back on that event, I am somewhat appalled by the cheek of us kids, just walking in, helping ourselves, making ourselves so at home. Fortunately, madam was very understanding; some people might not have been.

Later on, we found out that those pinewoods were known as "Corbett's Woods". The lady (madam) was, in fact, Mrs Ashby's sister who, although married and with a family, had kept her maiden name of Corbett, so she was Mrs Corbett. Complicated isn't it? Well it was to me.

One final thing to all this, about a fortnight later we received a message from Mrs Ashby via Hetty. The message was that the Corbett house was out of bounds to us. No fuss, no telling off, just that; stay away.

Well, that's the end of the first story – and they all lived happily ever after.

Story Two

As usual, we were wandering about; I couldn't tell you exactly where we were but roughly in the area of Twyford – you remember, with the ford and footbridge, and giant kerbstones.

You may have already gathered that it was very hilly in this part and there was always lots of water about, causing lots of streams. There were at least two fords that I knew of and the possibility of a third.

The three Elders had been told there was a lake in the area that they might be able to use for fishing later in the year. Personally, I had no interest. I was told I was too young to go fishing, by Nelly and Hetty; I'd only come along to keep them out of trouble.

It was springtime with all the spring flowers and fresh greenery everywhere. Possibly it was during the Easter Holiday break, and that's why we were not at school; the sun was shining – it was a lovely day – it was good to be out and about.

After a lot of searching, we found a lake, whether it was the one they were looking for I've no idea, but it's a lake, so be satisfied.

It really was a most picturesque setting. I was but a kid and even I could see that. There was a grand looking large house perched on top of a grassy hill; this grass was well kept and ran down to the edges of the lake.

It was quite a large lake; it needed to be because in the middle was a fair sized island. There was a footbridge to get across to the island; not just any old tatty footbridge, this was a lovely job – it had no handrail. But then you didn't need a handrail; it was so wide you would have had to be either drunk or a right mug to lose your footing and fall in.

Something I also remember most clearly was that this bridge was so well maintained - it was really well looked after. It looked almost new. I was most impressed by that bridge. If you think I've gone overboard in telling you about the bridge, just you wait till I tell you about the island.

It was the sort of sight that can almost take your breath away, 'cos there they were:

"A host of golden daffodils;
Beside the lake, beneath the trees, fluttering and dancing in the breeze."

Bill Wordsworth would have flipped his lid!

Most of my working life was spent in gardening and, as a result, I have attended countless flower shows and exhibitions and I have never seen anything come even close to that island, and I don't think I ever will. It was to my mind perfection.

The island was just one mass of yellow and, as Wordsworth says, all swaying gently together in a slight breeze.

We thought we ought to take a closer look, but we really ought to have known better; we never seemed to learn. Over that lovely bridge we went, no fear of falling. Once on the island it was nice to be standing there – there was room enough to move around provided you were careful.

Some of the stems had snapped in the breeze and the blooms were laying on the ground. We started to pick them up; might have been a better idea to leave them alone, but we didn't think anything of it.

We heard footsteps on the wooded bridge, and started to think we were in trouble, again. The footsteps belonged to a rather distinguished, smart looking gentleman who, as far as we could see, did not seem in any way flustered or angry.

As he approached he said, "Good morning lads." That sounded like a good start.

"Good morning, sir."

"What are you lads doing then, eh?" (Please note I want to come back to that remark).

"We are just having a look around, sir," said Billy.

"What a lovely place. Some of these flowers have got snapped off and we were just picking them up."

"I see. Yes, there has been a bit of a breeze." The gentleman then went on to explain – "My wife and I live in that house on top of the hill there, and we own this land and the lake. Over the years, the two of us have planted these daffodils so we can see them from the house; we don't like to see them picked. I understand that you were only picking up snapped ones so there's no harm done. Now, what do you intend doing with those flowers?"

It was Len's chance to speak up. He was a bit of a smooth talker. "Well, sir, we were thinking we might give them to the two ladies where we are billeted, because they are looking after us so well; it's a small thank you."

"Very commendable. Where are you staying then?"

Again, we went through the Ashby / Wicken routine.

"Well, make it up to a couple of dozen blooms, then off you go, because the sooner they are in water the better."

This gentleman walked with us back across that lovely bridge chatting all the way. At the far side he said, "Well, I may see you around again. You are always welcome, but please don't do any damage or pick any of the flowers. I hope the ladies enjoy the daffodils, I'm sure they will."

Len decided to push his luck a bit, saying, "Sir, later in the year would we be allowed to come fishing here?"

He thought a moment. "Come and see me nearer the time – must be off. Cheerio lads."

"Goodbye sir, and thank you." And, carrying the flowers, we made our way back to Wickens.

But, you know, Bill Wordsworth was right:

"For oft when on my couch I lie,
In vacant or in pensive mood,
They flash upon that inward eye
Which is the bliss of solitude,
And then my heart with pleasure fills,
And dances with the daffodils."

Thanks very much Mr Wordsworth. You really helped me out there. I couldn't have put it better myself.

Nelly and Hetty were very cautious about accepting the flowers once we got back. They thought we had pinched them from somebody's garden. "Oh, ye of little faith!"

But once we had convinced them that it was all above board (well almost), they seemed quite pleased at our little gesture.

Going back to that comment that the kindly gentleman made – "What are you lads doing?" The lady at the bungalow said almost exactly the same thing – "What are you doing?"

Why do people ask that when it is perfectly obvious what you are doing, in our cases:

1. Playing table tennis.
2. Gathering daffodils.

It's a silly question, but if either one of us had come up with a silly answer like, "I'm playing my Jews harp", or "we are painting the kitchen ceiling", we would have been told that we were being impertinent, cheeky or rude. But when you think you might be in trouble it's best just to try to humour them.

It's hard to know what to do with adults sometimes. Ah well, never mind.

That's the end of story two, and I'm sorry to say it didn't all end happily ever after because, sadly, the daffodils died.

At the finish of story two, you won't be too surprised to learn that we now move on to story three.

Story Three

By now, it's late summer and there's lots of fruit ripening on the trees, so it's "scrumping time".

Now the word 'scrumping' is another name for the stealing of other people's fruit and we didn't like the idea of that very much. What we preferred was "R.Q.T.L.P", which stands for Random Quality Testing of Local Produce, which sounds much nicer. After all, we had our good reputation to think of.

My playmate, Arthur Jay, had told me about a cottage near to where he lived that we didn't know about. It was set back off the roadway, so we'd missed it. But according to Arthur, the back garden had an apple tree with the best apples in the area, so we thought it ought to be tested.

We found no trouble in getting into the back garden through a big gap in the back hedge. Very careless that. We helped ourselves to these quite nice looking apples, shoving them down inside our shirts, which was normal practice. Now, I must admit that we were taking more than we needed, which was both silly and greedy. We had found from past experience that some people didn't like their fruit being taken away for testing; this bloke seemed to be one of them.

He saw us from an open window and was going off something alarming. Well, if he's going to be like that about it we'll leave, the sooner the better. As we reached the gap in the hedge he reached his back door. The chase was on! This was not a fair chase because us four lads were handicapped by shirts full of apples. It's not easy to run at top speed with pounds of apples bouncing around inside your shirt. (You should try it some time!). We got onto the roadway and bounced along in the direction of Wickens; the man followed – he wasn't giving up easily. The three Elders had enough sense to run straight past Wickens gateway; no point in letting him know where we came from.

From the sound of his footsteps he didn't appear to be gaining on me, but I dare not look round – just a case of keep going.

When I was about level with Wickens gate, disaster struck. My shirt came out of my trouser top; apples went everywhere. It was like bombs leaving an aircraft bomb bay. It was just an explosion of apples; and what did I do? I stopped to pick them up. As soon as I'd stopped I knew I'd made a mistake, so I just stood there breathless, shirt hanging out and in trouble.

Within two or three strides he was there behind me and I felt a hand on my shoulder turning me around to face him. I didn't know what to expect. I looked up at my captor; he too was breathless but grinning all over his face. "You're new to this aren't you?" he said. I just nodded.

"Come on, help me pick these up and tuck your bloody shirt in."

We collected the apples and put them in a little pile on the grass verge. I was hoping nobody would come out of the Wickens gateway or I'd have some explaining to do. The man then took me by the shoulders and said, "Look, if this ever happens to you again, keep running. Better still, if you want an apple come and knock on my door. If I've got apples I'll always give you one, alright?"

"Yes mister, thank you mister."

The man reached down and picked up about four apples, a bit bruised and scuffed but whose fault was that? He slipped these apples inside my shirt, gave me a very light, almost friendly clip round the ear, saying, "Go on, clear off."

"Yes mister, thanks for the apples mister. Goodnight."

"Goodnight." He went back home taking the remaining apples with him. I went to find the Elders and avoided entering the Wickens gate – end of story.

Now, the link in these three tales is that in each instance us four lads were, to a greater or lesser degree, in the wrong in what we were doing. But the three people concerned handled it so nicely. No ranting or raving and tantrums like others I have previously mentioned; just calm, quiet, understanding and common sense. It shows it can be done.

27. Mind My Bike

With the trilogy over, we are now back to the main plot, or as they say, "Meanwhile, back at the ranch."

The three Elders had been working pretty hard in their spare time doing fruit picking and any other honest way of getting enough money together for the bicycles that they were after. It's almost certain Jim was getting help from Mum, Dad and Gran with the odd postal order here and there. Same as I think Len and Billy were from their parents; I just had to sit and wait, and I wasn't finding that very easy.

By somewhere around mid-July all three were ready; I'm surprised that I cannot remember who won the race to get their bike first because it had become a pretty keen contest, but the main thing was they were all able to get their bikes roundabout the same time. Nor can I tell as to where the bikes came from; the only place I knew of in the area was "Old Sweeney Todd" at Chelwood Gate and I don't somehow think they would have gone there, I just don't know.

But once the bikes had arrived they were all pretty decent, quite adequate for what they wanted. They even had brakes and tyres, and pedals. It was decided that Jim need not get a carrier for his bike, so until my promised bike arrived from London Jim, Len and Bill would take it in turns to ferry me to and from school on their crossbars. So it might be illegal but Horsted Keynes didn't know what a policeman looked like; they were so good they didn't need one. This means of journey was not too comfortable but it was better than walking. You must remember that whenever anybody went out like that you had to carry your gas mask, always, and they often got in the way.

It wasn't too long before a letter arrived to say that on a certain day my Dad would be putting my bicycle on the train and it would need to be collected at Horsted Keynes railway station – I could hardly wait.

When the day arrived, Jim explained to Old Jonah about the arriving bike. "No problem," said he, "Pop out during the morning session, take Geoffrey with you and go and collect it."

It had been some years since I'd learned to ride a two-wheeled bike. My last holiday before the war at Hayling Island where my aunt lived, I'd learned on my cousin Colin's old bike and now I wasn't sure if I could still do it. There was only one way I was going to find out.

At the railway station the bike was duly brought out; it was quite a bit smaller than a standard size adult bike but that wasn't a problem because I wasn't an adult. It had been freshly painted, pale blue, and as far as I was concerned it was a smashing little bike – if only I could ride it. To start with it was all a bit wobbly but once I got a bit of speed there was no problem. It was like the old saying, "It's easy as riding a bike."

At school and at Wickens everybody had to come and look at 'my bike', and one thing's for sure, it was a lot more comfortable than the crossbars.

Having a bike made a vast amount of difference all the way round. We didn't have to leave so early for school in the mornings and, of course, got back quicker on the return trip. Doing errands didn't take so long; it was lovely. The most important difference was that it opened up a wide new range of places to explore – more trouble ahead.

Unfortunately, this was curbed to a large extent because the Battle of Britain was taking place, sometimes right over our heads. There were reports of enemy fighters strafing civilians, whether or not this was true there was no way of knowing, but Old George said he was shot at while working in the potato field. I'm not sure about that either, but I heard no reports of any casualties.

This meant that we were asked not to stray too far from the house, and it wasn't fair to moan about it. They were only trying to look after us as best they could. But regardless of the restrictions, it was so nice to be able to go out for a bicycle ride without going too far afield.

My playmate, Arthur, had a bike so we two went out and about quite a bit together particularly at the weekends. At that time of course there were far fewer cars on the roads. This was made even more so because of the rationing of petrol which came into force very soon after the outbreak of war, so bike riding was a reasonably safe pastime, provided you were careful.

The arrangement regarding Kitty and Mrs Ashby's bicycle was working out well. So was Kit's new school. She seemed to be doing extremely well there and liked it better than any other school that she had ever attended.

While we were actually at school the aircraft 'dog fighting' overhead did cause a few problems. We did, in fact, spend quite a few hours trying to have lessons while sitting underneath our tables instead of sitting at them.

Two senior boys used to have to sit on a chair outside the main door, whichever place we were using on that day. Their job was to be spotters and warn of any imminent danger close by. They had their own table to dive under just inside the door. One boy did mornings, one did afternoons. Brother Jim did the morning shift. Looking back on it, it all seems pretty comical now, but believe me it wasn't then.

There were at least two German fighter planes shot down by the RAF in our immediate area that I know of; there may well have been more. The first one, so I was told, crashed in the village pond, which was some way outside the village, not far from the Horsted Keynes railway station. This was the opposite side of the village to where we stayed so we had no need to venture out that way. I, for one, don't recall ever seeing this village pond. There's more to tell regarding the aircraft that came down into the pond, killing the German pilot, later on.

The second German fighter shot down crashed onto some scrubland at the Chelwood Gate end of Birch Grove, not too far from the Macmillan's house, but on the opposite side of the road.

As soon as it was possible, Arthur and I were up there on our bikes. There was a small group of people there, but there was not really much to see. Don't really know what I was expecting; it was all a bit of an anti-climax.

There was this dreary, dark grey aircraft. There had been a small fire and some general debris scattered around the aircraft all looking a bit charred, and that was it. Also, there was an over-officious armed guard who wouldn't let anybody within many yards of the plane, and would not answer questions. So we were unable to find out whether or not that pilot survived. It was a bit of a wasted trip really.

That's more or less the way things carried on for the next few weeks, ducking and diving, but trying to carry on as normal as possible.

The German fighter plane crashed into the field pond on Cinder Hill killing the pilot on 30th September 1939, the day before the end of the Battle of Britain.

28. Hamburger for dinner?

The dinner hut was a very important feature in our everyday school life; no matter whether we were at the village school, Nissen hut or community centre. It was always the case of back to the dinner hut for lunch / dinner, call it what you like.

The hut itself was a wooden structure, very like an army barrack hut. Very soon after us Londoners arrived, a brick built extension was built on as a kitchen.

The lady in charge of the kitchen and therefore in charge of catering was Mrs Lee, who was a pleasant lady and not one of 'The Frosty Brigade'. It is possible that Mrs Lee had children attending the village school but I can't be sure. Same as I'm not sure if she worked that kitchen single-handed or had a helper. Whether she had help or not, by and large the resulting school dinners were quite acceptable, for school dinners. But occasionally there would be a hiccup and things would not turn out as they should. For instance, sometimes during the winter months the so-called stew would look more like dumplings floating in an oil slick, but it was very rare.

There were always two sittings, first the village children, then us lot. It was almost certain that both sittings had the same meals, and there was no choice, take it or leave it.

During each sitting, a teacher would be there to supervise table behaviour, no drinks allowed, and strictly no talking. The teachers had drawn up a rota, alternating one day a village teacher, next day a London one, and each teacher supervised both sittings. The village head teacher, Mrs Morse, was on the rota, Old Jonah wasn't.

There is still some doubt in my mind regarding Mrs Morse. She had the look of a headmistress, and most of the time the manner and appearance to go with it. But just now and again it would slip. A couple of times going in or out of the school, through 'The Desiccated Churchyard', we would meet her and, if on my own or with another boy, she would always say "Hello" or "Good morning or afternoon", whichever it was, and you'd get a really lovely smile, not what I sometimes call cardboard smile, a nice warm one. It made me think that behind that stern exterior that we saw most of the time there was really a nice lady.

The two events I am about to relate both happened in the dinner hut, both whilst Mrs Morse was the supervising teacher, and as far as I can recall, very close together in time.

Earlier on I mentioned about the German fighter plane coming down near Horsted Keynes pond, and the pilot being killed. After a few days we heard rumours that the dead airman was to be buried in the church graveyard right next to the school. That didn't particularly bother us – suppose he's got to be buried somewhere – thought no more about it.

One morning it was our turn to use one of the village school classrooms. The lesson, whatever it was, was going well enough; the teacher was Mr Burbridge (Old Burb). Through the classroom window we saw some activity in the churchyard.

The class whispers were heard by Old Burb and he halted the lesson to say, "Yes, the burial of the German airman is now taking place in the churchyard. I wasn't going to say anything about it but seeing as how it seems to be having a rather unsettling effect on the class, maybe we should pause for a moment and talk about it. So, put your pens and pencils down a moment."

"There is an international agreement that covers situations like this. Each country agrees to treat the fatal casualties of their enemy with dignity and respect and most countries stick to that. As you are now seeing, we do. This airman may have lived in the countryside, or may have come from a town like Hamburg, a town that has been in our news a lot just lately."

"He was somebody's son and he won't be going home."

We all listened very intently; we were not being talked down to like children, which was very refreshing – it was also very moving.

He carried on, "He died serving his country; we should respect that. So I would like us, before you carry on with your work, to join me in respectful silence for a few moments."

There was complete silence in the classroom until Old Burb said, "Thank you boys, now quietly carry on with your work." This we did until lunch / dinner time. But for the remainder of that period the atmosphere was very sombre.

The lunch / dinner break for the village school children always started earlier than us, because they always had the first sitting, and by breaking earlier it saved us having to hang around waiting for too long. Nevertheless, there was always a slight wait.

Always there was some inter-school banter as they filed out. One of our mob would call out, "What is it today?" And an answer would come back, "Mince", or "Stew", or maybe "Sausage Pie".

"Any good?"

"Not bad."

But on the particular day we got the most unusual answer, "Hamburgers!" We couldn't wait to get in there.

As we waited, a boy with the name of Cheeseman and the nickname of Shanky – Shanky Cheeseman – was the school comedian, and he picked up on this. "Didn't Old Burb say something about that Jerry being a Hamburger?" The idea was planted.

When we were called in we had made our way to the top end of the hut near the kitchen area. The plates with the dinners already on them were waiting to be collected.

The system was, take a dinner, turn left or right, and find a seat at one of the long tables set out down each side of the hut. These tables would have knives, forks and spoons already set out down each side, thus making four rows of children – you could sit wherever you liked. This left the central area clear for the supervising teacher to pace up and down.

On this day it all went according to plan, but then it always did, when Mrs Morse was in charge.

Each boy took his seat and when the last boy was seated Grace was said, and everybody was ready to tuck in, but nobody did. We all just sat there and looked at our plates; nobody said a word, 'cos nobody was allowed to.

There on our plates was not the expected hamburgers but piles of meat, much more than we would normally get. Everybody seemed to be thinking the same thing. There were lots of looks going up and down and across the tables, plus a few funny faces being pulled.

Some started eating the potatoes and other veg, some of the braver ones even tried the gravy, but absolutely nobody touched the meat; it got pushed to one side, it got worked around; what it did not get was eaten!

It didn't take Mrs Morse long to see that something was amiss. She went to one boy, "Why aren't you eating your meat? We cannot afford to have it wasted."

"I'm not hungry Miss."

On to another boy, "And you, why aren't you eating it?"

"I don't like it Miss."

"Have you tried it?"

"Yes Miss, a little bit Miss." He lied.

So it went on, each boy she questioned gave similar answers.

Understandably, Mrs Morse was getting annoyed, as there seemed to have been no trouble with the village children. She then said, "Seeing as how none of you seem to be very hungry, you won't be requiring your sweet, pudding, dessert", whatever it was she called it. We always called it "afters". This was bad news.

Anyway, that was her threat, and still nobody made any move to eat any of the meat. Then Mrs Lee, who always kept a low profile, came out of her kitchen area into the eating area and approached Mrs Morse; they had quite a long talk.

What normally happened was, while we ate the first course, the sweets (afters) would be set out ready for collection as required. When everybody had finished the first course the teacher would give the OK and one from each table would go forward taking their dirty plate, knife and fork with them, scrape any waste into a container, stack their plates then collect a sweet and back to their seat. Once seated the next pair would do the same, until everyone had a sweet, then you could all start to eat it.

For some reason this had not been done on this particular day. Following the Morse / Lee chat, which seemed to have got quite heated, Mrs Lee suddenly turned away and went back to the kitchen and started putting out the sweets, telling the two boys at the top end of each table to make a start in collecting them. At that, Mrs Morse stormed out of the hut.

All at once it seemed very important to get the eating done with, get outside and be able to talk about what had happened. With sweets finished, Mrs Lee took it upon herself to dismiss us, also telling us, "Don't worry, it will all blow over."

Outside, everybody just stood around in groups, talking, mostly about the row and what would happen to Mrs Lee because she was well liked. Secondly, about the meat, and that was where I heard it said that we'd had "The hamburger for dinner."

Wonder what happened to all the meat we left? Was it re-used in some other way? Maybe it was given to local dog owners; if that's the case I hope nobody had a Dachshund. What Mrs Lee said proved right – it did all blow over.

The second dinner hut story is all about "afters", always my favourite part of any meal. You will recall that I wrote earlier that just now and again Mrs Lee had hiccup days. Well, I think the day I'm writing about might just have been one of them.

So far, everything had gone according to plan. Mrs Morse again in charge. We had all collected our sweets (still like afters better) and had been told we may start. The sweet was jam tart with either custard or some sort of syrup poured over it; I can't remember which. It doesn't really matter because nothing that you poured on this pastry would have softened it. If you think of quarry tiles with jam on, then you are beginning to get the picture.

Every boy was fighting a losing battle with this pastry (better not say tart). We only had spoons, and picking up with the fingers was bad table manners. As I pressed down on this jam tart, suddenly it went 'ping' and went flying up the centre of the table, much to everyone's amusement, except me. There was of course a lot of sniggering along the table which drew Mrs Morse's attention to the fact that something was going on.

What had happened was just the same as when you play 'tiddlywinks' with counters, and my "afters" had gone shooting up the table for about six or seven places.

It's a pretty safe bet that playing tiddlywinks with your afters is not considered to be good manners and is frowned upon. That's what happened to me; I was frowned upon by Mrs Morse. She quickly worked out what had happened, because mine was the only empty plate. Then she moved down the hut and when level with offending piece of pastry, leant over the shoulders of two boys daintily picking it up between her forefinger and thumb.

Then, holding it well aloft, moved down to stand behind me where, without lowering her hand, she let it drop with a loud 'clunk' onto my plate, saying at the same time, "I believe this is yours!" Neither the pastry nor the plate broke.

As Mrs Morse walked away, her back towards me, I quickly picked the jam tart up in my fingers and took a quick bite. This caused more sniggering, which in turn caused her to whip around a bit quickly, thinking that something was going on.

She looked at me enquiringly. I put on my best innocent smile – I'm very good at that – and I said "thank you", only to be told not to talk with my mouth full. You can't win with some people can you?

There was also another small incident worth telling; maybe not very important, but nevertheless something that stuck in my memory. It concerns not the dinner hut but the village school playground.

Whatever was happening every dinnertime we would all have to make our way to the hut, where we would have to wait around for the second sitting. If the afternoon's lessons were at the Nissen hut or community centre, then after having eaten our meal we would make our way to the appropriate place. It was usually during these trips to and fro that we would try our luck on "The Goat Run".

One of the village boys, I never knew his name; in fact, I never knew any of the village children's names. This lad was always involved in anything that was going on in the playground. He had a very loud voice and was always busy, busy, but he was not a bully. It was just sheer force of personality with him. As we stood waiting for our meal you couldn't help but notice him.

One Monday in mid-summer, as we waited to be called in, we could not help but notice something different about him. He was completely bald - his head had been shaved. This came as quite a shock to many of us; we had never seen anyone so young, completely bald. Nowadays you do see young cancer patients with complete hair loss but back then it was almost unheard of as far as I was aware.

The matter was being made worse as all the other village children would have nothing to do with him; he was completely on his own. He'd lost his charisma.

For a short while, he was at a loss as to what to do in this situation, then he had an idea. He just leaned against the wall of the school building and started to sing at the top of his voice, loud and clear. This went on right through our mealtime, and he was still singing as we wandered away in dribs and drabs for our afternoon lesson.

The next day was a repeat performance, from one song to another. He didn't have a particularly good voice, or a particularly bad one, but he did have a loud one.

As I've said, it was mid-summer and, at times, very hot. Now boys don't mind sitting down in the dirt, but you know what girls are like, fussy. So, some of the village girls asked permission to take two long benches from the school building into the playground, and permission was given.

As soon as the benches were carried outside, many girls rushed forward to sit down. On one bench there was enough room for two more people. So what does the wandering singer do? He strolls over to it and sits down, still singing. All the girls seated on that bench got up and walked away – he kept singing.

It stayed like that for a few minutes, then he stopped singing, moved the bench to the place that he wanted it, then he lay down full length on it, tucked his hands behind his head and resumed singing again.

This was the pattern for the coming days and weeks right up to the start of the summer holidays. It became so commonplace that we stopped taking any notice of it. Therefore, I cannot tell you how it resolved itself because I just don't know. But I have wondered at times how I would have reacted in those circumstances, quite differently I'm pretty sure.

Maybe you won't agree, but I think it took a degree of courage to do what he did, and I admired him for it.

29. Camping Out

All the way through the summer Nelly always seemed to be busy, all day long. This was due to making all sorts of jams as each variety of fruit became available. Also preserving whatever fruit she could; remember there were no deep freezers or fridges. Even if they had have been available there was no electricity in the house to run them on – it was almost Victorian.

In the kitchen there was a pantry where foodstuffs that were currently in use were kept. There was also quite a large larder in the corner of the staff sitting room. This was where all jams, and tins, jars of preserves and general food stores were kept. Also when the shooting season was on it was where any poultry and our own rabbits were hung while awaiting the pot.

One final thing in the larder worth mentioning. Once the Wickens chickens got into the full swing of laying eggs, a brand new dustbin was placed in the larder. This dustbin was then about three quarters filled with a jelly-like substance called "liquid glass", into which any surplus eggs were placed.

As I had it explained to me, the liquid glass formed a seal around the eggshell, thereby stopping the eggs from going off. All I can say is it seemed to work well enough.

Once the summer holiday break from school started we had a lot more time to kill. The aircraft activity overhead had reduced considerably and there was much less dog fighting.

The Ashby's were away a lot, nearly all weekdays and often weekends as well; we didn't mind, and I'm sure Nelly and Hetty didn't either. Much less work and cooking for them.

Then one of the elders, I don't recall which one it was, had an idea; I do wish they wouldn't have ideas, it nearly always ends up causing trouble.

This was the idea. Why don't we ask Nelly and Hetty if we can sleep on the terrace? That way we'd be sort of in the open, but sort of undercover. I kept quiet, there were too many 'sort of's' for my liking.

This idea was talked over for about three or four days. In the end it was decided nothing ventured, nothing gained, so, waiting for a moment when the sisters were on their own, without Aunty around, we all went in and put the idea forward.

They seemed a bit surprised at the request, but didn't chuck it out of hand straightaway. "Let's think about it for a bit", was their first answer. Well, that wasn't exactly a 'no', was it?

Next day during one of our mealtimes, Hetty came in to say they could see no reason why we couldn't sleep on the terrace. It would have to be midweek and, of course, the Ashby's would have to be away. Also it must be a dry night, and for one night only. One final condition was there must be no getting up and wandering around in the dark. Sister Kit was not in the least bit interested in all this planning.

By now the Elders had convinced me that this was a great idea and it was going to be fun. I'm afraid I was daft enough to believe them.

Really I couldn't see what all the fuss was about; all we were going to do was go to sleep on the terrace instead of upstairs in our room. It seemed to bring back memories to Jim and Len of camping with the Sea Cadets and The Boys' Brigade, and Billy just got carried along on this tide of youthful enthusiasm. He was nearly as daft as I was.

On the day of this scouting jamboree, there were things to be fetched and carried, so we were involved in doing the fetching and carrying. This consisted of two mattresses, one camp bed, and one pump up lilo, along with blankets and pillows.

During the evening the lilo was pumped up, but I don't remember with what. Beds were picked and made up ready. I was told I could have the lilo, but I wasn't too fussed about it. A big fuss was made about wearing pyjamas when sleeping outside, even though we were only half outside. Apparently, pyjamas was just not the done thing. Again, Nelly and Hetty agreed to shirts and shorts for the night; they really were being very good sports about all this.

After 'round up time' we were given the chance to change our minds about all this if we wanted to. But at this late stage nobody was going to be the first to back out. So "Operation Sleep-out" was on.

We all got ready for bed and got into our different types of bed, and I have to admit the lilo was very comfortable. We all talked for a while same as we normally did, but on this night I think it went on longer than usual. Then one by one we all fell asleep.

When I next awoke it was dark; I had no idea what the time was; I was cold and very uncomfortable. All the air had gone out of the lilo. I was lying on a solid, cold tile floor. I was not happy.

For a while I lay there not knowing quite what to do. Thinking to myself I knew this idea business would lead to trouble, and I can see why I was offered the lilo. Also, I remembered the final condition – "No getting up and wandering around". Well, if they think I'm lying here all night like this they've got another thing coming. "Come on everybody up! This is an emergency!"

The three Elders were not happy to have their beauty sleep interrupted and it took me some time to get them to understand just how dire the situation was. All I could get from them was, "What do you expect us to do about it?"

"I expect you to fix it. It was after all your silly idea, and two of you all supposed to be camping experts. I've heard enough about it during the last week, so do something!"

Then Hetty appeared; she did not present what you would call a vision of loveliness in her hairnet, dressing gown and slippers but that didn't matter a jot; help was at hand. As you would expect, her first words were, "What's going on? I thought we agreed no getting up and wandering around? I'm disappointed in you lot."

"All the air's come out of Geoff's airbed."

"Have you been fiddling with it?" Hetty asked me.

"No, I was asleep; we were all asleep, and I'm cold."

She sent two of the Elders into one of the rooms to get cushions while she went back into the house, returning very quickly with another blanket. The cushions were arranged to make a bed. I was told to lay on it, I was covered over and tucked in. Also I was told one more peep out of me tonight and all sorts of 'orrible things would happen to me. Nevertheless, I still think I said, "thank you and goodnight."

The Elders got back into their beds confirming the threats regarding 'orrible things.

"Well a fat lot of help you three were." I slept well.

Next morning, no big deal was made about what had happened. It was treated as just one of those things. In fact it was all treated as rather a big joke; everybody thought it was very funny, except me, oh and Aunty.

Aunty suddenly came out with the news that she had known right from the start that it was a silly idea and should never have been allowed to go ahead. Nobody took any notice; they hardly ever did.

Frequently I have to refer to the fact that we seldom knew what the time was and I think perhaps I should explain why.

Wristwatches in those days were nowhere near as robust as watches are today. Over-winding, broken springs and balance wheels were among the most common breakages and so easily done with the slightest little knock. Because of this, school children of that era almost never had watches. Too easily broken in the rough and tumble of school life.

With the coming of war it became almost impossible to buy a clock or wristwatch. The reason being the firms dealing in that line of work were doing what was called "war work". These clock and watchmakers were transferred onto making instruments for fighters, bombers, tanks, ships and submarines. The list is endless.

So, if you hadn't already got a watch by about 1940 you were unlikely to get one for the foreseeable future. The answer was to get your old clocks and watches repaired, and that's not as easy as it sounds. Spare parts were unobtainable and it was only through cannibalisation of other old clocks and watches that you stood any chance at all; if, and that's a very big if, you could find somebody capable of doing it who was not up to his eyes in "war work".

All people, men and women, if they were in highly skilled jobs, were not "called up" for the armed services if it was thought that their skills could be better used for the war effort in a civilian role. These people were told they had "reserved occupations", but these people could still be drafted to anywhere in the country that the Ministry of Labour saw fit to send them.

This group included farmers, fishermen, some in the building trade, and many much more highly skilled people too numerous to list, but I'm not sure about policemen, and particularly doctors who would have been needed both on the home front, as it was called, and in the services.

To take this just one small step further, all metals of all types were in desperately short supply, which meant after the first few months the buying of household pots and pans and kettles became a thing of the past, as was the purchasing of hammers, chisels and spanners. Times are getting hard boys. Our next stab at camping out came a few weeks later, and it's all a bit vague because I don't remember it anywhere near so clearly as our first adventure.

It all centres around that old caravan that I mentioned when we were in the bicycle manufacturing business, where we used to keep that old junk bike after

Jim had done his work on it.

The bike was long gone, dumped in somebody's field, and we often would go and sit in the caravan if it was raining ('cos it did sometimes) and we were in the way indoors.

Now, I'm pretty sure you are well ahead of me here. Yes, that's right, some clever clogs had the idea of sleeping in the caravan – here we go again.

Once again, Hetty and Nelly were not totally against the idea but it needed a bit more thinking about, mainly because we would be quite apart from the house by a fair distance. By now we were into the later part of summer and even with double British Summer Time the evenings were still beginning to draw in a little bit, and turn not cold but a bit chillier.

This, I'm afraid, is where it all gets a bit vague because I don't remember what we slept on. One thing is for sure, we wouldn't have been allowed to take mattresses to the van so I can only assume that we made up straw palliasses.

This caravan was quite small and if we were all going to lay on the floor we would just about fit in but it was going to be a tight squeeze. We had been given blankets, pillows and a torch. It was considered too dangerous for us to have an oil lamp; very wise.

We had also been given a deadline; I don't remember what it was, nine or ten o'clock. Up till the deadline we could change our minds and go back indoors and sleep in our beds. After the deadline it was "lock out". Seeing as how I've already explained none of us had a watch, we didn't know what the hell the time was; we had no choice but to stay out. Not that it really mattered; we had already decided that, come what may, we would stick it out – we had our pride.

There were times during the night when we might have regretted having pride. Nothing untoward happened; it was just a long, uncomfortable night. I don't think any one of us would admit it, but I'm sure we were all glad when it was over and we could troop back into the house. I never heard any more ideas about sleeping out; I wouldn't have wanted to do it again. It had killed the camping bug, I'm pleased to say.

30. Danger UXBs

Don't go thinking that because we were tucked away somewhere in the countryside for safety sake, that we weren't getting any bombs, 'cos we were. It's true that they weren't falling what you would call thick and fast, but they were falling.

Never do I remember one falling in the daytime; it was sometimes evening, but mostly at night time, and thereby hangs a couple of tales.

One evening, it must have been some time in October 1940, we'd had our normal day and evening and were all in our beds talking the way we usually did. It was dark outside so the last one to get into bed had to blow the lamp out and pull back the curtains, making the most of whatever moonlight there was. As I say, we talked for a while, then said goodnights all round and settled down to go to sleep.

Now, Jim had the bed nearest the window and quite suddenly he said, "There's going to be trouble tonight."

With one accord, Billy, Len and I sat bolt upright in bed.

"Why? What are you on about now?"

"There's going to be trouble tonight." Jim repeated.

"Yeh, we heard that bit, what's the matter?"

"I can see a star up there and it's got a red blob on it; that means trouble."

"There'll be a big red blob on you if you don't shut up and go to sleep."

"Well, come and take a look" said Jim, so we all got out of our beds and went to the window. Once at the window we could see it was a lovely clear night and there were hundreds of stars in the night sky. There was Jim pointing vaguely up into the sky trying to point out a single one with a red blob. We stood no chance of seeing this one star.

We were, I think, all convinced that Jim thought he could see it; he was not given to leg pulling and teasing. There was a very serious side to Jim, sometimes a bit too serious.

It was jokingly suggested that he borrow Mr Ashby's telescope. "You might be able to see it better." Jim didn't take that remark very well and tempers were getting a bit short. It was Billy, I think, who said, "Let's get back into bed, forget it, and try to get some sleep," and that we did. Except Jim, who just couldn't forget it and, although nobody answered him, he lay there predicting forthcoming gloom and doom all over the place, muttering to himself. Eventually, we did all get to sleep.

We were all awoken in the early hours of the morning by an almighty bang! It was still dark and once again no idea as to the time.

It really was a mighty wallop and it shook the door and windows. Once again, we all shot up in bed, not quite sure what to do; we didn't have to wait long. In almost seconds Hetty was there, along with hairnet, dressing gown and slippers, just as before.

She asked if we were all right, and getting four 'yes' answers, told us to pull the curtains across in case of any more bangs. This would help stop shattered glass from flying to some extent. We asked did she know what it was. "No, we may find out more about it in the morning." "If there are any more bangs tonight don't wait to be called – come down to the kitchen as quickly as possible. But I think you'll be alright now. Try to settle down again. Night."

As soon as she closed the door Jim started.

"I told you there'd be trouble tonight and you all just laughed."

"There was nothing any of us could do about it was there?" reasoned Billy.

"I know that but I told you." And to be fair, he had!

Eventually Len and Billy would go their own ways, but Jim and I were of course brothers for the rest of our lives. In the following years Jim never let me forget about his prediction of doom and gloom as forecast by the red blob star. The red blob means, I suppose, that I really can call it "that bloody star!'".

The most likely theory the next day was a German bomber on its return trip had a bomb that had not been dropped when over its target so had then dropped it anywhere on their way home. This one fell in the nearby woods. Pleased to report, nobody hurt.

The second story happened about the same time, not that it really matters very much.

It must have been a weekend because Mr Michael was at home for the weekend and had brought a young lady colleague with him. Also, Mr and Mrs Ashby were holding a small dinner party; I suppose it could have been somebody's birthday.

Things, as far as I could see, were ticking along quite normally, no kitchen panics. While Nelly prepared the meal Hetty would be putting the finishing touches to the dining table, us kids just keeping out of the way.

It was beginning to get dusk and George was bringing in lamps for the whole house. Hetty was doing her best to get lamps to as many rooms as quickly as possible. The only person allowed to help her was Kitty. Us scruffy boys wandering around in that part of the house with houseguests around was unheard of. Even dear little Kitty could only go into certain rooms.

As I've mentioned before, it took an awful lot of oil lamps to light that big house, and of course all blackout curtains had to be drawn in every room. It was no five-minute job.

On Hetty's umpteenth trip upstairs with lamps, once again there was an almighty bang and the whole place seemed to shake. This was followed at once by very loud screaming and the young lady guest ran from her bedroom into the passageway screaming her silly head off. You could hear her all over the house. Everybody thought she was injured, but she wasn't. The worst crime of all was that she was in her underclothes; that definitely lost her a lot of Brownie points, at least with Hetty it did.

Between them, Hetty and Mrs Ashby calmed her down and took her back to her room. I think Hetty was all for locking her in, she was so disgusted with her.

In due course, the other guests arrived and the dinner party went ahead as planned, at least they had something to talk about.

Also the next day there was a lot of joking about the incident. Us boys were teased about it's a good job we weren't upstairs at the time and seen this young lady running around in her cami-knickers; what would we have done?!

Personally, I'm glad I missed it. I have enough trouble with stuttering without going 'boss-eyed' as well.

There were many rumours of unexploded bombs, UXBs as they were called; particularly from the area of Dane Hill, which was slightly further south than we were. Just how many of these rumours were true was hard to tell, the numbers varied, depending on who you were talking to.

It may have been because of the route the bombers took, what we would now call the flight path. Whatever the reason, poor old Dane Hill had more than its fair share of UXBs.

The nearest one to Wickens as far as I was aware was in Corbett Woods, very close to where the Bennett family lived. That would be about a quarter of a mile away from Wickens. We didn't hear anything about all this until after it was all over; I don't know how big this bomb was.

When the 'Bomb Disposal Squad' arrived Mrs Bennett put the kettle on to make tea for the men. Making tea for soldiers had become something of a national pastime as soon as they arrived on the scene. But in Mrs Bennett's case there was method in her madness. In talking to the officer in charge she asked were they going to de-fuse the bomb or would they have to blow it up. His answer was he didn't know until he had seen it.

"If you can de-fuse it can I have the casing for a souvenir?" Mrs Bennett asked after another pot of tea. The reply was, "It depends on a lot of things – I make no promises, but I'll see."

For reasons that I know nothing about, in the end there had to be a controlled explosion. But the officer did give Mrs Bennett the largest piece of casing that was left. We all saw it a few days later. It was quite heavy, because it was quite large. One side of it was almost complete.

It stood in the Bennett's hallway as an umbrella stand and for a while was Mrs Bennett's pride and joy. Mark you, if bombs are falling all around I don't think that an umbrella is going to be much help, do you?

31. Then There Were Three

All during the summer, Billy had been getting letters from home saying that his mother was thinking of getting out of London for good. He didn't talk about his home life very much at any time, but we had gathered from the little he did say that they had some relatives in or near Hastings. There was more talk from him regarding Hastings than there ever was about his life while in London.

Also, we worked out that prior to evacuation Billy seemed to have already spent a fair amount of time in the countryside. He knew plants in the hedgerow, like Deadly Nightshade, Blackthorn, Wild Honeysuckle. Also, he knew what slow worms were and that snakes shed their skins, that rabbits thump their hind feet or paws as a danger signal.

So you will not be surprised to read that Billy was hoping against hope that if and when it came this relocation would be somewhere near Hastings. It was a somewhat sobering thought, Billy leaving. He had taught us other four (including Kitty) quite a lot about the countryside. As I've said right from the start of us four boys, there is no doubt Billy was the brainy one. Looking back on it now, I think that given the opportunity, and if things went well during the rest of the war, Billy had enough brains to go a long way.

Quite apart from anything else, we had been very close companions for nearly a year. It is possible that I knew Billy and Len better than I knew my little brother, Martin. Us five kids had bonded into a sort of family. There was an unwritten code, we didn't go around deliberately getting each other into trouble, and if one of us was in trouble the others helped out if they could.

In nearly a year, I can only remember one serious argument, and that was between Len and Jim regarding the makeshift bicycle, and even that didn't go on for long. That's not bad going, considering there were five of us. To a certain degree it was us against them. We all knew we were going to miss Billy.

You must remember that, as senior boys, Jim, Len and Billy were all fast approaching fourteen years old, the then school leaving age.

First a letter arrived for Billy saying that Mrs Behoe had rented a place in the Hastings area, as we'd all expected. It went on to say that, given a short spell to get settled in and sorted out, she would be sending for Billy. It didn't take too long for that second letter to arrive giving him a date and travelling instructions; what they were I don't know.

What clothes he had were packed into his little case; any surplus went into carrier bags, such as they were.

After all I've written about Billy, I'm really surprised at myself for not being able to remember him actually going. Him leaving the house and saying goodbye to Nelly, Hetty, George and so on, it's all a blur. But I do remember Kit, Jim, Len and I walking with him into the village where he caught the bus to Haywards Heath, where he had to catch a train. As we waited for the bus he promised to write, and Kitty said if he did she would answer it. But of course nothing happened; we never heard any more of him, ever.

As we four of us walked back to Wickens, Len turned to Jim and said, "Well, I suppose we're the next ones to go." He was half right.

Whilst on the subject of people leaving, it is worth mentioning that the numbers at school were now holding pretty steady. The German bombing blitz of London was well under way and parents obviously thought it safer to leave their children in the safety of the countryside.

A lot of the school's senior boys were like Len and Jim, fast approaching school leaving age, so come the end of the autumn term school numbers could drop quite dramatically.

It was about this time that Old Jonah asked boys to tell parents when they wrote home, that should any parent wish to leave a boy in school for another year they should contact him (Jonah). This was to try to compensate for the huge disruption to their education.

How many boys passed on that message we will never know. Most boys wanted to be shot of school and start earning money; I'm pretty certain Len did not pass on this message.

The people upon whom evacuees were billeted were sometimes called foster parents, because it was a bit like that as these people received an allowance per child per week from the Government. The allowances were:

- Ten shillings and sixpence (10/6d) for the first child.
- Eight shillings and sixpence (8/6d) for every child after that.

Today's (2013) money equivalents are 10/6d = £15. 8/6d = £12, not a King's ransom. (Source: National Archives Currency Converter). Whether this allowance would still be paid during this extra year was not mentioned.

My mother and father heard about this extra year and wrote to say they would be coming to see us as soon as they could arrange it. Although I can't be sure, I don't think either Kit or Jim told them, definitely not Jim, and I only wrote short notes to put in with Kitty's letters. But it really matters not! The main thing is that they knew.

It must have been some time in October 1940 when Billy left, I can't remember. Keeping track of time passing at Wickens was just as hard as when I had been in hospital; there seemed to be no good reason to keep track of it. Just as long as I didn't miss out on Christmas!

Then a few weeks after Billy's departure, came news like a bolt out of the blue. A letter from Len's parents said they were seriously thinking of taking Len back to London. As far as I was aware, no reasonable reason was given.

Everybody was very surprised at this, even I who was still only nine years old could understand why Billy had gone but nobody could understand this move.

The whole point of being evacuated was to get away from the bombing, and now when the London blitz was at its height they want to take Len back into it; how daft can you get?

As I've said before, when you are nine years old nobody asks your opinion or tells you anything. But from what I was able to gather, Mrs Ashby did write to Mr and Mrs Hawes explaining about the extra year offer and that she was quite willing for Len to go on staying there. But the offer was rejected as far as I could understand.

The general opinion was that it was Mr Hawes putting his foot down. Everybody had a very poor opinion of Mr Hawes since his one and only visit; it was something that was never talked about. It was 'gone with the wind'. But the general consensus was that Len was, or soon would be, old enough to go to work and be bringing in wages, and that was thought to be the main factor. Far be it for me to argue with that. All of us on the kitchen side of Wickens who had got to know him thought that, as soon as he could, Len would join the army and be like his elder brother, his hero.

Also, those of us that knew him well were going to miss him much more than Billy, who was a nice enough bloke, but always a bit aloof and had not too great a sense of humour. Whereas Len was a good salt of the earth mate, with a really good cheeky sense of humour; that's what we were going to miss about him the most. When we were feeling down, as of course sometimes we did, he would cheer you up – a great bloke. It would not be hard to imagine him being in his element in the army.

Within a fortnight Len was packing the few (the very few) things that he had. At the goodbyes Nelly put on a brave face, but poor old Hetty shed a few tears and said it was all so very wrong.

As usual, these goodbyes always seemed to happen on a Saturday so Kitty, Jim and I walked with him to the village to catch the bus, but this time it was a lot, lot harder. As we waited for the bus, conversation was very difficult. "Don't worry, when you come back to London we are bound to meet up some time aren't we?" We nodded, but wondered. By the time we returned to London our parents had moved out of that area, so we never did see or hear from Len again;

it was never quite the same at Wickens once Len had gone.

As promised, Mum and Dad came to visit soon after Len had departed. Even they, during their short visit, said that they could see the difference without Len there. They, like everybody else, liked him. It was usual on these visits that if Mrs Ashby was at home, Mum and Dad would spend a short while with her during the afternoon, in her study. When they came out they told Jim that they had been discussing the possibility of Jim staying in schooling for another year. It seemed that Mrs Ashby was quite agreeable, if it was all right with Mr Jones (Old Jonah).

So, they would be leaving early enough to stop and see Old Jonah during his Sunday afternoon parent surgery. Poor old Jim wasn't happy about it but the matter was out of his hands. We all had to move a bit quickly to catch Jonah because, as I've said, it was a long walk to the village. We did make it in time to catch him. Once my parents explained the reason for the visit, yes it was agreed Jim would be staying on.

When the bus for Haywards Heath came, Jim, Kit and I said our goodbyes and started to walk back to Wickens. By the time we got there Kit and I were in no doubt at all about how Jim felt about his new arrangement.

Speaking of new arrangements, with the going of Billy and Len there had been a shuffle around of bedrooms. This meant that Jim and I were moved out the big bedroom that us four boys had shared, and moved to a somewhat smaller room over the kitchen. It was a very nice room, quite big enough for us two – it overlooked the garden. Being over the kitchen it was warmer than our old room and, with winter almost here, that would be a blessing.

At this time Jim had started model making, so they put a plain table in our room for him to be able to work on. That sweetened the pill a little bit with regards having to stay on at school.

While all these comings and goings were happening, Kitty just carried on regardless. She was loving her schooling at Haywards Heath and would not hear a word said against it. Loving school? I always knew there was something wrong with that girl.

32. An Austerity Christmas?

It was at mealtimes that Kit, Jim and I missed Billy and Len the most. At the best of times Jim was not the greatest conversationalist in the world, whereas Kitty was! The trouble was most of her non-stop chatter was about "At my school this, and my school that", plus the latest sporting achievements of her new heartthrob, never saw him, don't remember his name, but he sounded like a right ninny. So Jim and I let her do the talking, we did the eating.

Things carried on in the normal routine; school, helping with the lamps when I could, still Sunday school on Sunday for Kit and I but only if the weather was dry, because it was a long walk to Chelwood Gate. As a concession, Jim was excused Sunday school now he was fourteen years old.

The weeks rolled by, the weather was getting colder and, once again, the word 'Christmas' started creeping into peoples' everyday conversations. That is always a good sign. Along with the Christmas word, there was another one, one that I'd never heard before; it was 'austerity'. I didn't like the sound of that word. Nearly everybody was saying, "It's going to be an austerity Christmas this year." It seemed to be the 'in' thing to say. It appeared to me that people were saying it without knowing what they were talking about. It was just the right thing to say, then walk away scratching their heads, looking bewildered (I know that feeling).

We started to hear of one or two things that would be going on in the run up to Christmas, maybe not quite so much as last year, but nevertheless enough to put that feeling in the air that is only there at Christmas time.

But there was also something else going on, something that we couldn't fathom out what it was. We didn't think it was trouble, we would have heard about it before now. But sometimes when we walked into the kitchen their conversation would come to a very sudden stop. They took to always closing the door if they were talking so as to have some warning as the door opened.

Yes, there was definitely something afoot – it was our job to find out what! As we got nearer to Christmas, Kitty's school put on some sort of show on a Saturday afternoon. She asked me if I would like to go with her and I did. After all these years, I can't say I remember too much about it but I do remember it was an enjoyable afternoon. What I remember mostly was the school; at the time the only word I could think to use was magnificent!

It really was a lovely school, mainly because it was quite unlike any school I had seen before. For that time it was a modern, very new looking building, plenty of room and light. This was very different from my concept of schools, my thoughts going back to the Victorian type buildings that were the schools I had attended in London. This school seemed to have all the things that our London schools never had, like a gymnasium, and a sports field with running track. It was very obvious why Kit liked it so much.

For me to go into Haywards Heath was a bit of an event; it didn't happen very often. So what with the school show and the school itself it was quite an afternoon one way and another. The ninny wasn't there, so I didn't get a chance to cast my eye over this superman.

We were still getting nowhere into solving of the mystery conversations – must try harder. But there were still things to do in getting ready for this austerity Christmas. Cards to write and send, because there were still Christmas cards to be bought even with acute shortage of paper, but these cards were not very large, and very flimsy. We also went out gathering chestnuts.

The Christmas pageants and concerts like we had been to last year were on again this Christmas. Like last year the same Sunday school teacher collected Kit and I so that we could go. Nearly everything seemed to have been scaled down a bit from last year. It was explained to us that many of the people who would have normally have been organising or performing in these events could well have been enlisted into the armed services, or doing more important work, like war work.

There were about the same number of parties to go to as last year, austerity or not it was all boiling up quite nicely. The "Big Mystery" was solved about a week before Christmas 1940. Whilst Kit, Jim and I were having our tea one evening, Nelly and Hetty came in and sat down in the armchairs. They said they had something to tell us.

It seems that Mrs Ashby had been in touch with our parents and asked if they would like to come to Wickens after work on Christmas Eve, stay Christmas Day and night, returning to London on Boxing Day afternoon. This would include brother Martin, of course, but also our sisters Phyllis and Daphne. Thus, giving our family a chance to get two undisturbed night's sleep away from the worry of bombing.

This was fantastic news. We could hardly contain our excitement! Surely there could not ever be a better Christmas present than that. It didn't need gift-wrapping. The really nice thing about this was that, although it was going to make extra work for them, Nelly and Hetty were nearly as excited as we were.

In my excitement in even writing this, I forgot to say that this very generous offer had gratefully been accepted, because apparently it didn't stop there. Due to the fact that Dad, Daphne and Phyllis had all got to wait till their work finished, plus the uncertainty of buses from Haywards Heath and the amount of luggage, including presents, Mrs Ashby would arrange for a car to collect them from Haywards Heath station. Also, the return trip on Boxing Day. All my parents had to do was let Mrs Ashby know the train times. This was Mr and Mrs Ashby's Christmas present to us kids. It was quite unbelievable. Now you know why I still believe in Father Christmas.

When the news finally sank in, we had all sorts of questions. What's going to happen about this, and what about that? "Don't worry. Mrs Ashby's asked us first. We think it's a good idea and we've got everything worked out – it's going to be lovely for you."

This gave that last week before Christmas a new momentum; we just couldn't do enough to help. We were all excited, but it went against the grain for Jim to admit it. He was just quite pleased. We used to see brother Martin every time our parents visited, but Daphne and Phyllis we had only seen once or twice in the fifteen months that we had so far been there. They both had boyfriends now, so had far more important things to do than visit little brothers and sisters, although Phyllis would write to me from time to time; there had always been a bit of an extra link between Phyllis and I – it stayed like that until she died.

The days ticked slowly by, there wasn't a lot we could do to help but what there was we did willingly. Christmas Eve arrived and I always think it's the best day of Christmas. There's always what I call the Christmas buzz around and you can feel it. This year it was worse than ever. All we could do was wait.

There was only one bedroom that had a window that overlooked the drive. That was Nelly's room, the worst bedroom in the house; very dark and dingy, with a sloping ceiling. As evening got round to about seven o'clock, I asked if I could go and sit at her bedroom window and watch for the car. She warned that I might get a bit cold up there. I said I didn't mind. "OK, off you go, but don't touch anything." I promised I wouldn't and off I went.

How long I waited I've no idea; it seemed like forever. Then at last I saw the dimmed headlights of the hire car pulling in through the front gate. They were here!

There is no way I can describe the next quarter of an hour, because I can't remember. Even as I write now, I can still feel the emotion of it and it's hard to write. There were hugs, kisses and tears, everybody talking at once, not much of it making any sense.

After a while, things settled down a bit. Nelly and Hetty came forward to say their 'hello's' to everybody. They had been standing back watching this joyful scene. I really do think that was their reward – they were just happy to be able to do it. God bless them for that.

Tea was made, and what would Martin have to drink? He was still very young. It was explained that the small dining room was to be 'our room' during their Christmas stay and we would eat in there on our own as a family. Everybody was offered something to eat and, once they had been shown where they were sleeping, we went into 'our room' where a fire had been lit. With food on the table and more tea on the way, we talked until quite late. Then off to bed.

To be quite honest, there is an awful lot of that Christmas Day that I don't clearly remember. Maybe because, in the main, we just sat around in that small dining room with a nice fire going all day, enjoying being together as a family. My mother's offers to help were very politely refused by Nelly and Hetty. They said, "You just relax while you can."

The only two things I can remember clearly from that day when we were all up and dressed and sat down to breakfast. Whilst we were eating it, and talking, 'cos there was plenty of news to catch up on, there was a light tap on the door and Mrs Ashby entered. We all went to rise out of politeness. "No", she said. "Please stay as you are and enjoy your breakfast. I only wanted to wish you all a Merry Christmas and I'm sure it will be for you all. If there's anything you need please ask Hetty." We all chorused our Christmas greeting to her and she said, "I'll leave you all to your breakfast. Enjoy your stay."

She turned, about to leave the room; reaching the doorway she turned back. "Mr and Mrs Sleeman, would you mind if I went and fetched my husband? I would so like him to see this family scene."

My father replied, "By all means, we would welcome the chance to see Mr Ashby, after what you are doing for us."

"Thank you. Just stay as you are, I'll be straight back with him."

In no time at all they were both back. Mr Ashby was his usual chatty self, apart from, "Good morning, Happy Christmas" I don't think he said another word. My father, though, stood up and went across to them and shook hands with both of them. He was pretty close to tears but made a little speech.

He was a very good talker, knew just the right things to say. Now I can't remember what he said; no doubt thanking them for their wonderful gesture of getting us all together for Christmas, but I do remember at the end him saying that, apart from anything else, what a bonus it was to go to sleep last night and not have to worry about any bombs falling. The Ashby's nodded, said goodbye, and left us to ourselves.

The other memory is that during the morning Mr Billings called in to see everybody, and he came in to say hello to mum, dad and the family. That was the only time I saw Mr Billings in any room of the house other than the kitchen or staff sitting room. He gave my parents a bottle of his homemade elderberry wine, explaining that he didn't know how we would be for a glass of something with our Christmas dinner and his bottle might help. He finished up staying quite a while because he and Dad always seemed to get on well and have a lot to talk about. He had his Christmas dinner with Nelly, Hetty, George and Aunty.

The rest of the day whizzed by. After the Christmas dinner, we were all allowed to have a little drop of the elderberry wine (except Martin) - even my Dad took a sip and he was a teetotaller. Anyway, after the meal Dad insisted that we do the washing up. It had been a really good Christmas dinner and Dad thought they had done enough for us; now we do something for them. They didn't protest too hard.

They sat in their armchairs. Kitty made tea for those who wanted it, the rest of us washed up a mountain of plates. Everybody seemed to be happy.

Christmas Day came to an end and merged into Boxing Day. It was cold because there had been a very heavy frost overnight. Despite the coldness, Dad wanted to go for a walk so Kit, Jim and I went with Dad. Mum, Daphne, Phyllis and Martin stayed in the warm. They spent the time chatting to Nelly, Hetty, George and Aunty (not that she'd have much to say).

The fire was still going in 'our room', lit by breakfast time. Nelly said she would do a light lunch for them before they left for home. The car was coming, I think, at four o'clock.

My parents didn't quite know how to thank Nelly and Hetty for the lovely, restful, family two days. Same as last year, they had given everybody a token thank you Christmas present, but they thought it hardly seemed enough so they asked them was there anything that mum, dad or my sisters might be able to get for them in London that they couldn't get in shops in Haywards Heath. If there was, let them know and they'd do their utmost to get it for them.

Neither Nelly nor Hetty could think of anything but then Hetty, always the bashful one, said, "Well, there was something. I wondered if I could ask you Mr Sleeman?"

Now you see there is something I haven't been telling you about my father. His hobby was breeding canaries; the type known as Borders, and he was very good at it. He would enter his birds in cage bird shows and had got to the stage where he could only exhibit his birds in championship classes. All my brothers and sisters had grown up with a canary background, even at nine years old I knew quite a lot about the rearing of young birds – we all did – we'd grown up with it.

Now Hetty knew this from hearing us talking, and as she now explained to Dad, "I've always wanted a singing canary but don't know enough about them to go into a shop and buy one. Would you consider selling me one of yours? One that sings nicely – I know I can trust you."

There was a long pause, then Dad answered, "Hetty, I wouldn't dream of selling you one of my birds." That pulled us all up with a bit of a jolt; it was so unlike Dad to talk like that. Poor Hetty went all red and flustered. Dad grinned. "But I'll give you one as a thank you. If you can wait till about June, the end of their breeding season, I'll have a bird that for some reason will be no good to me for breeding. You are welcome to one."

"Will it sing?"

"Yes, I'll sort you out a good cock songster. You have got plenty of time to be sorting out a cage, and Jim, Kit and Geoff know enough about its care to help you out." Jim, Kit and Geoff nodded as if somebody was pulling an attached string. This solved the problem for Mum and Dad as to how to say 'thank you', not only for Christmas but for everything.

Once lunch was over, my family started getting their bits and pieces together. Mum and Dad went to see Mr and Mrs Ashby just long enough to say a very big 'thank you'. In due course, the car arrived. There were the usual tearful goodbyes. We stood at Wickens gateway and waved our arms off until the car was out of sight.

It was sad to see them go but what a lovely Christmas we had had. Weren't we lucky?

Personally, I couldn't see what all the fuss had been about. If that was an austerity Christmas, could we order another one for next year please?

33. It's a Hard Life

It almost goes without saying that following our excitement at Christmas things seemed a bit flat afterwards, but then I think it always does. The coming of the New Year 1941 was a bit of a non-event. January was here and I shouldn't think that it's a month many people look forward to.

As far as I can recall, very little happened regarding Jim, Kitty and I during the early part of 1941 that is worth mentioning. There was a distinct possibility that I was becoming well behaved; I'm going to have to watch that – can't have rumours like that flying around - could ruin my reputation couldn't it?!

So, in this lull in events, I'm going to relate some of the things happening in the country at this time, of which you may not be aware. These things would affect everybody in some way or another and just had to be coped with.

Life was made quite difficult for strangers in any area because very early in the war all signposts and place names were removed. This included all place names on all railway stations. Every means of identifying the name of any place or area had to be removed.

We were all told that the reasoning behind this was to confuse the German army in the event of Germany invading this country. It was a brilliant idea and it would no doubt work really well.

The proof being that it totally confused and bewildered the British as well. This country was in danger of becoming a nation of wandering nomads, wandering around from place to place trying to find out where the hell they were. To make matters worse, we were given a lecture at school on this subject and we were told that if strangers stopped us and asked us the way to anywhere we had to pretend we didn't know. They might be German spies.

Whether or not this not giving strangers directions was a Government policy, I don't know, but it was repeated to us by Nelly and Hetty. Also I have spoken to other people of my age who were living in other parts of the country at that time; some of them also remember being told this.

This happened at a time when Billy and Len were still with us. We used to get stopped frequently on our way to and from school. It seemed to be such a waste of people's time, and petrol, at a time when petrol was rationed. We talked it over and, rightly or wrongly, decided to help people if we could. We were only kids but it seemed just a silly waste of time and petrol. If we didn't give people directions somebody else would. It seemed rude not to.

On the railways, passengers, as they were then called, would have to count the number of stops if they didn't know the route and hope that they got it right, because I was told that station staff were not allowed to call out the name of the station as each train arrived, but I cannot confirm this. Many passengers got off at the wrong stations unless there was somebody around to ask.

Another problem was so many things were rationed; as children, the everyday household things were not our concern. But, looking at the list now, there seems to be very few food items that were not rationed. Rationed to very small amounts per person per week. Even basic foodstuffs like bread and milk.

Three main foodstuffs that were never rationed were potatoes, sausages and fish.

From the children's point of view, sweets and chocolate – 2 ounces of sweets or chocolate per person per week, if you could find a shop that had any. Most chocolate went to armed services NAAFI. There were absolutely no ice creams to be had; they were things of the past. Regards fruit, there were only home grown fruits, which meant no bananas, oranges or lemons.

All clothing, boots, shoes, household linen, even handkerchiefs, were rationed.

Everybody in the country, even babies, were issued with an identity card and adults were expected to carry it with them all times, along with gasmasks.

Gradually, a national register of all citizens over the age, I think it was eighteen, was compiled to show who would be eligible for the armed services, and who for Government war work.

The blackout meant just that. There was no street lighting whatsoever, all outside lighting was forbidden. Not even the smallest chink of light could show or be shown from household windows and doors. Air Raid Protection Wardens (ARP) were very strict on this. "Put that light out!" became something of a catchphrase at that time.

Even traffic lights had hoods fixed onto them so only the smallest amount of red, orange and green showed. Just enough to control traffic flow.

All cars and bicycles' lights had to be dimmed to the point of being almost useless. Also, cars and bicycles had to have large white stripes on their front and rear mudguards. These were of Government prescribed size and had to be complied with.

Pedestrians were advised to wear something white; in fact, there was a Government slogan out at that time – "Wear something white at night."

They were also advised to carry torches, which was all very well if you could get batteries, which were like gold dust. Even then, the torch glass had to have a piece of thin paper placed under it to dim the light.

There were posters everywhere guarding against the dangers of speaking carelessly in public places and giving away important information to the enemy. "Careless talk costs lives."

There is one more item I feel I must mention. It was not rationed, it was completely unavailable, and the item is films for cameras. People that still had films would not use them unless it was something very important. For that reason, I have almost no photographic records of my evacuated time, which I regret very much. Private photos and snapshots were temporarily a thing of the past.

You might now be inclined to think that these measures were harsh, even draconian, but at that time they were really necessary; so the people used to have a little grumble, blame Hitler, then accept it and get on with their jobs. We'd got a war to win.

34. One Man Went To Mow

Meanwhile, back at the ranch, life was ticking along much the same as usual. Nelly still a-cooking, Hetty still a-waiting on people, George still a-lamp filling, Aunty, oh! - never mind her.

But I lie ('cos I do sometimes). It seems that if you look closely things are not quite normal, not with Nelly anyway. She's smiling at everybody, there's a spring in her step - she's in love.

She's forever writing letters and cards and wanting me to 'pop out' on my bike to catch the post. Now, at nine years old, I'd got a lot to learn about this sort of thing. But even now, looking back on it, I still can't imagine Nelly as a great romantic, but there she was all hearts and flowers. The letters had so many kisses on the envelope there was hardly room for the address and stamp. How soppy can you get? It was as much as I could do to touch these letters and cards, in case I caught it and I made sure nobody saw me put it in the post box.

This 'mush' she was writing to and seeing from time to time was the son of a builder who did small building jobs and repairs in and around the area.

One morning, Jim and I were getting ready for school - Kitty had already left. We went into the back yard to get to the bike shed. We saw Nelly talking to a young chap, thought nothing more of it. Having got our bikes out, we called out "cheerio" to Nelly, but she called us over and introduced us to him. Oh dear!

Poor Nelly stood there beaming at him as if she'd won first prize in a dozen raffles. I just can't remember his name; it's gone.

Now, I've been racking my brains as to how I can refer to this bloke in the future, because he will crop up again later on. He will be known as SBH, standing for 'Silly But Happy', because that's him to a 'T'.

As a builders' labourer, I could imagine him playing sandcastles but not mixing cement. OK, it's none of my business – it's her affair (pardon the pun), but she deserved better.

Anyway, Jim and I went across on this particular morning, said "hello" and a few words like "goodbye" and left them to do their own thing, but I don't think it was anything to do with building.

It was by now well into spring, and cycling to school on a lovely morning was no hardship at all; in fact, it was very pleasant. Most of the hedgerows and trees had their lovely nice fresh green shoots, and that leads me nicely onto a character that I want to tell you about.

Meet "Old Frank". Don't bother to say hello, 'cos he won't answer you. Now, Old Frank, as he was always known, was responsible for those lovely hedges that I just mentioned. He is the hedger and ditcher, or as some people would say, the roadman.

It was always a waste of time saying hello or good morning to Frank. On the very rare occasions that we got any response at all, it was only a grunt. Most times he would turn his back and completely ignore us. Maybe he was a dumb mute, nobody knew, but he could still have given us a wave. It was easier for us to think he was just a miserable old devil, but it matters not.

No matter what he was, this old chap was a craftsman and his work was immaculate. His hedges neatly trimmed and level; his grass verges kept trimmed to a reasonable height; his ditches cleared out regularly, with gullies cut to allow road surface water to drain into the ditches. He did a good job.

He had no fancy tools, just a bill hook and crook stick for the hedges, a small scythe for the long grass and a spade for the ditches. He never left the hedge trimmings lying around – how he got rid of them I don't know. The cut grass lay where it was and the ditch clearings were thrown into the base of the hedges.

When I see what they do to the hedgerows today I can honestly say that I find it quite upsetting. The main object of all this writing is an account of being evacuated. The last thing I want is to start a crusade on countryside welfare, but when I see what these so called hedge trimming machines, that cost thousands and thousands of pounds, do to the hedges, I am appalled.

If, as a young gardener, I, or anybody else, had produced work anywhere near as bad as that, we would have, quite rightly, been sacked instantly.

What happens today is not hedge trimming, it's hedge mutilation or massacre. These hedgerow butchers with their high technology fancy machinery may call this progress, but I think we are going backwards.

So, Old Frank, wherever you are stand up and take a bow. You may have been a 'miserable old sod' but that doesn't alter the fact that you were a star in your own right. Head and shoulders above today's highly trained 'whizz kids'. Well done mate, and thank you, I will always remember your work.

Well, I'm glad I've at last got that off my chest. Now let's move on to something else we used to see on our way to and from school. That's the gypsy caravans.

We used to see gypsies from time to time, at no particular time of the year. As Londoners, it was at first a bit of a novelty. It would be true to say that, to start with, we were a bit wary of them; didn't quite know what to expect. We had only heard or read stories about gypsies, or seen bits in films. Nearly all of it unflattering, so we tended to steer well clear. We didn't give them any trouble, nor did they us.

They would make camp on any wasteland, or on the roadside verge, if it was wide enough. Most times they would stay for two or three days before moving on. Their ponies would be hobbled and left to graze slightly further off. During their short stay, the gypsies would go around from door to door selling baskets, clothes pegs that they had made, also lucky heather and good luck charms. Most people would buy something from them; it was said to be bad luck if you said "no" to the gypsy sellers.

There was one time when a gypsy lady came to Wickens' back door and she had a small child with her, a toddler. As Hetty was busy elsewhere in the house and Nelly was in the kitchen preparing a meal, Nelly answered the gypsy's knock on the back door. It's highly probable that Nelly bought something from her. Nelly wouldn't want to invite bad luck.

With the back door open the smell from the cooking wafted towards the woman and child. In a voice like an old crone, the woman said to the child, "Smell the lady's lovely dinner cooking ducky." The toddler just looked very sad and forlorn and nodded. This touched Nelly, as it was supposed to do, "Wait a moment", she said, went into the kitchen and cut two large pieces of cake and took it out to them.

For this, she was given a gypsy blessing and was assured that good luck was just around the corner. It didn't work; it wasn't good luck around the corner, it was SBH, how lucky can you get?

With gypsies in the area, everybody was on their guard and extra vigilant, but to be fair I never heard of any troubles that were caused by them. But it was a good chance for some of the "old timers" like George and Mr Billings to trot out their favourite gypsy stories to us youngsters. Some of these stories were believable, some I'm not so sure about, but some of the things we were told about regarding what they would eat, things like hedgehogs and snakes, were believable because they went into so much detail. I never had the chance to prove any of this; the gypsies were never around long enough to invite me to dinner, I'm very pleased to say.

In the household there had been some sort of a rift going on in the Dilly family and, in case you've forgotten, that's Nelly, Hetty, George and Aunty. How could anybody forget that?

It was none of our business, so Kit, Jim and I had no idea what it was all about. It may well have been over this 'toy boy' of Nelly's, SBH, because all joking to one side, he wasn't a very impressive looking specimen. That may not have been the reason and, as I've said, none of our business, but all was not well in the domestic bliss of the Dilly's.

Poor old George was definitely being ganged up on by the two sisters. Us three kids just kept a low profile and our heads down. Once again, I have to use the phrase 'to be fair'. Nelly and Hetty kept us out of it and carried on just the same towards us. The same goes for old George; in fact he tended to spend more time with us and be even friendlier than usual. This, because his own family were not talking to him very much. Even when they did, in not too friendly a manner, old George was glad of us and Mr Billings for company. It wasn't very nice.

Of all of us, I think Jim had missed Billy and Len going the most, because those three were all the same age, so had a lot in common, whereas our interests were totally different because of the age gap. My playmate, Arthur Jay, and I could knock around together, but Jim had nobody. He didn't go fruit picking quite so often but, when it was still in season, he never missed an opportunity to go beating for the shooting; he liked that. It was through going beating that he started to build a friendship with Mr and Mrs Bennetts' youngest son, Ray. It seemed that they were both short of company of their own age so it seemed like an ideal arrangement. Whenever I'd met Ray whilst out he came across as a nice, friendly, helpful young chap, slightly older than Jim, but not much.

Now, Ray was a member of the Air Training Corps (ATC) and, from what Jim heard about it, he thought he would also like to join. Can't be sure, but I think they had meetings, or parades, two evenings a week and occasionally weekends. I've no idea at all where they had to go for these parades, or what they got up to once they were there, but it gave them somewhere to go and something to do two evenings a week.

Because Jim had no lights on his bike, he was not allowed to use it after dark. In the blackout it would have been extremely dangerous and, with all the aforementioned shortages, buying a set of lamps was almost impossible. The result was Jim had to wait until spring and longer, lighter Double British Summertime evenings. Once they arrived there was no holding him back and he joined the ATC.

One slight hiccup was that, again, because of all the shortages, particularly clothing, they were very short of uniforms so Jim would have to wait. He was,

I think, a bit disappointed but nevertheless he felt he was doing his bit for the country. After the first two or three weeks, having proved more or less that he intended to keep going, they issued him with a forage cap and hat badge.

Well, that's great isn't it? Forage cap and hat badge, no trousers - good job summer's coming.

Round about this time my own personal intelligence service (that means through being nosy) picked up a few things which led me to believe that we could soon be going back to London, which somehow didn't make sense. Although I would have been coming up to ten years old, I listened every evening to the BBC news, nearly all of it on the war and the bombing of British cities, including the London blitz, which had been going on nightly for months. Even I could see that going back to London rather defeated the purpose of being evacuated. Once again, my little brain was confused, so I decided to talk to Kit and Jim about it.

They told me that they too had been picking up vibes along the same lines and were as confused as I was. Fat lot of help they were. So we agreed to work together on this and exchange any information that came along. That didn't prove to be difficult, because there was none, and we began to think that we had got it wrong.

When they were ready, we were told what was going on. It seemed that our parents wanted us to go back to London, yes, but only for a day trip. They wanted us to see for ourselves what was happening to London. Also, I think to give some justification as to why we had been sent away from London, our home, and from them.

It seems Mrs Ashby was against the idea but our parents had stuck by their guns, a date had not yet been fixed, but it would be quite soon, and a Sunday, because of Dad's work.

Well, this was really something to get our teeth stuck into. As I've mentioned before, even going in on the bus to Haywards Heath was a bit of an event, but going to London? Wow!

One Sunday evening, we were all listening to the BBC evening news on Hetty's wireless. I remember Mr Billings had called in for some reason; he was in his best suit, being as it was Sunday evening. He was probably on his way to the pub in the village, but stayed on to listen to the news.

The very first item on the news was that German troops had crossed the border into Russia, thereby invading Russia. Even I could sense that this was important news. It was Mr Billings who broke the silence that followed by saying, "I think he'll find he's bitten off more than he can chew this time." How right he was.

Us three kids could only wait for news of our trip, not knowing what to expect, but looking forward to it anyway. As for Jim, his mind was ticking; he had a cunning plan but wasn't telling Kit and I what it was just yet.

35. There's an Old Mill by the Stream

While we three awaited our London trip, of course things carried on in their daily routine. The world wasn't going to come to a stop just because we were going to London for the day.

There was still some bother between George and his daughters but very slowly things did seem to be improving; doubtless it would soon sort itself out.

Things at Kit's school seemed to be going along well enough to keep her happy, which was a good thing.

It was much the same at Jim and my school; we were now down to three teachers – Mr Jones (Old Jonah), Mr Thew and Mr Gough. The use of the Nissen hut was becoming less and less; it seemed as though its use was gradually being phased out. With not quite so much chopping and changing of venues it was beginning to seem a bit more like schooling, a bit more settled. But the allotment was still going strong under Mr Thew's guidance.

It was all pretty dull during this period, no riots, no escapes, no nothing – we must be losing our touch. If we're not very careful, the villagers are going to start talking to us.

Whilst doing this writing two or three things have come to mind that are not grumbles or complaints about the village. They are just observations from that time and I feel I should mention them.

First, in my nigh on three years there I never saw a policeman, not once. Now we've all read at some time or another about 'the friendly village bobby'; well I don't think they had one, friendly or otherwise. If they had, surely with all the things that us naughty evacuees were getting up to he would have put in an appearance to give us a 'friendly warning'. Of course, he may have been working 'under cover' – I hadn't thought of that.

Second observation, there was, as far as I could see, no fire brigade, not that I ever recall one being needed. But even in the best run places fires unfortunately do occur.

Third observation, there seemed to be no ambulance service available.

This belief is strengthened because Nelly was coming back to Wickens in the blackout, following a trip out on her evening off. She tripped and fell, dislocating her shoulder. She managed to get back to Wickens, where her sister

The water mill – something to see and admire.
Photo: Author's collection

Hetty set about helping her. Whether the Ashby's were in residence or not, I can't remember.

The upshot of all this was that a chauffeur driven car had to be arranged from the village in the middle of the night. This to take both Nelly and Hetty to Haywards Heath hospital, where the shoulder was put back into place, then the car, which had waited, brought them back again. But I knew nothing of this until next morning, 'cos I was bye-byes.

One final observation, there must surely have been a local doctor, but in the time I was there I never heard of anyone speak about a doctor or where he lived.

This all seems to make Horsted Keynes look a bit like Shangri-La. No crime rate amongst the adults, and the children never naughty so they don't need a policeman.

Never careless, so they don't have any fires.

Never sick, so they didn't need a doctor or ambulance, except Mrs Silvester and her efficient kitchen-type clinic for us sickly outsiders. End of observations.

Outside school hours my playmate was Arthur Jay, but as I think I've explained before, he used to go to school in Haywards Heath, the same school as Kitty, but in the junior section. This meant that once at school I had to look elsewhere for my mates. The unlucky pair turned out to be brothers, John and David Jones. Both around my age, David was the same age as me, John a year older.

They came with the school in September 1939 and had been around all the time, but it was only recently that we had pal-ed on to each other. Because of the stuttering, I was still very slow to make friends but, whilst on the subject of stuttering, it was not as bad as it had been. This led me to be a bit more confident.

I'm not sure when it happened, but quite soon after arriving at Horsted Keynes, John (the elder one) had a nasty accident, falling from a high bank and cutting his head open quite badly. He had been in hospital for some time. It was some long time after that incident that we became pally but he still had to be careful not to overdo things. The three of us got on really well.

Sometimes when it rained it would be too wet to do our usual thing in the village school playground, so we would go for a stroll to see what we could discover.

As you went into the churchyard, on your left was a small pathway which led to a wooded area, maybe 'copse' would be a better word. This was where "The Tribe" had got ready for their raid; surely you remember that?

Now, for some reason I can't explain, I'd never been along this pathway and into this copse before; suppose I was just too busy doing other things, so it was breaking new ground for me.

On one of these walkabouts, John, David and I came across three, maybe four, canisters or cylinders laying in a pile in this here copse. They were khaki in colour, so we presumed they had been left, maybe forgotten, by an army training squad. Now, we had been warned over and over again, "Not to touch anything that we found that looks suspicious – it might be dangerous".

But we were only looking at these things so that doesn't count. By just looking at them we could see that whatever these things were they had been used – they were completely empty. We could see (without touching) that these cylinders were now just empty cases. So John picks one up, smells it and shakes it. At once he is in trouble.

A few small particles of whatever the substance was flew into his face and eyes and he was screaming in pain, and could not see. There was a small stream running through the copse and David and I led John to it, knelt him down to try and wash this stuff out, but the water only seemed to make matters worse. David and I were scared stiff and worried about John.

We guided him back to school, where Mr Thew took control with a, "I'll have a word with you two later". What was surprising was that there was no suggestion of calling for help, or getting John to a doctor (if there was one); it all had to be done 'in house'.

It was quite out of the question for John to partake in lessons that afternoon. He was allowed to sit in a chair with his eyes covered. As the afternoon wore on, John said that things were beginning to improve slightly.

The teachers decided, after speaking to us, that these were used tear gas cylinders. All three of us were given a good ticking off, but it was felt that the scare we had had was punishment enough. "Don't do anything silly like that again". "No sir".

At close of day, John's eyes were still too bad for him to be allowed to ride his bike back to their billet; it would not have been safe. So both John and David's bikes were safely locked away and David had to act like a guide dog. The next day John's eyes were a lot better but they looked red and sore. He said he could see reasonably well. At the end of the day he was allowed to use his bike to get to their billet. He was, as they say, 'recycled'.

Then on another jolly little ramble in the same copse. I don't know whether we had gone further than usual or whether we had inadvertently wandered around in a circle, but it doesn't matter all that much. We found ourselves standing on the top of a quite high embankment and we were looking down onto a very old watermill.

This was the first watermill I had ever seen and it had the same effect on me as those 'golden daffodils'. It was quite lovely in a rustic sort of way; as if you'd stepped into a time warp and been taken back many years.

Now you are thinking that we went charging down the bank and started messing about, got ourselves into trouble again. Well, you are wrong, so there!

We stood and looked at this mill, we admired it, talked about what it did. We then turned and walked away; there's a surprise.

Now I've heard that a painter called John Constable painted 'The Water Mill'. Well, I wish he had come and painted this one. The paintwork was in a terrible state. All cracking and peeling. A couple of coats of undercoat and a nice gloss finish would have made a world of difference. Maybe he was too busy doing war work. But even if he had been kind enough to paint it, he would have been wasting his time, because after the war somebody demolished it, which to my mind borders on criminal. But at least that's something they can't blame on the evacuees. Or can they?

When I was older, in fact, married with two children, I took them to Horsted Keynes to show them around the place I often talked about. We spent much time looking for that old mill; now I know why we couldn't find it. It had so impressed me; I wanted them to see it. I'll write more about my re-visit later on. Right now, I'm getting ready to go to London.

36. A Day Return to London

This is another part that I have not been looking forward to writing, but not for the same reasons as the Mrs Ongar saga, but because I fear that I may lack the words and writing skill to adequately portray to you what I saw and felt on that day. All I can do is to give it my best shot. Here goes, wish me luck.

The first part is easy. The big surprise that Jim had been keeping to himself was that he would be going to London in a full ATC uniform. Because Ray Bennett had been in the Corps much longer than Jim, Ray had a uniform, which he agreed to loan Jim for the day.

On the Sunday of our trip we had no trouble in being up and ready on time. We had to walk to the village and be there in time to catch the first bus into Haywards Heath. I just don't know what sort of time that would be.

What happened about train tickets, again, I don't know. Whether or not tickets had been sent to us, or whether Jim or Kit were given money to buy tickets at the station, it doesn't really matter. We had tickets and the journey to Clapham Junction went without a hitch.

Our school friends who had already done this journey had told us about the large number of barrage balloons that we would see; they were not kidding. From the outskirts of London the sky was full of these enormous silver balloons as far as you could see. Hundreds of them, all facing the same way, blown by the wind or breeze. If the reason for their being there was not so sinister it would have seemed almost decorative.

Once at Clapham Junction, our Dad was waiting on the platform with little brother, Martin. Hugs and kisses all round, then quickly on a bus bound for Queenstown Road, home, it was a lovely feeling.

On the bus, Dad explained that Gran was away for a short while. She'd gone to visit her sister in Taunton, Somerset, to get a small break from the bombing. She was really sorry to have missed seeing us, but sent her love and had left us some money. The money was fine but I'd rather have seen Gran.

This is where the words start to fail me, because I just cannot describe my feelings as we climbed those stairs into our old flat. Small it may be, Wickens it wasn't, but it was home!

Again, hugs and kisses from Mum, Daphne and Phyllis. There was lots of talking and laughing and there was lots to see.

Walking down Queenstown Road from the bus, we had already noticed some changes. At the top end near Lavender Hill some shops had been flattened by bombing. Most of the remaining shops had no shop windows. Many of the houses, nearly all flats, had no windows either. The chapel on the corner was gone as well.

On the pavement outside each house, the Ministry of Defence had built air raid shelters, one for each house. They were, of course, very sturdily built and each one would be about the size of a present day bus shelter.

The MoD had put doors on but Dad was a pretty good handyman and had put a better one on so as the shelter could be locked up when not in use. He also built in two bunk beds for Daphne and Phyllis, with a child size camp bed for Martin. There was just room enough for three chairs for Mum, Dad and Gran when she was there. That's how they slept night after night.

He also ran cable down from the flat so they had electric light in the shelter; they also had a wireless. All this we were of course shown.

While Dad and Martin had been meeting us, Mum had been preparing some lunch. But before we could sit down to eat that, we had a whole list of people that wanted to see us. People who lived in Queenstown Road and had seen all of us growing up.

So we went on a whistle stop tour of Mrs Bond, Mrs Gough, Mrs Humphreys, Mrs Gokey, Mr and Mrs Quitingdon and our old friends, Mr and Mrs Bangeebango and daughters.

At each stop it was exactly the same routine. "My, haven't you grown?" "Aren't you looking well?" "Are you being looked after all right?" "Take care of yourselves." At each stop they would have found hidden reserves of sweets and chocolate that were pushed into our bag and, in some cases, money. This was all beginning to look like a very good idea, maybe we should do this more often. At nearly all the stops there were tears as we said goodbye. I wish they wouldn't do that.

Back to the flat for this lunch. It was like old times sitting around that kitchen table with all the family, hearing Dad's canaries singing in the back yard because he always kept them outside in the open air.

Straight after lunch we went out again. My sisters, Daphne and Phyllis, were told they didn't have to come if they didn't want to. But Dad made it quite clear that when we went to catch the train to return he wanted everybody to be there to see us off. Long face from Daphne, Phyllis didn't mind.

So, leaving Daphne and Phyllis behind, the rest of us set out for the Elephant and Castle. 'The Elephant' as it was known.

The trip to 'The Elephant' was light-hearted and I was not aware of noticing any particularly bad bombing, just the odd bomb site here and there. Even those should not be brushed aside too lightly; they meant heartbreak and hardship for some poor souls. The reason we were not seeing much out of the windows was due to the fact that all the bus windows were covered with a green protective mesh. This mesh was to stop splintered glass flying and causing injury. A small hole was left in the centre so passengers could see where they were and when to get off.

One other reason was that we were giving our full attention to Mum and Dad.

It was so good to be out with them again in London.

There was no way of me knowing what to expect when we got to 'The Elephant' and I was not ready for it. The word 'surreal' is not a word I like very much and I try never to use it, but in this instance I'm going to because it's the only word that fits the bill.

At 'The Elephant' as we stepped off the bus it was as if I had stepped into a bad dream. One of those dreams that you try hard to wake up from and can't. We stepped into utter devastation! There was nothing to see but piles of bricks and rubble.

This is where I struggle to describe what I saw, because if I had not actually seen it with my own eyes I would never have believed it. It was the stuff nightmares are made of.

There were vast areas of what had been shops and houses flattened. Just an odd segment of walling left standing here and there. These bits of walling would sometimes have a battered doorframe loosely hanging from them.

The piles of rubble were not just bricks; there was broken furniture, broken doors and windows, bits of old shop counters, shoes and some clothing. Most strikingly in all this debris were the building's roofing timbers sticking out like fingers pointing to the sky. Much of this timber was charred through burning, in some cases still smouldering.

There were a few ARP wardens on these rubble sites, attempting to dampen down in the worst places, by using stirrup pumps. You could not but help smelling that smell of things smouldering.

We started to walk slowly along the pavements. Dad was the only one doing any talking. The rest of us were a bit 'shell-shocked'. Whether or not Mum had seen anything as bad as this before I've no way of knowing but she was certainly very quiet.

As we walked along, there was a lot, and I mean a lot, of broken glass underfoot. As you put each foot down there would be a nasty crunch as small pieces of glass crunched into even smaller pieces. Father kept talking.

My most vivid memory of that visit to 'The Elephant' was as we came to a road junction. There on that corner had once been a tailor's shop. 'Had once been' are the right words, because it wasn't there any longer.

There was a low ridge of wall about a foot high running along what used to be the shop front. This ridge had once supported the shop windows, for displays. It had been quite a large shop. Where the shop windows space had been were the display tailor's dummies. Some broken, some partially burned, others with partially burned display suits on them. Nearly all of these dummies had been knocked or blown over and were just lying there in the debris. They looked too much like bodies for my liking; it was somewhat grotesque.

My father, for reasons only known to himself, stepped onto one of the rubble piles to pick up a roll of suiting material that lay there smouldering. He held it out for us to see. My mother became very worried. "Oh don't do that dear, somebody might think you are looting", she said. "Yes, I suppose you are right", he replied, throwing the roll back onto the pile of rubble. As he did so, a small shower of sparks flew off the roll.

At what I imagine was the back of this tailor's premises there was just the corner of one room, two walls at right angles to each other that had somehow miraculously been left standing. It looked as if it could have been 'the staff room'. The walls went up to ceiling height, except there was now no ceiling. On one wall there were some hooks to hang hats and coats, with one unclaimed coat waiting to be collected. On the other corner wall there was some sort of work service with a teapot and teacups still in place. Waiting for someone to make the tea. It was all a bit eerie.

On the far side of this vast area of devastation some way away, there was a row of buildings with shops on the ground floor. As far as we could see they appeared almost undamaged by the bombing, apart from the windows had all gone and the shop fronts all boarded up. Everyone had painted on the boards, or had notices up saying "Business As Usual". All except one trader who wanted to be different. I don't remember his exact words but, roughly, it was "They Won't Close Me Down!" Fantastic.

What enhanced this surreal feeling was the normality of the people walking about. They were going about their Sunday business as if there was nothing wrong. It made me feel like running up to them and shouting, "Can't you all see what's happening here? Do something about it!" But you see I suppose to them it was now normal. They were used to it. Us coming in from the country weren't.

After that tailor's shop on the corner, I just don't remember any more; I'd seen and had enough. In truth, I was a bit scared, not for Kit, Jim and myself, but for the people that had to endure this bombing night after night. People like my family. Whether we walked around for much longer I've no idea; if we did, then I don't remember it.

The next thing I do remember is being on the bus back to the flat. Our Dad was trying very hard to cheer us up and jolly us along, without much success.

Mum had prepared a special tea which we all sat down to before leaving for the train. When we all left the flat to go to The Junction, I didn't know it then but that was the last time I would ever be in that 'small but dear old flat'. I shall write more about it later.

The 'goodbyes' this time were a lot harder; now we knew what was happening to London we were more anxious. As our train pulled in we were told not to let down the window and lean out; it was too dangerous. "Yes Mum". Dad found us an almost empty carriage and we, and our bag crammed full of sweets and chocolate, piled in, then through the closed window we stood and waved and no doubt cried as the train slowly pulled away.

The only other occupant, sitting in the far corner facing the engine, was a young naval officer. He was reading a book. He looked up, smiled, said "hello" and went back to his reading. We settled down in our seats. Kit and Jim next to each other, I sat opposite them. We all went into deep thought. There was almost no talking between us, even Kitty was quiet. We were, I'm sure, reflecting on the experiences of that day, because I would like to think that it had affected all three of us in one way or another.

It was Jim who broke this spell of silence by getting up to reach the bag that held our supply of sweets and chocolate. From it he took a smaller bag of boiled sweets, opening it, offered the bag towards Kit, she took one, then my turn. He then hesitated for just a moment, then took a step across the carriage and proffered the bag towards the young officer.

"Excuse me, sir, but would you like one of these?" The officer looked up and smiled.

"Thank you, that's very kind." He took a sweet, but before putting into his mouth said, "Have you children been visiting your family?"

"Yes sir."

"Is everything all right?"

"Yes, thank you sir."

"I'm very glad. Thank you again for my sweet."

Jim ventured. "Take another for later on."

"No thanks, one's enough."

With that, Jim went back to his seat, the officer back to his reading. Kit, Jim and I went into deep meditation.

My own thinking was about the German boy that we had been asked to befriend when I was in the fever hospital, remember him? Name of Max. He seemed like such a nice boy. But now it could be his father, uncle, even his big brother bombing our London and other cities. Then it dawned on me that on Hetty's wireless I had heard that our bombers were bombing Berlin and other German cities as well. Did that make us as bad as them? I just didn't understand the logic of what was happening.

Adults were very quick to lecture us children about the hardships of war, about how everybody must go without because of the shortages; about the dangers and the suffering. Us kids could see that. You couldn't escape it if you tried. What nobody ever tried to explain in simple language was 'why are we at war'?

'What's it all about?' 'Why are we fighting the Germans?' Why?! That was my recurring question, why?!

It didn't take long for the train to reach Haywards Heath. How Jim knew when we got there, I don't know. As the train pulled in we stood ready, taking care not to forget our bag of goodies. The train stopped and Jim went to open the door and couldn't, and slight panic set in. The officer, who we'd said goodbye to saw the problem. "Here, let me do it," he said, dropping his book and coming to our rescue, but even he had trouble with it and had to let the window down, reach through and open it from the outside. He then jumped down onto the platform and helped Kitty and I down; Jim refused any help.

"You all set now then?"

"Yes, thank you sir. Thanks for your help."

"That's all right." He then shook hands with all of us and wished us good luck. Getting back in the train as the window was open, he slammed the door then lent out of the window. It was a bit like seeing a friend or relative off. As the train started to move he raised his hand in a sort of half wave. "You children take good care of yourselves. Bye." As it pulled away Kit and I waved, Jim came to attention and gave a very smart salute (I wish I could have done that). The officer smiled and tried to return Jim's salute, but leaning forward as he was it wasn't easy.

Why I have remembered that young naval officer for the rest of my life I have never been able to understand, but remember him I did, very clearly. Maybe it was his dignified friendliness. I hope he made it safely through the war.

With the train out of sight we picked up our treasure trove, left the railway station and went across the road to the bus station, awaiting the next bus back to Horsted Keynes. There was very little being said between us.

On arrival at the village, we started the long walk to Wickens. As to what the time was I've no idea, but with Double British Summertime there was no danger of it getting dark just yet.

If the object of this trip was to show us why we had been sent away, as far as I was concerned it worked. Speaking for myself, I had learned that war is not a game of soldiers to be played with bows and arrows. War was pretty serious stuff, in fact downright dangerous. Underneath those piles of rubble we had seen there could have been people, or the remains of people.

In nearly everything I do I try to extract some humour, but there is no humour in this.

The Geoffrey Sleeman that was plodding wearily back to Wickens was a somewhat different one that had stepped out eagerly and excitedly that very same morning, because during that day I'd done a lot of growing up.

37. "It's 'im"

Following the trip to London, things took a little while to settle down again, at least as far as I was concerned. It was nothing serious, just some difficulty in getting back into the everyday routine, back to normal, whatever normal was. Maybe that is what Mrs Ashby had feared; maybe she was right.

But after a while, I did start to pick up the threads again. When questioned about that trip, I remember I didn't like talking about it very much. Letters from home were more eagerly awaited, just to know everybody was all right.

In a strange way the London Blitz was having a knock-on effect on our school. At the beginning of evacuation, when things in London remained quiet, a lot of parents had taken their children back to London. So our school numbers dropped quite dramatically. When the Blitz commenced and thousands of people became homeless, some families decided to move out of London altogether for the time being.

Some came to the Horsted Keynes area and, being London children, the village school didn't want to know them. So they came to our school, such as it was; we made them welcome with a sort of fellow feeling.

It didn't matter that they didn't come from Battersea, or even from our side of the River Thames; they were Londoners and that was all the qualifications you needed to get into our school.

In nearly all these cases it was whole families moving together and renting empty houses in the area. Some had some pretty scary stories to tell, but most didn't want to talk about it. In a lot of cases the fathers were either in the armed forces or away on war work. In this new intake were "The Harvey Brothers", my future friends, but it didn't happen overnight.

Their names were Brian (slightly older than me) and Arthur (another Arthur), who was slightly younger than me. They had been bombed out of their East End homes twice. Their father was in the army and their mother had decided enough was enough and had rented an empty farmhouse.

We didn't get to know each other straight away; being 'the new boys' they were a bit cautious to start with and tended to keep to themselves. New school, strange routine, new to the countryside, we'd all been there and knew that feeling. As I've said before I was, at that time, very slow to approach people because of the stuttering. Never knew how people would react, so I kept my distance.

Then, one day as I was cycling back to Wickens from school, I was overtaken by the school car; the one that we never qualified for. As was normal practice, he tooted his hooter and I waved and, as usual, all the kids in the car waved back. One of the faces I saw was the youngest Harvey, Arthur, and he was waving. Right, I'll have to look into this tomorrow. Where's he living around here?

Next morning on the way to school the school car passes, toot-toots, and both the Harvey boys were grinning out of the car window.

During break time, I approached Arthur and asked him where they were living, to be using the school car. He explained that his mother and her sister (Arthur's aunt) were renting the farmhouse at Birch Grove Farm. This was news to me because I'd never heard of Birch Grove Farm. It seemed that it was tucked away on land somewhere between the house where Arthur and Mrs Jay lived, and the Twyford area. It had somehow escaped my inspection; I'll soon put that right.

During our chat, Brian had come across and joined in. We three were getting on quite well. I started to explain where Jim, Kit and I were billeted but they already knew. The other kids in the car already pointed it out to them.

It wasn't too long before we were arranging to meet up in the evening and they would show me where they lived. Then I would give them a tour of Wickens' grounds.

As in many cases these two brothers were nothing at all alike. In Brian's case he was dark haired and well built, very shrewd, confident and streetwise, with a good but cheeky sense of humour. Whereas Arthur was fair haired, very slight in build, a touch on the shy side, not so confident as his brother, but a bit more brainy, very likeable; a good footballer, too good for me to play with.

When we met in the evening they took me to the farm. It was just as you would imagine the average farmyard from those days being - farmhouse, barns, pigsties, chickens running around.

It seemed that the arrangement was that Mrs Harvey and her sister (both of their husbands were in the army) were both bombed out so were sharing this rented farmhouse. The sister had two girls, Nonie who was about Kitty's age, and Audrey, about two years younger. So Brian and Arthur had mother, aunt and two cousins in the house with them. Complicated isn't it?

They had the farmhouse, one shed and a very small piece of ground right opposite their front door. The farmyard, barns and pigsties remained under the control of the farmer. On my first visit the pigsties were empty.

Right from the word go it was obvious that Mrs Harvey (the boys' mum) didn't like me one little bit. Yes, I know, it's hard to imagine, but would I lie to you? You will no doubt have gathered from your reading that I was a really lovely little chap, but there's always a 'but'! I wasn't Mrs Harvey's idea of a lovely little chap. What's more, she didn't bother to hide it.

When I used to knock on that front door of an evening, I used to pray that anybody would answer the door but her. If, by some unfortunate chance, it was her, I would ask if the boys would be coming out this evening. She never once answered me. There would be a withering look and a grunt, then turning away sharply, she would shout at the top of her voice, "Arfur, it's 'im!" Charming.

Never at any time was I invited in. If my big toe had accidentally strayed across their threshold, I'm sure it would have been stamped on, but I was careful, and it didn't.

Looking back over it, I can see that if they'd been bombed out twice they probably didn't have much in the way of furniture, but a smile and a friendly "hello" costs nothing. But smiles and Mrs Harvey were not compatible. I never saw her smile. She was a very severe looking lady and she scared the pants off me.

Her sister, however, was much more pleasant and if she answered my knock she'd smile, say "hello", then call to Arthur or Brian, "Your friend's here", and add to me "They won't be a minute." That's a bit more like it.

By the looks of things, these two families had already been here for some weeks before they started attending school, getting settled in and things sorted out. They'd already started keeping rabbits in hutches, and some chickens.

It may have been just bad luck, but in their short time there they'd had one rabbit die. They had a cockerel; he died as well. They had buried these 'pets' in their piece of ground right opposite their front door. In each case the 'pets' were left with one foot still sticking out of the ground and Brian considered it good luck to shake hands with the cockerel's claw every time he came out through the front door.

Seeing as how I was never invited in, I therefore never had to come out, so I could forego this practice, so I took my chances with my luck.

The two girl cousins, Nonie and Audrey, tagged along and joined in whatever us boys did, but with Nonie was only sometimes, and with Audrey it was always. Looking good was the main focus of Nonie's life. To be fair, she made a good job of it, because she was an attractive young girl, but not very bright.

But Audrey, who was also quite attractive, couldn't have cared less about what she looked like. She was quite clever and brainy and wasn't worried about that either. Her main object in life at that time was to prove to us boys that she could be as good as us in everything we did; maybe even better, and the trouble was, she could do it, in some things. She was a good sport.

Soon after I started going to play at the farm, I took Arthur Jay along with me. It wasn't fair to abandon him. We'd been mates for some time now. After his first visit he wouldn't even go and knock on the front door, it was left to 'Muggins'.

The problem was this gave us two Arthurs; one of them had to go, so we had a meeting about it. It seemed a bit harsh to bump one of them off. Not only that "The Wicked Witch of the North" wouldn't have liked it at all if we took away her "little Arfur", would she?

It was Arthur Jay who came up with the answer. He explained that at his Haywards Heath school, most of the boys there called each other by their surnames, so he was used to being called Jay, so that was decided upon. So:

Arthur Harvey was called Arthur.

Brian was called Brian.

Arthur Jay was called Jay.

Geoffrey was called all sorts of things.

One evening, in answer to my timid knock, my prayers were answered; it wasn't her, it was Audrey. "Hello", she greeted. "Just having some tea. See you by the pigsty in five minutes".

You see, underneath all the 'tomboyishness' she was a romantic at heart. Meet me by the pigsty in five minutes. Talking of pigsties, soon after I started going to the farm the farmer had bought some piglets and put them in the stys. The girls thought they were sweet; I wasn't so sure. I still had memories of escaping from those man-eating pigs a few months back. They were all right as long as they stayed in their stys. There were about eight of these piglets and, for the first few days were the focus of attention. But they smelt and were noisy. They lived like pigs, but I must say that I always got a more hearty greeting from the pigs than I did from Mrs Harvey.

When the gang arrived at the pigsty after finishing their meal, Jay (the old Arthur) and I pointed out that there was one short; a piglet was missing.

"Yeah, the little weakling died", explained Brian.

"We asked Mr (whatever the farmer's name was!) if we could have it and bury it with the others by the front door. Din't yer see it just now?"

"No, I'll have to look next time."

By this time we'd had a good nose around, in all the barns and outhouses and found out what's what. There was one big barn that had a hayloft with an upper door from which you could throw out hay or straw; in this case it was straw, loads of it.

On the lower floor was a tractor's trailer, so us kids, including the two girls, dragged the trailer out of the barn and placed it under the hayloft trap or door. We then threw out enough straw to fill the trailer, nice and thick. Then we took it in turns to jump from the hayloft into the trailer, making a hell of a noise as we did so.

We were going great guns when the sister (Brian and Arthur's aunt) came out and stopped us. She said it was far too dangerous and somebody was going to get hurt. Not only that, but farmer what's-his-name wasn't going to be too pleased with what's happening to his straw. The aunt was very nice about it; in fact, even saw the funny side to it. She said she was half tempted to have a go at jumping herself! But no, it was just too dangerous.

She made us put all the straw back into the loft. She even helped us clear up all the mess we'd made. The trailer was put back in the barn, but not forgotten. That trailer was to be involved in some of the greatest fun of my entire childhood. Watch this space.

By the time we'd done all that, the time was getting on a bit. Nobody knew exactly what the time was, but nobody really cared. We knew it was too late to go too far afield that evening.

The farmyard had a big five bar gate, so we just swung on that and sung all the songs of the day, mostly army ones. "Bless 'Em All" was our favourite. Once the Harvey family were called in Jay and I went back; him to his home, me to

Wickens – it had been a fun evening.

The next time I approached the Harvey's front door I paused, not only to say my usual prayer, but also to look at their 'pets' corner graveyard'.

There they were, the feet of their dearly departed sticking up through the soil.

Now just stop and think a moment about what they had outside their front door ...... Claw, Paw and Trotter ...... sounds more like a firm of very dodgy solicitors to me!

38. Things That Disappear In The Night

It is difficult to fit the next events into any specific time during this writing, because it happened not once but at pretty regular intervals, starting some time in 1940 and continued right through until the time I went home to London.

We'll start at the beginning in 1940. In those days we were still walking to and from school. On our way to school in the mornings, everything would be quite normal; just a nice quiet walk through the countryside, but by the time we returned in the afternoon Corbett Woods would be transformed into an army camp. There would be hundreds of soldiers swarming all over the place, like an ants nest.

There were tents, lorries, staff cars, dispatch riders, motorbikes and always a couple of large mobile sheds, always padlocked. From the road we could always see smoke from a fire, but never managed to get close enough to see where it was coming from.

The first time this happened it was a big surprise and caused a fair amount of excitement amongst us. It will come as no surprise to you to read that we went to investigate these goings on.

We were never allowed into the woods whilst the troops were camped there, but many soldiers would come to the perimeter to talk to us. The main questions were, "Were we local kids?" "What part of London did we come from?" and "Where's the nearest pub?"

Our main question was, "Do you have any badges or army buttons you don't want?"

In most cases any soldiers that came from London would be called over to have a chat, not that I'd have much to say, but it was all different from usual and quite exciting to see so many soldiers at once. So, next morning, we were on the lookout for them and, as we went along, we called out and waved to any that we saw. Then we'd have a chat with them on our way back to Wickens after school and this became a daily routine, waving and talking.

On the fourth morning, on the way to school, they had gone; vanished, overnight. During the night they had pulled out, absolutely everything was gone, except their rubbish and litter. We could see where the tents had been, we could see the tyre tracks and wheel marks. We never heard a thing and Wickens was only set back a little from the road.

We were quite stunned, but this was to be the format over the next couple of years. They would come, take over the Corbett woods, stay for three, maybe four, days then pull out, but always silently at night, like an army of ghosts. Never did find out who cleared up all the mess after them.

Those were the "here today, gone tomorrow" type camps, that happened more frequently as the war went on. There was at least one, possibly two, camps in the Danehill area that seemed as if they might be there for the duration of the war. If the wind was blowing from the right direction we could hear some of the bugle calls when we were in the Ashby's garden.

One afternoon it was our turn to have use of one of the village school classrooms. So Old Burb was once again taking a class of us junior boys there, with Old Jonah and Mr Thew in charge of senior boys at the Nissen hut and the allotment.

We were well into the lesson, working quietly away like the well-behaved boys that we were. Suddenly a voice from a boy sitting near the window piped up.

"Excuse me, sir, but there's a soldier in our playground, and he looks as though he's lost." Old Burb moved over to the window and, unbeknown to him, so had all the boys; all peering over shoulders to get a good look.

The solder was there all right, and seemed to be somewhat perplexed as to what to do next now he'd got there. He turned to face the school building, maybe looking for the entrance. As he turned, a shout went up "That's my Dad!" And from the front of the pack Tom Greensmith came pushing and shoving, fighting his way to the classroom door. Chairs went flying in the mad rush to get outside to his dad.

Other boys went to follow, but Burb stopped them in their tracks. "Leave them, this is their moment", he said. Having given them a reasonable time to have said their hello's and got over the excitement to some degree, Burb went out and shook hands with Tom's father, had a short chat, then told Tom to get his coat and go with his father.

This had, of course, caused great excitement in the classroom, but Old Burb came back in and said, "Well, come on get back to your work."

It turned out that Private Greensmith had been posted to the camp at Danehill. But because of wartime security, troops were not allowed to give the addresses or locations of the places to which they were posted. So, neither Tom nor his mother had any idea whatsoever as to where he was. All his, and all the camp's personal mail was censored and any information that was a security breach would be deleted or sometimes cut out. Mail being sent to him (any soldier) would have to go through British Forces Post Office (BFPO) which ran a sort of Post Office Box No. system. It could sometimes prove to be a long, slow process.

When Tom's father was, by sheer good luck, posted to Danehill, he was able to work out that they were only a few miles apart.

The first opportunity he got he went to the village and found the address at which Tom had been billeted. The people (foster parents) were very helpful, but explained that Tom was at school and directed him to it. You know the rest.

On the day following the joyous meeting, Tom was back at school. We were all together at the Nissen hut. During the morning, Old Jonah sent for Tom and told him he'd heard about his father being in camp at Danehill. He added that if Tom got the chance to spend more time with his father he was to take it, regardless of school hours. But if ever Jonah found out that this privilege was being abused, it would be stopped.

These more permanent camps, I suppose, were good for local trade, and business, certainly the pubs. But they brought their fair share of heartbreaks, not least than to Jay's mother, Mrs Jay.

As I have said before, Mrs Jay was an attractive, friendly, outgoing lady and she took to befriending (for want of a better word) soldiers, mainly sergeants.

Where and how she met them I don't know. I come back to that old saying, "It was none of my business."

The trouble was she took it all so seriously. Each one she met was the love of her life, who was going to keep in touch when he got posted then come back when the war was over and marry her.

When the light of her life did get posted, she waited each day by the front door, waiting for that letter that never came. Surprise, surprise! Within a week the tears would start.

We've all heard the saying, "There'll be tears before bedtime". This was one of those cases where the bedtime came first and the tears came later. But she never learned; even at nine years old I could see she was being very silly, but it wasn't my place to say anything and I kept out of the way as much as possible.

There was another thing that used to occur from time to time regarding soldiers that's worth mentioning.

We would occasionally come across soldiers wandering around on their own. Sometimes they looked quite smart, but some looked decidedly dishevelled. They were always lost and would ask us for directions to the nearest bus or railway station, or bus stop. Now they could, of course, have been German spies but all we wanted to do was get away from them as quickly as possible, so we would direct them either to Chelwood Gate or Horsted Keynes and let the people there sort it out. They were bigger than we were.

The reasons we were given by these soldiers were varied and inventive. One soldier had been dropped off in the woods miles from his camp and was having to make his own way back to his camp as an initiative test.

Another had been left behind when they broke camp, to clean up the mess. Then he had to catch his company up under his own steam. He'd got lost; could we help?

One was asleep in the back of a lorry and fell out, and he didn't know where the lorry was going to. So they went on and, because we were kids, we were expected to believe them. Pull the other one mate!

They were almost certainly deserters; people said we should report them to the authorities, but even if we felt inclined to, what authorities? The nearest we saw to authority was an occasional air raid warden or the postman.

There will be another tale regarding soldiers, but it comes a bit later on.

Meanwhile, back at Wickens, things plodded on in its exciting daily routine. During the summer months, George didn't need much help with the oil lamps, because they didn't get used much.

From time to time, Hetty and Nelly would take it in turns to have a few days off and would go to some friends in London. These trips were always arranged when the Ashby's were away, so as not to leave too much work for the one who stayed behind on duty.

Whereabouts in London these people lived I've no idea. Their name was Webster and every Christmas that we were there they sent all of us presents. Even though we never ever met them. That makes them nice people as far as I'm concerned.

These trips would only be for three or four days, but during one trip Hetty did find time to go and see Mum and Dad, which was a nice thought. Don't remember Nelly doing it though.

There were some quite large afternoon gatherings at Wickens during the summer. Nothing on the same scale as the garden party, more afternoon tea get-togethers. They were big enough, however, to warrant the London maid, May, coming down to help. Having her around was like a breath of fresh air – she was fun.

The only way I was allowed to help was to open the front door and, if any guest wanted to get rid of a coat, or a gentleman a hat or an umbrella, it was my job to take it from them. These items were put in the small dining room on a table. I was supposed to remember what belonged to whom. If I got it right I might get a pat on the head and "Who's a clever boy then?" If I got it wrong, I got a dirty look.

It was never very clear to me what these gatherings were all about. They were not formal meetings, more likely fund raising events, but it was none of my business anyway.

As Dad had promised Hetty, he brought down a canary for her once his bird-breeding season was over. She was dead pleased with it and had acquired a nice roomy cage. It was just what she'd always wanted. It was a good deep yellow and a good songster. We helped her through the first few weeks regarding feeding and watering; there wasn't really much to it. It was given some silly name like Joey, but Caruso would have been more apt. Boy, he could sing! More about him later; that's the bird, not Caruso, the great singer.

On the schooling front, things were definitely improving. We were not being chopped and changed around quite so much. This was due to the fact that the Danehill Nissen hut seemed to be being phased out, and we were going there less and less. But at the moment Mr Thew still had the allotment going strongly. Just now and again boys in my age group would be allowed to go to the allotment to help out.

Things seemed to be ticking along nicely at Kit's school and she was still having no problems there. But then I always think you didn't get too many problems at school if you were reasonably clever. The problems start if you're not too bright.

When I was at school, as I've already said, I spent my time with the Jones brothers. Outside of school hours it was with Jay and the Harvey's. On both these fronts, I was managing to keep out of mischief and trouble; must be getting old.

This summer of '41 was just like every other summer, ticking away all too fast. It was as we were approaching the summer holiday break that we were told one Monday morning that Mr Jones (Old Jonah) would be retiring at Christmas, owing to ill health. Young children don't tend to notice things like people's health, but even we had noticed that he had slowed up a great deal and spent much less time teaching.

We were told that Jonah and his family would not be returning to London but staying in the village. Also, we were told that neither of our present teachers would be taking over as Headmaster. A new man from outside would be brought in, and we would be kept informed. This was sad news, because Old Jonah was very well liked and respected and was going to be a difficult act to follow, at least from the boys' point of view. All we could do was wait and see who the replacement was and what he was like, in the New Year.

There were only a few senior boys whose parents had taken up the offer of staying on in schooling for the extra year. Because of their extra age (even if only a little bit extra), they were given extra responsibilities, which quite naturally they enjoyed. So these days Jim was not feeling too bad about having had to stay on. In fact, I think he was quite enjoying it, but wouldn't admit it.

39. The Cresta Run

During the summer of '41, most of my spare time was spent in the company of "The Harvey's". We seemed to have developed a routine that suited us all. They appeared to have had certain jobs to do for their mother and aunt. Meanwhile I would still help George where I could, even though there was very little to do on the lamps in summer; very often just change one used one for a topped up and clean one, then have one big go at them all once a week. But whatever, I felt the need to be there, after all George was still giving me pocket money every Saturday morning.

So, Brian, Arthur, Jay and I would meet up most afternoons. This usually meant me having to go and knock on the dreaded front door; for, although three of them were known to Nelly, Hetty and George and were always greeted kindly, they didn't like knocking on Wickens' back door any more than I liked knocking on the farmhouse front door. Seeing as we played more at the farm than Wickens, I was the one who pulled the short straw. Lucky old me!

Again, there seemed to be a routine about it. During the afternoons we would wander far and wide, exploring just about everywhere – tree climbing. But I don't remember us getting into too much trouble. We spent quite a lot of time down at the ford at Twyford. Remember that? The ford with "The Bridge of the Flying Cyclists". There were lots of minnows in the stream and we used to enjoy splashing about there.

Also, occasionally, soldiers would bring their army lorries down to the ford to wash them off. Whether they wanted it or not they got our help. Our little 'war effort'; then in return we expected a ride back to the farm. It was dead against army regulations, but who cared?

After we'd all had our respective teas, we'd be let loose again, which meant another prayer and knock on the door. About this time, with all the door knocking I was doing, I was probably doing more praying than the Pope!

Now, the farmyard, as I've already explained, had more or less what you'd expect in a farmyard - shed, barns, pigsties. It was surrounded by quite a substantial hedge all around the yard. The entrance was a large, very strong five-bar gate, which we used to swing on and sing at the end of each evening.

On the other side of the hedge the ground rose fairly sharply into a sort of hillock, too steep to be cultivated; it had become a copse, but was quite large. There was a nice wide track going into the copse but it was quite a steep incline. To the side of this track there was one tree that had one of its branches that had died. This branch stuck out over the track way and looked horrible. None of us liked the look of it, so it was decided to try to hack it off.

This was no small task, as this branch was somewhere between four to six inches thick. Now, Arthur said he'd seen a hatchet in one of the outhouses and went to fetch it, but it didn't work, even with the hatchet – it was too much of an effort to reach the branch. We were all just too short.

Then Audrey had an idea. "If we was to get the trailer out of the barn and pull it up here, we could use it as a platform; then we could easily reach." The farmer didn't know it but it was very kind of him to lend us all his gear.

We got the trailer out and pulled and pushed it up the incline to the tree; but, being on an incline, it started to roll back down again, so we turned it sideways across the track and put blocks behind and in front of the wheels. It worked beautifully and we took it in turns to hack away at the offending branch with that tiny hatchet.

We didn't give up easily, but after three, maybe four, evenings we seemed to be getting nowhere, so we gave up.

Admittedly, we were disappointed but another plan was beginning to take shape, because each evening as we went to put the trailer away, we were having difficulty in controlling it on the downward slope. There was only the tow bar to steer with and that was a bit cumbersome and awkward.

Whose idea it was I don't remember; if I did I'd give them a medal. "Why don't we push it up the hill and ride down?" See what I mean? What a great idea! By folding the tow bar back we had some degree of steering. We gave it a trial run and it worked, well more or less. On the first evening of those rides, we were running out of time. So we put the trailer away in the barn, knowing full well that we would have it out again next evening.

The next evening I didn't have to knock on the door. They were already outside waiting for Jay and I; we were all eager to get going. We decided to start off from the same place as the day before, and to all have a turn at driving the thing.

To start off with it wasn't too alarming, depending upon who was driving. The slope we were using was not too steep at that point, so we were able to get in a few practice runs and find out the good from the bad drivers. We used the hedge around the yard as a crash barrier (good job it was substantial).

We all had to agree, much to her delight, that Audrey was the best driver, followed by Brian, then Arthur and me about equal. Whilst Jay was so bad we had to take his 'licence' away and ban him from driving, which didn't seem to bother him one little bit.

From here on we progressed a little further up the slope with each ride, which of course made each ride longer. It was quite hard work pushing and pulling that trailer up that slope time and time again, but we didn't care – this was fun!

We all felt that we were losing a lot of enjoyable ride time because the trailer was taking so long to build up momentum to a good speed. By the time we got really going we crashed in the crash barrier. Something had to be done about that so we agreed that on each run one of us would stay off the trailer so's to be able to give a running push until enough speed had built up; then at the right moment dive onto the back of the trailer. It was a bit like the cresta run or the bobsleigh, but without the snow and ice.

This manoeuvre was not without its dangers, because with the driver trying to steer the thing the rest of the crew had to help drag the pusher aboard. They were never too fussy about where or what they grabbed hold of, resulting in some very loud shrieks and some watery eyes. Audrey was not allowed to do any pushing. Enough said.

With every run the rides got both longer and faster. Audrey did a great job with the diving; she was like Queen Boadicea in her chariot – nothing and nobody was safe.

How nobody got hurt during these escapades, I really don't know. Well, Arthur did get a bit hurt, but that doesn't count, 'cos he makes a lot of fuss.

It was his turn to do the pushing off and he wasn't a very stockily built boy; a bit on the slight side. As he pushed he somehow lost his footing, or tripped over his own feet, something stupid like that. By now he'd let go of the trailer and on the downward slope he was running faster than he'd ever run in his life before. His arms were flaying about like windmills and his legs were all over the place. This was not poetry in motion! Watching him, we knew we wouldn't be able to keep going like that for long. He didn't, and soon another red skin bit the dust.

"Don't worry about him – we'll pick him up on the way back", and we carried on with our ride. We couldn't have stopped anyway, even if we'd wanted to.

Once we'd crashed into that poor old hedge and had our usual little chat about the ride, we thought that we just about had enough strength in our legs to push it up for one final ride of the day. On the way up we came across Arthur, still sitting on the track, grizzling. (See, I said he made a fuss). The trouble was he wasn't really hurt. There wasn't a lot of blood, just another spit and dirty hanky job. The funny thing was that always seemed to work – don't know why somebody didn't patent it.

Anyway, after the last ride of the day, and we'd got Arthur to smile again, we put the trailer back in the barn and went over to the gate for "evensong". We sung 'Roll Out The Barrel', 'Bless 'Em All' and 'We Don't Know Where We're Going Until We're There'. That would be about the time the Harvey's were called in and it was time for Jay and I to leave.

At Birch Grove Cottage Jay would peel off and go into his probably weeping mother. I would carry on a few more yards to Wickens.

As I walked those last few yards, I realised that although I wanted to go back home to London, Mum, Dad, Gran and the rest of the family, I didn't want it to happen just yet! Because I was having more fun than I'd ever had in my life before. The freedom I was given at Wickens would have caused my mother to have a fit. The same goes if she had known some of the antics that I got up to.

These two statements, "I want to go home" and "I don't want to just yet" are, in fact, contradictions. But I was learning that part of the growing up process shows you that life can at times get complicated.

40. The Order of the Bath

So, today's lecture is on personal hygiene. Not mine, good Lord no! Soldiers' personal hygiene. Some of the troops in camp had been given the order of the bath. Now, giving an order is one thing, but sometimes putting it into practice is a whole new ballgame. Many officers don't understand this; they are, after all, only officers. So let Geoffrey tell you how it worked out in actual practice.

By now, we were in the autumn of 1941 and it seemed to me that as the days got shorter, which of course they did, even with Double British Summer Time, that didn't stop it being winter, and cold, and long dark nights. Well, as this happened it seemed as if more 'in camp' activities were put on in the evenings for the troops. Things like 'camp concerts'.

It also seemed that quite a big thing was made of these concerts. They were supposed to boost the troops' morale; whether it did or not, your guess is as good as mine.

On these occasions some of the local dignitaries would be invited as guests of the Commanding Officer, and these guests would dine in the Officers' Mess prior to the concert. The result was that Mr and Mrs Ashby quite frequently received invitations to these 'camp concerts'. A car would come and whisk them off for the evening.

Although this meant a much easier evening for Nelly and Hetty - no evening dinner to cook and serve – they were not at all happy about it, particularly Nelly. She had visions of somebody hiding in the woods and, once the evening was in full swing, this someone could flash a signal to a German bomber waiting overhead and boom! The whole camp blown sky high. This was, I think, the fears for their jobs and home more than anything else.

More than once I heard her say, "You wouldn't catch me going there!" Well, there was no need to worry dear; I don't think you are on the CO's invitation list.

Following one of the camp concert evenings, Mrs Ashby came through to the kitchen (a most unusual event). She explained that during the camp dinner she (Mrs Ashby) had been asked if she could help out with a little problem of getting baths for some of the troops.

To cut a long story short, she had agreed that for the following few weeks, on a fixed day, a few soldiers would be coming along in the afternoon for baths. She quite understood this would cause some slight disruption, but in these troubled times "we must do all we can to support our brave lads", and all that guff.

They were told that there would be three, maybe four, soldiers and Mrs Ashby was sure this wouldn't cause too much trouble. She added as she left the kitchen, "Both Mr Ashby and I will of course be in London, but we are quite sure you can both manage". With that, she left.

Neither Nelly nor Hetty were exactly ecstatic over this news. In fact, quite the reverse. But they couldn't do anything about it. It wasn't their house and they weren't paying the bills. All they had to do was clear up any mess that occurred.

The 'bath day' came and the two sisters were not in a happy mood, nor was aunty. As I left for school on my little blue bike, I casually asked, "Do you think any of the soldiers will still be here when I get back from school?"

"I sincerely hope not", was my short, sharp answer from Nelly. The sooner I left, the better.

School over, I dashed back to Wickens as quickly as I could. I didn't want to miss any of the 'fun'. On arriving, I walked into the staff sitting room hoping to see at least one soldier, but there were four. They said hello and asked all the usual questions; I thought that some had had their bath and were sitting around waiting for their mates. But I was wrong.

Nelly and Hetty had used their loaf to a certain extent and moved the big table that us kids eat from. They'd moved it to block off the larder door that was in the corner of the room. This was where they kept all the provisions.

That staff room was full of smoke and nobody in the Wickens household smoked, so it didn't go down too well. The soldiers had taken over the armchairs; well they had to sit somewhere. There were papers, books and comics all over the place. That didn't worry me, so long as they left the comics behind when they went.

After a few moments of talking to the soldiers as best I could, I went into the kitchen. The kitchen door was closed; that was unusual. They were in a right old tizzy.

It looked like Hetty was on the verge of breaking into tears. It appeared that, whoever detailed these men for baths, had sent not three, not four, but eight!

Some of the more cheeky ones had been making remarks to Hetty about was she going to wash their backs for them. Also about meeting her in the village pub for a drink. Just really cheeky banter, but Hetty was no good with remarks like that and, as usual, went bright red. This only made matters worse and she got herself into a right old 'ooh hah'.

Poor Nelly was stoking up the Aga as if it were the boiler of 'The Queen Mary'. The soldiers were running off so much hot water the Aga just couldn't keep up. Aunty had gone to her room (best place for her), George was nowhere in sight.

The soldiers arrived on time with an NCO in charge. Being the NCO, he took the first bath and most of the hot water. He also took far too long. When he was finished he cleared off leaving the other seven to sort it out for themselves.

As time was getting on, Jim, Kit and I had to have our tea in the kitchen, which was no big deal. All three of us had, I think, worked out it was going to be an evening to be very careful what you said and did. Better still say nothing at all.

I was so good that evening - I was almost angelic. Didn't like it very much, and promised myself I wouldn't make a habit of it.

They were not all wisecracking smart arses; two or three having had their bath and about to leave, tapped on the kitchen door to say thank you. One I remember him saying, "You've no idea how nice it is to feel half human again". The rest were just, "Cheerio darlin', see yer down the pub tonight. Don't be late, 'cos I just can't wait".

This all went on until somewhere turned six o'clock. There were complaints about the water running cold, complaints about no tea being offered and no ashtrays. It was not a happy household.

As the last one went, everybody heaved a sigh of relief and the kettle was put on for Nelly and Hetty mostly to have a calming cup of tea.

While that was being done, Hetty felt safe enough to venture into the sitting room. She opened all the doors and the one window to get rid of the cigarette smoke. As she opened the sitting room door leading into the hallway, we all heard her give a little cry. After a short while she came back into the kitchen; she looked ill. She had gone almost white. She was changing colours so quickly she was like a chameleon, going from pink, to red, back to pink, then to white. But, joking aside, she looked really pathetic and she was carrying what looked like a dirty piece of rag in her hand.

She said to her sister, "You should just see what they've done in the bathroom – it's a mess".

"What's that in your hand?" asked Nelly.

"It's one of our hand towels. I forgot to take two of them out and they've used them to clean their boots on".

We all went through to see for ourselves. The flooring in the hallway was parquet and the short stretch between the sitting room and bathroom was just one mass of scratches from the studs on the soldiers' army boots.

Quite apart from the two towels, which had been used to buff their boots, to do this at least one of them had put his boots up onto the rim of the bath causing scratching on the bath rim.

On top of that, everything that you would normally leave in the bathroom, like soap, flannels, nail brush, toothpaste, toothbrushes, all of these things were gone – even the toilet roll!

In all the time I was billeted at Wickens, this was when I saw Nelly and Hetty at their lowest ebb. As far as I can recall, nothing was said. They just shook their heads, turned and walked away; Hetty again very close to tears. All this with the prospect of more soldiers next week to look forward to.

By the following week, I can only presume that the camp had been contacted, because only five arrived for baths, and this time Nelly was in charge.

First, the bathroom was cleared out of all 'nick able' stuff. Second, no smoking allowed in the house – "If you want to smoke, outside in the yard".

Third, all boots to be removed and left in the sitting room. "If you don't like it, you can leave without a bath".

It all went a lot smoother, but they still hated it. But it didn't carry on for much longer. There may have been a third week, but I'm not too sure about that. Maybe this batch of soldiers were moved on, but I think Mrs Ashby might not be quite so quick to volunteer the next time.

What happened about the scratches, I don't know. Whether it would have been possible at that time to get them repaired or removed, again I don't know, but I doubt it. Even so, I would have been at school and wouldn't have known about it. Maybe they were just camouflaged, or maybe we just got used to them.

But with nobody around to nick the soap, I had to start washing again. However, within a few months soap rationing started; that helped me out a bit. Somebody 'up there' loves me.

41. Farewell Jonah

After the incidents of the soldiers' bath time, things became rather dull. Sister Kit was as always full of chat, mostly about her school. It seemed that they were putting on a Christmas pantomime. None of the pupils were going to be in it; all parts were taken by members of the teaching staff. It was to be held on the first two Saturday afternoons in the New Year. She was really looking forward to seeing her tutors make fools of themselves. Kit asked me if I would like to go with her; I said, "Yes please" (always very polite).

There was a bit of a mystery about Jim though. He still went off once or twice a week to his ATC meetings but he was still going to school. He was now an old man of fifteen, still at school. When one day I asked him what was going on, he told me to "Mind my own business"; that wasn't very polite, was it?!

One of the main talking points at school was the forthcoming retirement of "Old Jonah" at Christmas. Also, and more importantly, what his replacement would be like. Lots of rumours, lots of guess work, but nobody knew for sure. Old Mr Burbridge ("Old Burb") had gone back to London. Soon there would only be Mr Thew, Mr Gough and "The New Bloke". If Mr Thew and Gough knew anything about the New Year replacement, they were keeping it to themselves.

The departure of "Old Jonah" was going to be quite a loss. He was going to be a hard act to follow. He may not have been the world's greatest teacher or headmaster, but somehow in our situation he seemed to be the right man in the right place, at the right time. He seemed to feel a great responsibility towards us; it was his job to look after us and stand up for us. This he did to the best of his ability on quite a few occasions. All of us would be sorry to see him leave.

On "Old Jonah's" last day in charge things were much more relaxed than normal, because by now we were functioning something like a normal school. But on this last day, all that went out of the window. The morning just seemed to whizz by; it was after all the last school day before the Christmas holiday. We had assembly and sang a few Christmas carols, then just killed time until it was time to go to the dinner hut. There, Mrs Lee had made a great effort to brighten the place up a bit with a few Christmas decorations. As I've said before, Mrs Lee was a really nice lady, who worked her socks off doing the best she could for all the kids, village and Londoners.

After the meal it was back to the Nissen Hut. I always thought that the Nissen Hut was Jonah's favourite place out of the three. It was there that it all started on that first shambolic day. It was also where Her Majesty the Queen came to visit his school, so it seemed right that this is where it should end.

During the afternoon, Mrs and Miss Jones came in; we all knew them slightly, but they never once got involved in school affairs, or interfered in any way. They were well-liked, nice ladies, and well respected.

Soon after their arrival, a strange gentleman walked in. Entry of "The New Bloke". At this point, Mr Thew took centre stage, made a short speech about how much we were all going to miss "Old Jonah" and he actually used those words "Old Jonah". There was a small presentation to "The Jones Family" from the teachers and boys. Don't know where the money came from; nobody asked me for any.

Poor "Old Jonah" tried to make a speech, saying he would liked to have carried on and see us all back to London, but it was too much for him and he had to give up.

Step forward again Mr Thew, and introduce the new headmaster, Mr Bellamy. He made a very short speech saying he was "looking forward to working with us. There may be a few changes, but for the time being just go away and have the best possible Christmas". Then we were dismissed.

Verdict on the new bloke – he didn't seem too bad, but far too early to make a real judgement.

As we left the hut "The Jones Family" stood at the door and shook hands with every boy. Both Mrs and Miss Jones were crying, so were many of the boys, and I am not ashamed to say I was one of them. This was no way to start Christmas.

The Jones family never went back to live in London; they bought or rented a cottage and became residents of Horsted Keynes.

On the home front, things were much the same as always. The two sisters took their short breaks every now and then. In case you were wondering, "Silly But Happy" was still the love of Nelly's life and I was still popping to the post-box quite often.

The most exciting thing to happen about this time was that Hetty got given a kitten. Whether they were having trouble with mice in the kitchen, I don't know, but Hetty had some friends who ran the post office at Dane Hill. One Saturday morning I was asked to ride out there on my bike and collect something. I wasn't told what. This 'something' was to go into a shopping bag that hung from my handlebars.

This was a bit of an adventure as I'd never been this far along Dane Hill before, nor had I met these people, a Mr and Mrs Butler. They made a lot of fuss over me when I walked into the post office and told them who I was.

The 'something' turned out to be this kitten; it was pure white. It was just dropped into the shopping bag and I was sent on my way. The trouble was I had to stop very frequently because the kitten kept clawing his (I think it was a he) way up the inside of the bag and sticking his head out. So I had to shove him back down to the bottom of the bag and quickly pedal on a few more yards. It took ages to get back to Wickens. I walked a lot of the way holding the top of the bag closed. They called him Snowy – that's not what I called him!

But he was fun to have around and to watch him playing during those long dark evenings.

Because of these long dark evenings, play with Arthur, Brian, Audrey, Nonie and Jay was restricted mostly to Saturdays. Of course I saw Arthur and Brian at school but lessons got in the way.

One Sunday evening Hetty turned on her wireless to listen to the six o'clock BBC news. When it came on they announced that Japanese bombers had attacked the Americans' base at Pearl Harbour. There were extracts of President Roosevelt's speech; it may have been a transcript but I'm pretty sure it was a recording of the speech; I always thought he had a very distinctive voice.

This was good news for this country; after months of America sitting on the fence Japan had pushed them off and made up their mind for them. England was not alone any more. Better late than never. For some months, the mood and morale of the country had been improving; America coming in with us was the cream on the cake. It may take a bit of time, but we were going to win, absolutely no doubt about it.

One little fact that I noticed; it's not important but I'd like to mention it. With both events, Germany attacking Russia, and Japan attacking Pearl Harbour, both of these were announced on the six o'clock news, both on a Sunday evening. As I say, not important, but strange.

Some other good and very welcome news was that the continuous nightly bombing of London had stopped. Now there were only occasional spasmodic raids. It was hoped that the Blitz was over.

We were fast heading towards Christmas. Now I've got some very bad news for you. The Christmas of 1941, I can't remember a thing about it. For quite some time this worried me a bit, but I think I've worked it out now.

Our first Christmas at Wickens in 1939 was new, strange and different. Because of this, in a strange way, it was also exciting.

The second Christmas with Mum, Dad and the family staying for two nights, I'll never forget that.

By the third Christmas, Kit, Jim and I had now been there two and a quarter years. Being at Wickens seemed to be the norm; I regret to say it but it was beginning to seem as if Wickens was our home.

Can you remember every childhood Christmas spent at home? And I think that's what happened.

If it had been a rotten Christmas I would have remembered it, so I must assume that we had the usual round of parties, and outings, and a jolly good time. But it would have been nice to remember it.

What I do recall is the New Year. The Ashby's gave a New Year's Eve party for all their friends. Quite a big affair. This meant May coming from London to help out. As usual, Kitty was able to help much more than Jim or I, but we helped when and where we could. When there's something like that going on there's always a buzz about the place that I always enjoy.

As a special treat, I was allowed to stay up until midnight; I'd never been up that late before.

They had to rely on good old Hetty's wireless for Big Ben to strike midnight. You couldn't move in the staff sitting room, there were so many party guests in there. I went and sat on the back staircase in the kitchen, which was always my favourite spot – fourth step up.

On the stroke of midnight, all hell broke loose. I'd never seen anything like it, and I was not impressed. After a while, either Nelly or Hetty said, "OK, you've seen midnight, time for bed". Good idea, and I climbed the few remaining stairs to the bedroom that I shared with Jim

When I woke up next morning, it was 1942.

42. Tar very much

With Christmas and New Year safely tucked away, all we had to look forward to now was January, which never exactly fills me with glee. What a dull, miserable month it is, and February's not much better; but at least it's a bit shorter. Why can't we start the year in April, just in time for my birthday?

As arranged on a Saturday early in the New Year, Kit and I went to her school in Haywards Heath to see their Christmas pantomime. It was an extra treat for me because trips further than Horsted Keynes or Chelwood Gate were very few and far between.

It almost goes without saying that Kit enjoyed the panto much more than I did. She knew all the cast and enjoyed seeing her teachers involved in some slapstick comedy. A lot of the humour was very much "in school" stuff so went right over my head. Nevertheless, it was a good show, and fun, and I was really glad I went.

Starting school again after the Christmas break was a bit of an unknown factor, with Bellamy lurking in the wings. For the first few tentative days everybody was on their best behaviour just watching to see what happened. Not very much did. Where it came from I don't know but Mr Bellamy soon acquired the nickname, "Ding Dong".

He told us that he was not very happy about us having to keep moving between three different learning sites; very unsettling. He was going to try and do something about it – he soon did.

At the end of his first week, he still came across as "alright". He was a bit tighter on discipline, but I would say he was firm but fair. Within about three weeks he had stopped the use of the Nissen Hut, which was still pretty basic. The allotment would be kept going until the end of the growing season. More use would be made of the community centre, which was a much more school-like building. Well done Ding Dong!

Part of the deal regarding the use of the community centre seemed to be that the girls, who since the very start had been having their lessons in a villager's front room, would now be amalgamating into our school with us. If you remember, Kitty had been one of them at the very start. These girls were the sisters of the boys in our school. There were now only about six or maybe eight girls left. Can't speak for anyone else, but it didn't bother me. We had long since lost our identity as Heathbrook Boys' School, so what did it matter?

It appeared that Mr Thew and "Ding Dong" got on very well, but we were not too sure about Mr Gough. There seemed to be tension between them. This seemed to be confirmed when we were told that Mr Gough would be returning to London at Easter.

Another thing I found out about that would be happening at Easter was that Jim would finally be leaving school. There is, as far as I know, no reason to believe that this had anything to do with "Ding Dong" coming. It was just time to leave. This also meant he would be leaving Wickens and I assumed going back to London.

Also, Kitty had reminded me that she (Kit) would be leaving school at the end of the summer term, because by then she would be fourteen years old. But there was plenty of time to worry about that – we were still only in January.

Soon after the start of the New Year term, Kit came back to Wickens one evening with the news that her school was going to put on a "Music Festival" and she was going to be in it. Now there's a surprise. But it really was no surprise because Kit had quite a good singing voice, as we were all to find out to our cost during the next few weeks and months (watch this space).

The subject of Jim leaving school wasn't being talked about at all. As usual, nobody asked my advice; they never learn do they? Having been told once to "mind my own business", I never asked, so I didn't know anything, and I was a bit miffed about it.

Slowly, and it did seem very slowly, we got through the months of January and February. It seemed to be a time of nothing major happening and everybody keeping their heads down and getting on with their jobs.

As Easter got nearer, Kit and I were able to find out some news regarding what Jim was doing. For some reason I never have understood, he wasn't going back to London. He was going to have to leave Wickens and move in with the Bennett family. Whether or not it was thought by Mum and Dad that he ought to be around to keep an eye on Kit and myself, I don't know. If that was the case, it was rubbish; I could have managed quite well on my own if I'd had to. Other young boys had, but nobody asked Kit or I.

When Jim did leave school and move out of Wickens it wasn't a big wrench; he was only a few yards down the road. His leaving left me with a bedroom to myself for the first time in my life. Hanging on the wall of that bedroom was the banner that Jim had had to carry for our school on evacuation day – white with black lettering:

LCC 695
Heathbrook School

So, "Then there were two".

Sometime soon after Easter, Mr Michael was home for a few days with his parents. This, as usual, caused Kitty to go floating around on a cloud. He was always very busy about the place, always fixing or repairing something or building something. Very different from his father, Mr Ashby, but full of his mother's energy.

This particular weekend that I have in mind there was something leaking, but I don't remember what it was.

Having looked at this object, Mr Michael decided that the answer was to seal it with tar, and by some stroke of luck he happened to have some. He explained to me that rather than just put tar over the hole, split, or crack in this "what-ever-it-was", it would be a better idea to pour in enough tar to form a complete film over the entire base. Thereby make a complete seal (he said hopefully).

So, he set about building a small fire in the yard in front of the scullery. Once this was going strongly he found some sort of receptacle, put some tar lumps in and waited for it to melt.

Most people seem to think that melting tar is a very nice smell, and yes it is, but you can have too much of even a good thing. This was one of those occasions. There was a gusty breeze and it was blowing the smoke into the house and everywhere. Once again, Mr Michael was not the most popular young gentleman, and it was going to get worse.

Quite oblivious to all this, Mr Michael just carried on regardless until he'd finished his repair to his own satisfaction, then cleared away his gear – job done.

Next morning, Hetty went to feed the canary and change his water and there he was lying at the bottom of his cage – The Great Caruso was dead! He'd gone to that giant bird aviary in the sky.

It would, I think, be an over-statement to say Hetty was upset, but she was understandably "bloody annoyed". This was because there was very little doubt that the tar smoke was the cause of the death.

To his credit, Mr Michael did come round to see Hetty and apologise as soon as he heard what had happened. He also offered to replace it with another bird. But, no, Hetty said, "I'll make do with my little cat". My Dad also offered to give Hetty a replacement bird at the end of the breeding season, but Hetty gave the same answer, although with Dad her thanks were more sincere. My Dad was also annoyed, but then he didn't have a very high opinion of Mr Michael.

Myself, I think that the refusal to a replacement bird was because the novelty of having a canary had worn off. Adults can be just like children sometimes; they're just a bit older.

At the start of "Geoffrey's New Year" (April), Nelly told me that when it came around to my birthday in a few days' time would I like to find out if Jay, Audrey, Brian and Arthur would like to come and have tea with me. It would not be a party, just tea, and then out to play. They were to ask their parents first as Nelly didn't want to be the cause of any trouble.

This was no big deal for Jay, because he'd had tea a few times before and I'd had meals with him and his Mum. But for the other three this tea invite was a big deal; they'd been in and around the garden and grounds with me, but never inside the house.

My birthday that year (my eleventh) was on a Sunday, so they came to tea on the day before, the Saturday.

How much Audrey, Brian and Arthur enjoyed it I don't know. They were somewhat over-awed by it all, even though we ate in the staff sitting room, but I knew that feeling; remember, I'd been there. They really were apprehensive and watched everything that Jay and I did, then they followed suit.

Nelly laid on a super tea and both she and Hetty fussed around trying to chat to the kids and put them at their ease, and to eat up. As I remember, it went off pretty well. When tea was over and we were about to go out, there were four well rehearsed "thank you for having me's". Once outside, there were also at least three very big sighs of relief. I think they enjoyed it – I hope so – they were really good mates.

In spite of these gestures of friendship to her sons and nieces, not only by me but also Nelly and Hetty, I still only got growls and scowls from "The Wicked Witch of the North", and I still hated knocking on that front door.

In the meantime, Jim was calling in to see us about twice a week to make sure we were alright. He didn't have much to say about his digs at the Bennetts', but then Jim never did have much to say about anything.

There was a brick making factory somewhere at Dane Hill and he had got a job working there, doing what I've no idea.

Soon, Mum and Dad were coming for one of their visits and we were all looking forward to that.

As usual, I was behaving myself, whilst Kit was driving us all nearly barmy practising her songs for this forthcoming music festival.

43. The Picnic

The next incident that I am going to relate is so silly that even now I can hardly believe that it really happened. It rates very, very highly in the list of most ridiculous things that I have ever been asked (or told) to do. You make yourself comfortable and see what you think.

It all started one bright sunny morning somewhere around late May, early June. There was just Nelly and I in the kitchen and we were talking. Why I wasn't at school, I don't know, but I wasn't.

"Do you know Aunty's going away for a week's holiday?" Nelly asked.

"No, that's a surprise. Where's she going?"

"She's going to see and stay with an old friend of hers. She's going next week."

That was an even bigger surprise. Aunty's got a friend, poor devil, but I didn't say that to Nelly.

She went on, "With Aunty away, and Mr and Mrs Ashby away, that's going to make things a bit easier for us for a few days."

"Yes, I suppose it will." I had the feeling that this conversation was leading us somewhere; I was right.

"So Hetty and I are each going to give ourselves an extra day off – don't tell anyone, will you?"

"By the sounds of it, there won't be too many people about to tell, will there?"

Still, Nelly kept going, "We were talking about it yesterday and Hetty mentioned that she would like to visit Ashdown Forest, but doesn't want to go on her own. Would you like to go with her and have a day out?"

"Yes, alright, I don't mind going."

"We could make up a picnic for both of you. Wouldn't that be lovely?"

Somehow, I got the feeling that something was going on. Nelly was trying too hard to sell this idea. I wasn't as daft as I looked, fortunately.

So, Hetty and I were going to have a picnic in Ashdown Forest next week, and I wasn't to tell anyone. Now I've never been mad about picnics – too many wasps, ants and flies, but you know me, anything for a quiet life.

The following week Aunty duly went on her holiday and a day was set for this picnic. There had been no mention of Kitty coming on this picnic and even now I couldn't work out why.

When I woke up on "Picnic Day", it was simply pouring with rain and this rain looked like the forerunner to the end of the world. All around it was as black as your hat, or Aunty's hat.

So, as I went downstairs into the kitchen, I was quite confident that the promised picnic was off. Oh dear, what a shame, never mind. But I was in for a nasty shock – it was still on!

No matter how much I protested and pointed out that it was pouring with rain. Nelly insisted, "It will clear up soon. It will be lovely in Ashdown Forest, and you will have a lovely time." But I was not convinced.

By the time we were kitted out and ready for this lovely picnic, it looked as if we were going on an Antarctic expedition. The first stage was the long walk to

Chelwood Gate to catch a bus to Ashdown. As Nelly waved us off, all smiles, I'd bet you any money you like that "Silly But Happy" was waiting nearby to slip indoors and spend the day with Nelly. Don't ask me where Kitty and George were – I don't know.

We were already soaking wet by the time we reached Chelwood Gate and caught the bus; there wasn't much chat between Hetty and I. During the bus ride, I wondered where Hetty had in mind to go and eat this picnic because it was far too wet to eat it anywhere outside. It was still pouring with rain and looked like continuing.

Wrong again. We got to Ashdown, Hetty found the forest; well, you couldn't very well miss it. We walked into the trees and stood in a mini quagmire, with rain cascading onto us from the trees, and Hetty started handing out sandwiches. Before you had a chance to eat all the sandwich, it was getting soggy; we were soaked.

It really was the most ridiculous situation to have put us in, quite daft. We didn't bother about a drink – we were already waterlogged! Eventually Hetty said, "Come on, I've had enough of this", and we left the forest.

We came to a main road and started walking along it. How (or whether) Hetty knew where we were going I don't know. Remember there were no signposts during the war. Because of petrol rationing, there was very little traffic. A small minibus type van came along. It stopped, asked where we were going and would we like a lift. All the talking was left to Hetty. The driver opened the rear doors and we gratefully got in. There were seats down both sides, so we had somewhere to sit. As we went along Hetty whispered to me that this minibus was used for moving the patients from the local mental institution about. It somehow seemed fitting that we should be in there!

Perhaps the driver thought that we were a couple of escapees from the institution. He tried talking to Hetty but didn't get much response. As we rode along, in what turned out to be quite a long ride, Hetty was rummaging through her handbag. She pushed some coins into my hand and whispered, "When we get out give this to the driver and say 'thank you'". OK, I nodded.

We came to a town, the driver stopped and we got out. I did my 'thank you' bit and off went the minibus. Whether the money was really a thank you, or a bribe to let us go, we will never know. It was still raining. To this day, I cannot be sure of where we were, but I've always assumed it was East Grinstead. Hetty preferred shopping in East Grinstead as opposed to Haywards Heath. We made our way to the bus station. Good, I thought, we're going back to Wickens. Wrong yet again. It seemed Hetty was only finding out times for later on. It appeared that we mustn't get back too early.

Having found a suitable bus, at a suitable time, we started walking again. Hetty was looking for a shop, so was I; a shop that sold arks, because arks were not on the rations yet, but they soon would be if this weather kept up. At last we found what Hetty was looking for; a nice little teashop. We went in dripping water all over the floor. We had tea, toast and cake and made it last as long as possible. Then out to face the elements again – still it rained.

Then Hetty had an idea. We could go to the cinema; it will be dry in there – I had my doubts. We reached the cinema and went in regardless of what was showing. There was plenty of room inside and we took seats right on the end of the row, and used a third seat to pile our wet Macs and coats on.

It was fine to start with, just nice to be sitting down, and out of the rain. Personally, I didn't have a clue what the film was, or what it was about, and I didn't care very much. Then we noticed steam coming off the wet clothes we were wearing; it was like being in a sauna. We seemed as though we were watching the film through a fog; I was fed up – we both were.

At regular intervals Hetty would leave her seat and emerge from the mist, clean off her steamed up glasses, and take a look at the cinema clock, because if we missed that bus there'd be no more till the monsoon season ended.

We left the cinema in plenty of time to catch that bus. As to whether it was still raining, I don't know, I was past caring. As to what we'd seen in the cinema, I don't know that either. I just wanted to get back indoors. It's quite a long bus ride from East Grinstead to Chelwood Gate. Fortunately we didn't have to change buses; then that long walk from Chelwood Gate to Wickens.

There was no way I could guess what the time was as we did that walk, because it had hardly been daylight all day, and talking was down to the minimum, but eventually we reached Wickens.

As we entered the back door, Nelly came rushing forward to meet us. "Oh, there you are! I was wondering what time to expect you. Have you had a lovely day?" I said, "No". Hetty made no reply at all; she just carried on as though her sister wasn't there – cut her dead.

"You must get out of those wet clothes", Hetty said. "I'm going to run you a hot bath in the downstairs bathroom. You go and get your pyjamas and dressing gown. While you are bathing downstairs, I'm going to bath and change upstairs". "And you", she said, turning to her sister, "can do something useful like warming us some soup, and getting us a hot drink. We are soaked". With that, she turned away and left Nelly standing. I shot upstairs out of the way.

The soup and drink were very welcome and it was nice to be indoors and warm; even the bath felt good. But the meal was eaten in stony silence, and I was glad to be excused from the table and go up to my room to bed. As I lay there trying to forget the day, I realised that I still hadn't seen Kitty, all day. But she turned up the next day – no idea where she'd been.

The next few days were a bit tricky. Nelly and Hetty were only talking to each other when they had to; even then it was short and sharp, but they had to get their act together when Aunty came back from her holiday. They needed a united front when she was about.

Looking back on it now, it still seems a pretty grim day out; but let's look on the bright side, shall we? Because it could have been worse you know. They could have sent me on a week's holiday with Aunty – Heaven forbid.

You see, I told you it was going to be silly didn't I? Now, why don't you go and put the kettle on?

44. The Sound of Music

The time was slowly ticking away and we were into June. It was time for my parents to come down for another of their visits. They always brought little brother Martin with them. At his age we noticed a difference in him every time we saw him. Gone were the baby and toddler days; he was a proper little boy now. The trouble was Kit, Jim and I didn't know him, and he didn't know us.

On their arrival, Jim, of course, joined us for the usual picnic lunch in the garden. Nelly and Hetty always supplied cups of tea on these occasions. The day took its normal format; the only difference being that we had all been invited to the Bennetts' place for tea. I hadn't known about that.

But what I was expecting was for Mum and Dad to have an afternoon meeting with Mrs Ashby and I don't remember that happening. You see, Kitty was due to leave school at the end of the term (when the summer holidays started) and as far as I was aware no decisions had been made as to what was going to happen then; a bit strange.

After spending the best part of the day at Wickens, we caught up on family news and happenings. Also, Kitty was going on and on about this music festival that her school was putting on. You'd have thought that she was the only person in it. Anyway, after all this, and when Mum and Dad had said their goodbyes to everybody, we all wandered down to the Bennetts' for tea. As I've explained before, it was not too far.

Our parents had not met any of the Bennett family before, so there were a lot of introductions to be made; all very boring. There was a lot of talk; I've no idea what they were talking about. I'd been told to be on my best behaviour, and that takes my full concentration. Nevertheless, I do recall a great deal of interest being shown, particularly by Dad in the large section of bomb casing that Mrs Bennett was using as an umbrella stand in her small hallway. As I remember, we had a very nice tea, plenty of chat and laughs. But I think Dad enjoyed it the most, talking to Mr Bennett. Dad once told me he would like to have been a gamekeeper if he'd had the chance.

With one eye on bus and train times, all too soon goodbyes had to be said; this done with all the usual "You must come again, and stay longer next time". We all left and took Mum, Dad and Martin to the village to catch the bus.

As we walked back having once again said our goodbyes, I asked Kit, "Did Mum or Dad say anything to you about what's going to happen when you leave school?"

"Nope. I haven't got a clue", was her reply.

It is difficult to be precise about the timing but within two or three weeks Jim called in to Wickens to tell Kit and I that he was leaving the brick factory and the Bennetts' and going back to London. He went into no details as to why.

It all happened so suddenly that it came as a bit of a shock; not only to Kit and I, but also to Nelly, Hetty and crew. Their general opinion was that there had been some sort of falling out.

My view is that Jim found things so different living at the Bennetts' place as opposed to life at Wickens. As I have written earlier, Jim could be a right "fuss-arse" about neat and tidiness. Now I have no wish to say anything nasty regarding "The Bennetts'"; they were always friendly, helpful and kind to us kids, but with all the goodwill in the world, compared to life at Wickens they were a bit rough and ready. I'm sad to say it, but it's true. It was, I think, too much of a 'culture shock' for Jim to handle, so he left.

Whenever I saw any of the Bennetts' after that, they were just the same as always; nice, friendly people – so no harm done, thank goodness.

Often, in this writing, I mention one of our teachers, Mr Thew, a nice man, good teacher - king of the allotment, you may remember. He could be a bit short tempered, but then I suppose we gave him plenty to be short tempered about. He played the violin about as well as Old Jonah played the piano, which is not saying much. His favourite piece of music was "All Through the Night". Trouble was he liked to play it all through the day as well. But when the chips were down he was well liked.

He and Mrs Thew were billeted with a farming family at a farm that was about halfway between the village and Wickens. The farmhouse was set back off the road but could clearly be seen. When I was out playing during the weekends I would sometimes bump into them. Out of politeness, I would feel obliged to talk to them; I was never very pleased to see them coming towards me.

Let Geoffrey tell you why.

First, let me make it quite clear that Mrs Thew was a very nice friendly lady. Small in stature, quietly spoken, almost timid. The problem was she had to keep touching me as we spoke. She would push the hair off my forehead out of my eyes, she would brush fluff off my shoulders that wasn't there in the first place; with her handkerchief she would rub away smut spots on my face that were never there either. If I was by chance wearing a tie, that would be adjusted and patted down – I hated it.

Whilst all this was going on, Mr Thew would stand slightly behind her, grinning his head off at my discomfort. When he thought enough was enough he would come to my rescue by suggesting that it was time to move on.

Even then it wasn't over and it was always the same ending. She would put her hands on my shoulders and say, "Promise me that you will be a good boy".

"Yes, Mrs Thew". What a cheek! I think that remark was quite uncalled for.

You should know me well enough by now to have worked out that I'm always good; well, sometimes anyway. Remember Mrs Thew; she pops up again a bit later on.

In the meantime, the time for this music festival was rapidly approaching; so too, for that matter, was Kitty's school leaving date, soon after the festival. But Kit didn't seem to be too worried about that. She didn't seem to be able to think beyond this festival; it seemed to be her only concern.

There would be a "ring-a-ding-a-ding" here and a "hey nonnie no" there, and "Nymphs and Shepherds" all over the place, as well as an endless supply of non-stop chat. In the end, Hetty agreed to go to this festival, I think only to try and shut her up. But it was hopeless. It seems that I agreed to go as well, but I don't remember saying a word.

Some of the songs that Kitty sang over and over again in the weeks and months leading up to this event, I can still remember the tunes and most of the words. There was one that I remember particularly when the weather is very, very cold:

"When icicles hang by the wall, and Dick the Shepherd blows his nails". Then another line, followed by:

"And milk comes frozen home in pails".

It always makes me grateful for central heating.

At last the "Big Day" came and Kit went off to the school that morning in a great state of excitement. I didn't think I'd ever seen her that excited before.

It appears that I wasn't at school that day, but don't ask why, I don't know. In due course, Hetty and I followed on to Haywards Heath in the afternoon. I wasn't expecting too much from this trip.

But I was wrong. I hate to have to admit it, but it was fantastic. Even I knew that they had rehearsed their little socks off, and it paid.

The programme (if that's the right word) consisted mainly of singing, but there were one or two instrumental pieces by small groups. But when they sang, you could feel it at the back of your neck. One rendition of The Skye Boat Song I will never forget; they sang like angels. Stand up kids, and take a bow!

Neither Hetty nor I begrudged the time spent on that trip. It had been really most enjoyable. But when Kitty got back to Wickens that evening she was quite emotional. Yes, it had been a great success, yes, it had been fun, but now it was over. Her bubble had burst. All she had to look forward to now was leaving school in two or three weeks time, leaving all her friends behind and not knowing what was coming next. Not surprisingly, that didn't cheer her up very much.

There really was beginning to be some concern at Wickens as to what our parents wanted to do about Kitty leaving school.

Then, about a fortnight before the summer holidays started, a letter arrived from home telling us that both Kit and I would be going home to London for good. Another letter had been sent to Mrs Ashby explaining this. We were going home.

But we would not be going back to our old flat in Queenstown Road, Battersea. The indecision over the last few weeks was due to the fact that Mum and Dad were house hunting. They had at last found what they wanted, in Wandsworth, near the Common. It was a large five bedroomed house, with a nice bathroom (oh dear) plus a garden. They would be moving shortly, then we can go home.

This would mean Kit could get a job and I would be starting a new school; my little brother, Martin, was now old enough to start school, so he would be starting at the same school, at the same time, at the start of the new term after the summer holidays.

For the first time in my life I understood the meaning of "bitter, sweet". Yes, I wanted to go back to London and be with my family, but I was going to miss Jay, Audrey, Brian and Arthur. Then there was Nelly, Hetty, George, and to a lesser extent, even Aunty and Billings. After nearly three years of being looked after by them, they seemed as much like family as anybody else.

Now I understood Kitty's feelings about leaving all her friends behind. But there was nothing we could do about it. If we could cope with being evacuated, I'm sure we could cope with being de-evacuated (I just invented that word).

However, I feel I must add that although I could fully understand the reasons for moving, I was deep down inside very disappointed not to be going home to our old flat. It had been the dream and the focus of the thoughts about going home. The image had been in my mind so many times and now it was not going to happen. Later on, I want to return to this subject.

Now what lay ahead was new house and new surroundings, new school, new people; just like being evacuated again. Nothing ever seemed to stay the same for very long, but I suppose that's life.

45. An Interesting Development

Just as I was about to settle down to write the concluding pages of my story, there has been a very interesting development; one that I think quite amazing and that I really must tell you about, because it is, I think, a very interesting little detective story in its own right.

It relates to the incident regarding the German aircraft being shot down during the Battle of Britain, and the subsequent burial of the German pilot in the village church graveyard.

Now, I must just briefly explain to you the procedure as I have finished writing each chapter. Upon completion, I pass each finished chapter onto a colleague who lives in the next village – his name is David Bland. He has agreed to monitor my writing to check against things like: any passage being too long-winded and boring; to check that it all makes sense; also to check that I've not gone 'over the top' in the parts where I've grumbled a lot; and maybe to pick up any silly mistakes that I've missed.

Having done this, David then passes it on to be typed.

Now, when David read the chapter about the German airman, he rather thought that I had not made some of the details clear enough and suggested one or two changes. Upon reflection, I agreed and was quite happy to do a re-write. But what I did not know was that David thought to himself that it would make much more interesting reading if we could find out what type of aircraft it was that had been shot down. Furthermore, if we could come up with the exact dates of

Geoff remembers the excitement of the children when they heard of the German fighter plane crashing into the pond, killing pilot Albert Sander. He was shot down in a dog fight over Cinder Hill Farm.
Photo: Courtesy of the Commonwealth War Graves Commission, Cannock Chase Military Cemetery UK Area

these happenings, well, so much the better.

As I was not in a position to supply this information, David set himself the task of trying to find this out, if he could. He likes doing this sort of thing and is very good at it.

The first move was to 'log on' (I hope that's the correct term) to the website for Horsted Keynes. In his search through the information relating to World War II, he came across reports of the Heathbrook School evacuees arriving in the village. As he worked on through this information he came across:

"No enemy aircraft were shot down in the Parish during hostilities."

Oh dear!

But he wasn't too worried about this because, having done this sort of research before on other projects, he knows that such mistakes are not uncommon.

So, David's next line of enquiry was to contact the Church Warden of St Giles' Church at Horsted Keynes. The Warden's name, Mr James Nicholson.

Speaking to Mr Nicholson, David explained that he would be grateful for any information that Mr Nicholson could give regarding the wartime German pilot that was buried in St Giles' churchyard.

The reply was, "Sorry, but I think you've got the wrong place. There is no German pilot buried in our churchyard".

Oh dear again! But this time with a little bit more concern. What was going on here?

Our David was not having a very good day was he? But he's not the sort that gives up easily; he's a real little terrier once he gets his teeth into something.

Patiently, David told Mr Nicholson the story of the German aircraft being shot down, how this dear little evacuee saw the burial through the classroom window and now hopes to write about it.

Just as patiently, Mr Nicholson listened to this endearing tale, but at the end said, "Sorry, can't help you. I know nothing whatsoever about it."

When it was suggested that a search of the church records be done, because any help at all would be greatly appreciated, for some unknown reason the Warden seemed reluctant to do this.

Still, David persisted until in the end Mr Nicholson said, "Look, just hang on a minute and I'll have a quick word with my wife and find out if she knows anything about this." There was a pause and the sound of a conversation taking place in the background.

When Mr Nicholson came back on the line, he said, "Well, I don't know if this helps you, but Mrs Nicholson has heard tell that some time in the 1960's a body was exhumed from the churchyard. It was taken away and never returned, but she knows no more than that. Could this be your man?"

This was, of course, quite exciting but a little more information was needed to make it really useful, so David still persisted.

Could the Nicholson's think of anybody in the village who might be able and willing to help? Again, Mr Nicholson was most helpful. Yes, he did know of at least one senior citizen who he thought might be able to help. However, he would like to speak to him first before getting him involved. That seemed fair enough, so David gave his telephone number and waited.

A few days later, the expected telephone call came. It was good news. Mr Nicholson had spoken to the gentleman, namely, Bob Pelling, and he was able to confirm that a German airman was buried in St Giles' churchyard during the Battle of Britain in 1940. He had a good memory and was willing and eager to help; he would be awaiting David's call.

Phew! Big sighs of relief all round. At last we had somebody who could corroborate my story.

So, with profuse 'thank you's' to Mr and Mrs Nicholson for their immense help, David got Bob's telephone number and made the call. From what I've been told,

David and Bob Pelling seemed to hit it off right from the word go. Again, David had to explain about my evacuee status and what we two were now trying to do with the writing.

Our project seemed to catch Bob's imagination and he offered to help in any way he could. He went on to explain that in the 1940's he was the 'errand boy' in the village store. Now, I do vaguely have an image of an errand boy in my memory, but to say I remembered Bob would not be true.

He went on to say that he actually saw this German aircraft coming down, and it crashed into a pond at a place called Cinder Hill. Now, I'd never heard of Cinder Hill until David spoke to me about it. It appears to have been about 2 miles outside the village.

The German airman was killed in the crash and was buried in St Giles' churchyard a few days later. Unfortunately, Bob was not able to give us any exact dates, but he might know a man who could.

He further explained that at some time in the 1960's the body of the German airman was exhumed and taken to the Cannock Chase German Military Cemetery, Staffordshire.

The cemetery was for German service personnel who were killed in action in this country; also, any German prisoners of war who died whilst in captivity.

At this stage, he was unable to help any further but he thought he might be able to help once he had seen his friend, Tom, who, like David, was very interested in this sort of subject.

The trouble was that this telephone conversation between David and Bob was taking place at the height of the cold, frosty, snowy weather in December (2010). Conditions underfoot and road wise were very bad right across the country, so Bob made it clear that things would have to wait awhile until travelling around became a little easier. He would ring David when he had some news.

While we waited, I got on with my writing and, of course, Christmas. David did his own thing and planned his next move.

His next move was to telephone the Cannock Chase Cemetery to see if he could find out any more information from them.

So, once again, he had to launch into this heart-wrenching tale about this dear young evacuee, who at the tender age of eight was wrenched away from his home and the bosom of his loving family. This was done by an anxious government, who whisked him off to a secret location deep in the countryside to keep him safe and out of reach of the German aggressors.

His older sister and brother were allowed to go with him, to look after and protect him. They were all told not to speak to strangers in case they were German spies.

Nevertheless, the secret was leaked and when Hitler found out where he was hidden, Hitler sent his Luftwaffe after him!

This action resulted in at least one German aircraft being shot down and the pilot killed on the mission.

David concluded, "We are now trying to write a book about all this. We have reason to believe that the pilot is buried in your cemetery and were hoping you may be in a position to give us some information. Can you help us at all please?"

The gentleman, who had been quietly listening to all this, had kept quite calm. Not a single sob came down the line. He seemed to be very interested and would help if he could.

"Do you have the plot number?" he asked.

"Er, no."

"Then, I'm very sorry but we can't help."

He went on to explain that they had over 5,000 German graves in their care and to find the information David wanted without a plot number could not be done.

After some further discussion David found out that it might be possible to have a photograph taken of the grave if we could come up with a plot number.

At that point David left it at that and waited to see if we heard from Bob.

It was 2nd April 2011 when Bob telephoned David. He had been to see his friend, Tom Irlam, and Bob had some news.

Like everybody else, Tom was interested to hear what David and I were trying to do, but in Tom's case it was slightly different because Tom could and would help.

He had told Bob that the aircraft we were interested in was a Messerschmitt 109 and it came down into the pond at Cinder Hill on 30 September 1940. The pilot was Alfred Sander and he had only just reached 23 years of age.

That was not the end of Tom's information. He went on to say that when Airman Sander was buried in St Giles' churchyard he was in Reserve Area, Plot 1, Grave 1.

There was no precise date regarding the exhumation, only that it took place somewhere between May 1962 and October 1963. The final resting place is in Cannock Chase – Cannock Chase German Military Cemetery, Staffordshire.

Also, Tom had the Cannock Chase plot number. There was also a message from Tom that, should David care to telephone him, he would be pleased to speak to him.

Of course David telephoned Tom, first out of courtesy to say thank you (he's a very polite little chap is David) and second, out of interest. But we still have no idea where Tom got the information from.

No amount of 'thank you's' will ever be enough to thank Bob and Tom for their interest and help

Now that David had the Cannock Chase plot number, he contacted them again, thinking that getting a photograph of Airman Sander's headstone would not be too difficult. This was not the case!

It seemed that permission would have to be given from a higher level.

This meant David making a series of telephone calls and in the end speaking to the Manager, or Superintendent of Commonwealth War Graves Commission. He listened to the well worn story and not only gave permission for the photograph to be taken, but also permission for it to be used in any publication that might result at some later date.

In due course, the photograph was emailed to David.

By the sounds of it this Manager and David had quite a chat, because he explained that the cemetery at Cannock Chase was not only the resting place of German personnel from WWII but also from the First World War. In fact, some of the WWI graves are those of crew members of Zeppelins that had been shot down (not many people know that).

I do not wish to take any credit for all the fact finding involved in this story; I had nothing to do with it, but I would like to give my sincere thanks to the following people who helped me to at last find the final resting place of that German airman.

My thanks are to:

Mr Bob Pelling of Horsted Keynes

Mr Tom Irlam, also of Horsted Keynes

Mr & Mrs James Nicholson, Church Wardens of St Giles' Church, Horsted Keynes

The Management of the Commonwealth War Graves Commission

The ground staff of the German Military Cemetery, Cannock Chase, Staffordshire

And last, but by no means least, my very good friend, David Bland (The Terrier).

The reason I am so grateful to the aforementioned people is because now the incident of the German pilot being buried in the village churchyard has somehow changed, but it is difficult to explain how or why.

It seems somehow to have become much more personal. This airman now has a name.

As I've been writing these pages, one phrase has kept passing through my mind, along with all the other words I've written. That phrase is the response that we give during prayers at Remembrance Services.

"We will remember them."

Do we only remember our own gallant dead, or do we also honour our fallen enemies as well? It's an interesting thought and one I've never stopped to think about before.

But from hereon, during any future Remembrance silences, I'm pretty sure that along with several other names that pass through my mind, Alfred Sander's name will be included.

Surely that is what Christianity and going to church is all about, forgiving.

46. Going Home

It all happened a long time ago, and I cannot be as sure as I would like to be, but I can't honestly say that I remember being as excited about going back to London as I thought I would be.

As I've already said, it was going to be all change again, and I was leaving a lot behind. But there was nothing I can do about it, so I'll have to get on with it, won't I? I was back to my normal state of mind - confused, again!

It was arranged that we would leave Wickens one week after the school summer holidays started and it would be on a Sunday. Once the letter had arrived telling us that we would be going home, it left us with three weeks to go. Two of those weeks would be at school.

Of course I had to tell the Headmaster (old Ding Dong) that I would not be returning at the beginning of the autumn term. By now, our schooling was being carried out full-time in the community centre and we were down to two teachers, the Head and Mr Thew.

On my last day at school there, Mr Thew called me over to him during the lunch / dinner break.

"Your last day with us Sleeman."

"Yes sir."

Foxwood, Elsynge Road, Wandsworth – a new home to come to on return from evacuation.
Photo: Author's collection

"Looking forward to going home?"

"Yes sir."

"You know the farm where my wife and I are billeted, don't you? You go past it every day."

"Yes sir, I know it."

"As you go past this afternoon after school, will you please call in there to see my wife? She would like to say goodbye to you. Will you do that?"

"Yes sir, of course I will. Thank you sir."

"Don't forget."

"No sir, I won't."

Oh dear, I was not looking forward to this one little bit. I bet you any money you like there'll be tears.

Towards the end of the afternoon session, Mr Bellamy (give him his full name) told me to get my things together, and get my bike. Then everybody came out into the forecourt and I had to shake hands with all the boys and both teachers. It was both embarrassing and touching. This was a practise that Mr Bellamy did for all boys when they left to return to London. They then waved me off as I rode out of the forecourt. Last words from Mr Thew, "Don't you dare forget to call in to see Mrs Thew."

"No, I won't sir, goodbye."

The farmhouse was about half way along my journey to Wickens, set back off the road, with just a track leading to it. I'd never been to this place before.

Having leaned my bike against the wall, I timidly knocked on the front door. When a lady answered I explained that I'd been asked to call in to see Mrs Thew.

I'm afraid you've lost the bet because, even before Mrs Thew reached the front door, there were tears in her eyes.

"So you are going back home to London", said Mrs Thew.

"Yes Mrs Thew."

"I'm not sure I agree with that, but I suppose your parents know best."

"Yes Mrs Thew." (You can see I was always full of chat).

"We are going to miss you."

"Thank you."

"Will you promise me that if there are any more bombing raids you will go to the shelter and keep safe?"

She wasn't crying, but tears were rolling down her cheeks. I didn't know what to do or say. She continued.

"If you should ever come back for a visit, like some boys do, you will be sure to call in and see us, won't you?"

"Of course I will Mrs Thew. You've both been very kind to me." With that, she threw her arms around me and gave me a very big hug.

"Help, what's going on here? I'm being hugged by a teacher's wife!" She released me from this bear-like hug and grabbed my wrist and pushed some coins into my hand. "Buy yourself something from us", she said.

It was time to go. I said "thank you" and "goodbye" and walked over to get my bike, and as I did so took a quick peek at the coins in my hand. Five bob! At that moment, I forgave her all her sins, because five shillings was an enormous amount of money for a child to be given. It would be equivalent in today's (2013) money of more than seven pounds (again I have used the National Archives Currency Converter).

As I cycled away she stood at the front door waving and calling out, "Goodbye, take care." I looked back when I reached the main road. She was still waving; I waved back. She watched me along the main road until a clump of trees cut off the view.

This gave me doubts about the wisdom of going back to London. At five bob a hug I could have been on a 'nice little earner'.

The last week at Wickens was not one of the most enjoyable ones. It was spent going around to the few people who might want to say goodbye. But, in the main, I spent as much time as possible with Jay and the Harvey brothers.

The last play day with them was not much fun. We talked about keeping in touch and getting together again, but that's all it was, talk. On the Saturday evening, Ray Bennett called in. I'd missed him when I had called in to say goodbye to his family. He had always had a really good catapult that he knew I admired and he'd called in to say goodbye and to give me his catapult as a going away present. Even now I think that was a lovely gesture.

Come the "Going Home Day", Kitty and I were told not to try meeting the bus, but to stay put. We wondered if perhaps Dad had once again been offered the use of Mr Cole's car because suitcases, or some sort of bags were needed, as we now had far more belongings to take home from the few meagre bits and pieces with which we had arrived.

So Kit and I waited impatiently for something to happen. At somewhere around midday, the hire car from the village pulled into Wickens' driveway and out stepped Gran. Well I for one was very surprised. I thought it might be either Mum and Dad or just perhaps Dad to do the final honours. But no, as I say, it was Gran. She arranged for the car to come back to collect us at a time somewhere around 2.30pm.

Whether or not Nelly and Hetty were surprised to see Gran and not my parents, I've no way of knowing. If they were, they didn't show it, not to me anyway. While Nelly made some tea and sandwiches, Hetty helped Gran pack our belongings into the cases that Gran had brought.

There was plenty of time after the Ashby's had had their lunch for Kit and I to go and say our goodbye's to Mr and Mrs Ashby and thank them for their extreme kindness over the last three years. As usual, I let Kitty do the talking; saying goodbye to the Ashby's was not the hard part. The worst was yet to come and I was not looking forward to it.

The car duly arrived and the cases were loaded. It was time to say goodbye to these wonderful people who had looked after us for nearly three years. They could not have done a better job if we had been their own children. By now, Mr Billings had joined the group.

Aunty was as usual cold, aloof and formal. Dear Nelly and Hetty both cried and, for the one and only time in three years, gave us both a hug and kissed us goodbye. When I said goodbye to dear old George, we were both so upset neither of us could speak. We just hugged each other. I loved that dear old man. Saying goodbye to Mr Billings was not so hard, even though he too had been very good to us. By now, all I wanted to do was get in the car out of sight. I never saw any of them again.

It took some time for Kit and myself to calm down. Having given us both time to sort ourselves out, Gran started telling us about the new house. She then asked us if we remembered her (Gran) seeing us off at Clapham Junction three years ago. Did we remember? Were we ever likely to forget?

The car didn't stop at the village green as I expected it to. Gran had arranged to go straight through to Haywards Heath Railway Station. We were going home in real style.

Once on the train bound for London, Kit's and my spirits began to rise. At last it was getting exciting. The journey didn't take too long and very soon the train was pulling into Clapham Junction.

Now Gran got a porter and told him we wanted a taxi. Wow! Gran really was going to do it in style. I'd never been in a London taxi before. Remember how I arrived home after coming out of the fever hospital, in the fish van!

The new house was not far from the railway station, so it didn't take long to get there. As the taxi pulled up, there was the house. Yes, it was a fine house, three storeys high and with the most unlikely name of "Foxwood".

The front door flew open and every member of my family came rushing out to greet us. We were home.

What happened next I'm not too sure about. In all the excitement, the memories have become a bit blurred, but doubtless we were shown over the house and all its many rooms; and of course the garden – that was to become my father's pride and joy for the next few years.

Two of the rooms were still empty because, having come out of a small flat, there was not enough furniture to go around. Although they had got some furniture in the two weeks since they had moved in, some rooms would have to wait.

This was a complete turnaround to the usual problem of not enough room; now there was almost too much.

That "Homecoming Day" teatime was like a big party. Mum had pulled out all the stops and laid on a bumper tea. As I sat at that meal table with Mum, Dad, Gran and all my sisters and brothers, I realised that some of my happiest memories of my childhood were about family mealtimes when we were all together. That is what I had been missing and thought were gone forever, but now they were back. We had a lovely family evening, talking about the house, Kitty finding a job, Martin starting schooling and me re-starting school in a few weeks time.

That night as I climbed up the stairs to the top of the house (in the blackout) to a nice little room that I would be sharing with Jim, the thought crossed my mind that this was pretty good.

Before I go any further about relating my feelings about being home. I do feel the need to go back a bit and write about my feelings regarding our old flat in Queenstown Road.

There was no doubting that our new home was a lovely big house, but it was not the place that I had been looking forward to returning to for three long years and I have to say that I did feel somewhat deprived.

All through my life, when I have lived in a place and been happy there, as and when I leave I have always said a mental "goodbye" and "thank you" to the old home. It may sound silly to you, but that's me!

The last time I left our old flat was on our day trip to London to see the bombing damage. When I left I didn't know it was going to be my last time, so I didn't say my goodbye and thank you, and it bugs me.

My memories of growing up there with my parents, brothers and sisters are extremely happy, particularly the Sundays when Dad would be home all day.

The meal times were real family times with us all sitting around a large kitchen table, with father entertaining us with his stories of what had happened to him during the past week. It's almost certain that some of these stories weren't true, but that didn't matter one jot. He was a very good yarn teller.

If any of my older sisters or brother Jim had managed to get to the cinema during the week, they would be encouraged to tell the rest of us about it. The meals seemed to go on for hours.

By moving, I feared that all that was gone forever. Happily, I was wrong.

Sadly now, all my brothers and sisters have passed away, and I have only one remaining link with those Queenstown Road days.

This vital link is a lady who, in those days was a young girl named Patsy Smith.

Now, my mother used to look after young Patsy whilst her mother went to work. It helped Mrs Smith and it helped my mum, who needed this extra money that she got paid, so everybody was happy.

Before school started, Patsy would be around to us from Silverthorn Road, bringing her day's meals in a big tin box. She would eat with us, play with us and listen to Children's Hour with us. When it was time, she would go home.

She was ours during the weekdays, but her parents' evenings and weekends. This went on for years, how many I just don't know.

If Gran took me out anywhere for a treat it was almost certain that Patsy came too; she was a couple of years older than me, but we were good pals. It became that she was like a member of our family and that's still how I think of her, an adopted sister.

Came the war, and Patsy was evacuated to an aunt in Norfolk. She never came back to London to live and we rather lost touch. But in the 1960's, whilst my wife, Shelagh, and I were on holiday in Norfolk we set about tracing her, which we successfully did.

Since then, we keep in touch, every birthday and Christmas there's a card plus a letter. We haven't seen each other in years, but she is without doubt, in time, my oldest friend, and my only remaining link with those happy days.

The next few weeks were spent not only in finding my way around our new neighbourhood and getting to know the people, but strangely enough getting to know some of my own family again as well.

My mother wasn't the sort of lady to fuss over people; she either didn't believe in it or she wasn't very good at it. Never managed to find out which. But for those first few days of being home she really did try her best to show us that she was pleased to have us back home.

It was the same as when we first arrived at Wickens. We soon picked up a routine and we soon picked up the routine at home, albeit very different from the Wickens one. The greatest blessing proved to be electric lighting.

Now I was back home I did not have that same freedom to roam around that I'd had in the countryside; firstly, because it was not my mother's way to allow it. She always wanted to know where I was and what I was doing. The second reason was the still possible danger from German air raids.

It was a period of settling in. One of the most welcome pleasures was to be able to go to the cinema. During our three years away, I'd only been once (that's not counting "The Picnic" one, 'cos that doesn't count).

During these weeks I listened to try to solve the mystery as to why Gran had come to fetch Kit and I home. You see, my brothers and sisters and I had always been brought up to believe that whatever one's parents said or did was always right. That's the way children were brought up in those days.

But I was beginning to have doubts on that score. There was no way that anybody was going to convince me, either then, or now, that my parents were right in not coming to collect us. They should have come down, no matter how busy they were, just having moved.

They owed the people at Wickens a personal sincere thank you for all they had done for their children for three years. Also, for making them so welcome on their visits.

Whether or not there had been some disagreement regarding our returning to London, I don't know; nothing was ever said to me. Nevertheless, and I hate to have to write it, but I think my parents were totally wrong and out of order. Having brought us up to always say "please" and "thank you" and be polite, they themselves fell short and I was surprised at them.

It was, I suppose, part of my growing up process that I was starting to get opinions of my own. Not always in line with other peoples. That has been bothering me for years and I'm glad to get it off my chest.

Whilst I've been ranting on here, Kitty has been looking for a job. It didn't prove too hard to find one, as an office junior. She will be going to evening classes to learn shorthand and typing. Her workplace is close enough to home so she can get home for lunch.

As the school summer holidays came to an end the prospect of starting at a new school drew closer, although for me it was a schooling re-start. For my little brother, Martin, it would be his first day at school.

On the first day of the autumn term our mother took Martin and I along to Plough Road School to enrol us - the infants for Martin and the senior boys for me. The moment that we walked through those school gates on that first time, that was the moment evacuation ended as far as I was concerned; it was over. Anything that happened from hereon, my friends, would be another story for another day.

47. The Aftermath

Just when you were thinking, "Well, that's the end of that", now for once it's your turn to be wrong.

You see, in the subsequent years two or three things happened that link in with what I have been telling you. The story, such as it is, would be incomplete if I didn't relate them to you. Anyway, I've got one or two points to make before I close, so you haven't got rid of me just yet. Better luck next time.

There is no reason to go into a lot, if any, details about the rest of my schooling. Only to say that I, like my brother Jim, stayed on for an extra year, until I was fifteen. The reason was the same, to make up some of the backlog caused through being evacuated.

By the time I left school the war was over and everybody was trying to sort themselves out and get back to normal. My brother Jim was in the army in Germany, Kitty was steadily progressing through the ranks in her office job and my first job was with a garden nursery nearby in Wandsworth.

Some mornings as I was working with a gang of others tending the plants and shrubs, I would see a gentleman who looked very familiar walking along the main road outside. Admittedly, he was some distance away but I was pretty certain that it was "Old Burb".

At last my curiosity got the better of me and I asked the foreman if I could go across to the fencing and check. "Alright, but don't take too long about it." I ran over.

"Excuse me sir, but you are Mr Burbridge, aren't you?"

"Yes young man, but I don't know you."

I explained who I was and that my brother Jim and I had been evacuated in 1939 with Heathbrook School.

"Well, of course I remember all that," he replied, "but I'm sorry I don't remember you or your brother."

"That's alright sir, there were quite a lot of us. It's just nice to see you again, and looking so well."

We talked for a few moments, me with one eye on the foreman. Then I said, "You might remember teaching two of my uncles in the 1920's; Norman Porter and Alfie King." His face lit up. "Now I know who you are!" he said.

After that, whenever I was working near the roadway and he went past he would always wave his walking stick above his head and I would wave back. This carried on until I went to do my two years of Army National Service in 1950. By the time I came back to resume my job, there was no sign of Mr Burbridge. He was a nice man and a good teacher, and he helped me a lot.

For the next little incident we have to 'fast forward' into the 1960's. I can't be more exact than that.

By now, I have progressed through a few jobs, always in gardening, plus a five-year period of self-employment.

Then in 1960 I obtained the position as resident Head Gardener for two of the Inns of Court, namely the Inner and Middle Temples in the City of London. My wife, Shelagh and I had a nice flat in the Inner Temple, with our young baby daughter, Kerry, and later on our son, John.

One early June afternoon, I'm working planting a bed of tuberous begonias in one of our major flowerbeds right outside 'The Inner Temple Dining Hall'.

As I worked, a voice from behind me said, "Excuse me, but could you tell me where Hare Court is from here?"

As I turned to face the voice, there I saw a smartly dressed gentleman and I directed him to Hare Court. He, in turn, thanked me, made some comment about the begonias and turned to find his way to Hare Court.

As he did so, I said, "You are Mr Michael Ashby, aren't you?" He spun back round, his jaw dropped open, surprise written all over his face. "How the hell do you know that?" he asked.

Then I had to explain that I was the youngest of five children billeted onto his mother and father at Wickens during the war. Also, I remembered being taken for rides by him (Mr Michael) in his Aston Martin sports car.

He was, of course, very surprised at this meeting and wrote down full details regarding myself, Kitty, and my brother Jim. Also as much information as I could supply regarding Billy Behoe and Len Hawes. He said he would be seeing his mother (Mrs Ashby) within the next few days and would pass on all this information to her.

He explained that having become a doctor, he then went on to train as a psychiatrist and often had to visit the four Inns when called in to give advice on some cases, so he would keep his eye open for me in future. Well, I don't know if he saw me, but I never saw him again.

There's one other little meeting but I'm going to hang on to that for a bit. But I am going to use the incident regarding Mr Michael as a link to write about Wickens and the people that lived there.

In the years between coming back to London and my leaving school to start work, I twice wrote to Mrs Ashby asking if it would be convenient for me to go and visit for the day at some time.

On both occasions she replied that now was not a good time. The first occasion I can't remember the reason; the second was that Nelly was getting married and they were rather busy. Mentally I wished Nelly all the best and good luck. If she was marrying old "Silly But Happy" she'd need all the luck going. But I digress.

What I really want to say is that during our period of evacuation Mr and Mrs Ashby were 'officially' the people to whom we were billeted, because they owned Wickens. We will forever be grateful for what they did.

But there can be no doubt at all as to where the main onus fell. It was Nelly, Hetty and George who had the work and responsibility of looking after us kids on a day to day basis. It would be ungracious of me not to mention Aunty and "The 'At"; also Mr Billings, whose patience I tested to the limit.

There just are not enough words that would say an adequate thank you, and believe me I've tried hard enough to find them.

For some time now I have wondered whether any of the Government allowance that "The Ashby's" got paid got passed onto "The Staff". At least some of it should have been. But we come back to my old catchphrase, "It's none of your business Geoffrey."

Apart from coughs and colds, none of us children were ill during our stay there. When in later years I heard and read some evacuation stories I realise how very, very lucky we were. Words just fail me.

They got very little thanks and they got no medals, but Nelly and Hetty, plus thousands of country housewives throughout the country, did as good a job as anybody else during the war, and in some cases better.

It rather reminds me of a quotation from one of the poems by John Milton:

"They also serve, who only stand and wait" (Sonnet 16). How very apt.

There is one thing that I've written earlier, that I now wish to correct and clarify.

At the very beginning of this writing under the heading 'Evacuation', first paragraph, I wrote, "Many lives would never be the same again."

What a damn silly thing to write!

Nobody's life was ever going to be the same again. There was absolutely nobody, no matter who they were, or what they were, or where they were, that could have escaped the effect of the war in some way or another. Some to a far greater extent than others. Not only in this country, but Europe, where things were even worse. The effects of the war were worldwide; it went on for too long for this not to happen. There was too much death, pain, suffering and destruction.

In my own personal case, the same as thousands and thousands of people, there were too many goodbyes and far too many of those goodbyes were forever.

This error on my part has been bothering me somewhat and I just wanted to put the record straight.

48. Horsted Keynes Revisited

With my job with the Inner and Middle Temples going well, and our two children getting bigger (as children have a habit of doing), my wife Shelagh and I decided I should learn to drive, then we would buy a car.

So, by 1966 we had our first little car and were able to go further afield if we felt like it.

One sunny Sunday I thought it would be a nice idea to take them to the scene of all my crimes, namely Horsted Keynes. A picnic was packed (bringing back wet memories) and we set off. It would be alright, the sun was shining.

On arriving at the village green, as far as I could remember it looked almost exactly the same, but I did notice that at the top end of what we used to call Church Lane the old blacksmith forge had been closed. Many happy hours had been spent in there, just watching.

We went down Church Lane; it still seemed pretty steep. I wanted to show them the "goat run", but that was gone too. The steep embankment was still there but they had removed the ridge that was the goat run – spoilsports.

Down to the church into the 'desiccated' churchyard. My wife wanted to look for the German airman's grave. She'd heard me tell the 'Hamburger' story but I'm not sure she believed it. But I had a pretty good idea where the grave had been and without too much effort we found it. We also found the grave of the village school head mistress, Mrs Morse. It seemed so strange to be back there again.

We went through the churchyard into the village school playground and the memories came flooding back. Of course, this all meant nothing to our two children, but I think Shelagh was finding it interesting. I was in a world of my own, just remembering and wondering what happened to everybody.

Next, I tried to find "The Old Mill" because even as a youngster I had been impressed at the sight of it, and I wanted to see it again for myself and show Shelagh and the children. Being the eldest by two years, I thought Kerry might learn something useful by seeing it.

But no matter how hard we looked we couldn't find it, and I was really disappointed, so we moved on.

Since starting this writing, I have found out that the mill was demolished after the war. Whoever was responsible no doubt came up with a very good reason as to why it should go; but I think to have knocked that mill down was almost a criminal act.

We then left the village and headed for Birch Grove and Wickens. As we drove along not too much had changed. There were a few freshly built houses and bungalows on route, but that was to be expected.

When we reached Wickens, I stopped outside. Apart from the surrounding trees having grown larger, it all looked much the same, but it looked as if Mr Billings' ramshackle old shack had gone – no big surprise.

After a while we moved on. The children were asking when do we picnic. We went to Twyford and I looked for the old chapel that had been used by Twyford School. Couldn't find that either – I wasn't having a very good day, was I?

On down Twyford Hill where our 'make do' bike had clanked down all those years ago. At least in the car the ride was a lot more comfortable, and this time I had my eyes open!

When we got to the ford, I was able to show them "The Bridge of the Flying Cyclists". This seemed like a good place to have our picnic, so we found a nice spot in a nearby field. With the sun shining and being warm and dry, it didn't seem right to be having a picnic.

Once we'd eaten, we let the children play by the ford. We could keep an eye on them as they tried to catch some of the minnows, just like I had done. While they played, I reminisced quite a bit; must have bored Shelagh silly.

We doubled back on the same route, past Birch Grove Cottage, where Arthur and the tearful Mrs Jay lived; one final look at Wickens and back to the village.

For some reason I cannot explain, I didn't go to the Dane Hill location but went straight back to the village. As we turned into the village I saw Mrs Fry's sweet shop, and I just had to stop.

To my surprise, it was open. Remember it was a Sunday afternoon. Once I saw it was open I knew that I had to go inside, so we all got out of the car.

The instant I opened the door I knew nothing inside had changed. It was the same old bell on a spring fixed to the top of the shop door. It was like walking into a time warp. A lady came down from rooms above the shop to serve us. She was pleasant, but remote because we were, after all, strangers.

We let the children choose some sweets for themselves and Shelagh and I bought something to chew during the drive home, and I paid. Upon receiving my change I suppose I was a bit slow to move and the lady asked:

"Was there something else you wanted sir?"

"Er, no thank you. Sorry, but I was miles away. I was just remembering, you see I have lovely childhood memories of this shop."

At once the remoteness was gone; suddenly this lady became alive and interested.

"Were you brought up around this part then?"

"Well, yes in a way. I was a wartime evacuee for three years, from London."

"What, here in this village?"

"I went to school in this village, but was billeted in Birch Grove, with Mrs Corbett Ashby."

"Did you know she was made a Dame a few years ago?"

"Yes, but to me she will always be Mrs Ashby."

"How lovely."

"I remember this shop being run by a Mrs Fry. She was very good to us kids; would often let us off the odd penny or two if we didn't have enough money."

The lady's hand flew to her face. She was so excited she didn't know what to do.

"This is still Mrs Fry's shop! I help her with it. She's upstairs now – she's very old." (I think she said ninety-three). "Oh, she will be excited when I go up and tell her!" she continued.

"We do occasionally get some of you ex-evacuees come back to see us. It's so nice to think that you haven't forgotten us. Do you keep in touch with any of the others?"

"Apart from my sister and brother, no I'm afraid I didn't."

"That's a pity. We have often talked about trying to organise a reunion for you all but we don't know how to do it." (This was before computers and websites). "Do you remember many of them?" she asked.

"Yes, quite a lot."

"We used to see a lot of them going past the shop door. There was a little lad with a blue bike. Do you remember him?"

"Yes."

"Do you really?"

"Yes." Then, with my voice cracking up I said, "It was me."

By now this poor lady was nearly having kittens. She looked across to Shelagh because I'm not sure she really believed me, and to be fair it was one hell of a long shot.

It was a very emotional moment as far as I was concerned, and I think Shelagh was caught up in it too. She nodded to confirm my claim to being "Blue Bike Boy". I was choked up.

"Oh, I can't wait to get upstairs to tell Mrs Fry. How lovely you've come back and brought your children with you." This lady was bobbing around so much I thought she was going to wet herself!

Anyway, I'd had enough and wanted to get out of the shop, so we said our goodbyes. I don't remember what was said. As soon as we were out of the shop door it was bolted behind us, and the closed sign went up.

Can't you just imagine her legging it up those stairs, shouting, "Look out Mrs Fry, he's back!"

When we all got into our car, Shelagh asked, "Are you alright?" I replied, "Just give me a couple of minutes and I will be."

That was enough for one day, so with a slow drive back past the village green, The Crown pub and that lovely old blacksmiths forge, we left Horsted Keynes and all its ghosts behind.

49. The American Invasion

This is the final incident that is connected to my evacuation. The trouble is that in relating it you might start to think that I've lost the plot. This is because I shall have to mention the Four Inns of Court, also the American Bar Association (ABA).

What have they got to do with being evacuated? Nothing, just trust me and hang on in there and Geoffrey will explain it all to you.

In 1970, the ABA decided at their Annual Conference that the following year's conference (1971) would be held in England, for some reason best known only to themselves.

The English, Four Inns of Court, namely Grays Inn, Lincolns Inn, Inner Temple and Middle Temple, upon hearing this, decided jointly to act as hosts to their American legal colleagues. The timing of this visit was to be July, and the duration was to be one week.

A number of lectures and meetings were arranged, each hosted in turn by one of "The Four Inns". Also, the Four Inns were each hosting four grand dinners in their halls on four consecutive evenings, which meant that each of the American delegates would dine in all four of these great halls during their stay here.

Nobody on the staffs of the Middle and Inner Temples could remember anything like this ever happening before. Months of work and planning went into it and, although the Four Inns were working on this together, there was still a very keen rivalry as to who could put on the best show and outdo the other three.

On the final day of the visit, the Four Inns were to hold massive garden parties in their large gardens, all to be held at the same time. For these garden parties the delegates could bring a guest. Nobody was sure what sort of numbers we were dealing with, but it went into hundreds.

As I was responsible for both the Middle and Inner Temple gardens, this meant that I had to have both of the gardens looking at their best on the same day.

In my 36 years working there, this was the one and only time that I was ever asked to do this. There is no denying that it was a tall order, but that was my job, so stop moaning and get on with it!

In the one-upmanship stakes, the Middle Temple had a definite edge when it came to the garden parties. This edge being that, as an ex-Honorary Treasurer of the Middle Temple, Her Majesty the Queen Mother had agreed to attend their garden party, which was an afternoon function.

There followed a whole series of meetings with the marquee hire firms; also the outside caterers. This with regards to the positioning of the two marquees; also, what the arrangements would be for the delivery of all their equipment when the time came.

If you did not cooperate with these people, you did so at your peril.

We had a well rehearsed routine for getting ready for special events like garden parties and wedding receptions. This routine would 'kick in' ten working days before the event.

The last few days were always hectic because not only was there our own work to do, but with the 'tent riggers' coming in to erect the marquee, somebody had to be around to keep an eye on them, because they would not respect your garden; all they wanted was to get the thing up as quickly as possible and be away. If not watched, and stopped, they would start driving trucks and lorries all over your lawns.

Once the riggers had finished, the caterers, tables and chairs and all their other equipment would begin to arrive, under the same rules, "No vehicles on the grass". This did not make me popular. Also, the working hours were long, because I could not lock up and finish for the day until they had finished what they wanted to do.

But somehow it always seemed to work out alright, and now looking back on it I quite enjoyed it.

They would keep you on your toes right up until literally the last few moments with requests like, "Have you got a small hammer and some tacks or drawing pins we can use please?" or, "Can we borrow a small step ladder for a short

From left, Sir Harry Philimore with Geoff and Shelagh Sleeman at the Middle Temple in London in 1971, awaiting the arrival of the Queen Mother. Geoff and Shelagh were presented to the Queen Mother in recognition of his work as Head Gardener at the Middle Temple and Inner Temple, and for his part in organising the garden parties for the American Bar Association in 1971.
Photo: Author's Collection

time?" "Have you got a ball of string and some scissors?" and even requests for a couple of aspirin, and first aid plasters, and many others.

They seemed to think that us gardeners were magicians that could produce anything out of a top hat, and "abracadabra" most times we could.

Tent riggers I could cope with, caterers also I could cope with, but on the morning of each event the firms doing the flower arranging would arrive. Nine times out of ten they would prove to be "A real pain in the bum". Very little was ever right for these ladies. We were always glad when they were finished and gone and everybody else could get on with their jobs. They always wanted to change everything around. Enough said.

On the "big day" by about noon I could think of nothing else in either garden that needed doing. Anyway, it was only fair that we should fade into the background and let the caterers get on with their job. So, leaving a volunteer on duty in the gardeners' shed to deal with those last minute requests, I sent the rest of my team home.

What I haven't yet told you is that two days before these garden parties the Middle Temple Treasurer said he was so pleased with the way their garden had been prepared that he had decided that I, along with my wife Shelagh, were to be invited to attend as guests. Also, during the afternoon we were to be presented to the Queen Mother. This as recognition and appreciation of the work that had been put into the preparation for the event.

Also, it was thought that it might be handy to have me there in case any of the guests were to ask any horticultural questions, which in fact some did, mainly regarding rose growing.

Having been able to finish at a reasonable time left me plenty of time to shave, shower and smarten myself up for the garden party and presentation. We had been advised that Shelagh should wear a suitable dress, with a hat and white gloves. For me, a dark coloured lounge suit, and wash my wellies (joke).

We had also been briefed that at the moment of the presentation Shelagh should curtsy and I should bow. All set, off we go.

At this point, I'm afraid I have to make some rather dull explanations as to how things work within the Four Inns of Court.

If and when a barrister becomes a bencher of his Inn, any title that he might have is automatically dropped, and within the confines of the Four Inns this barrister, regardless of their gender, then becomes "Master", followed by their surname.

So, whether Mr, Mrs, Miss, Sir, Lord or Lady, Earl or Dame, they all become Master 'So and So'. It puts everybody on the same level.

Now, Sir Harry Phillimore was a Middle Temple bencher. He was the bencher to whom I was answerable regarding Middle Temple garden matters. Because of this, Master and Lady Phillimore were also to be presented to the Queen Mother. The Master Treasurer would present the Phillimores and then Master Phillimore would, in turn, present Shelagh and I.

Phew! Sorry about all that; hope you understand it all.

As Shelagh and I stood and awaited the Royal arrival with Master and Lady Phillimore, I was doing some remembering.

My mind went back to November 1939 when the Queen Mother, who was then the Queen, had come to visit not only our school but also our school allotment. Also, I remembered that because of that Royal visit, my gang and I were accused of lying, and banished to our room without dinner or tea.

As I remembered, I also wondered, dare I remind Her Majesty of her wartime visit to my school and our allotment? Explain to her what followed and suggest to her that at the very least she owed me a dinner.

Don't worry, I wasn't daft enough to do it, but can you imagine the stir it would have caused if I had? Wouldn't it have been fun?

When the moment came, the presentation itself went very well. It was short and sweet. Just a brief conversation regarding the problems of getting a garden ready for such a big event. The Queen Mother congratulated me upon the way the garden looked and moved on – I'd lost my chance.

But there were two incidents during the garden party that I particularly remember as amusing that I would like to relate to you, both concerning our American guests.

Upon the Queen Mother's arrival, the Royal car drew up at a garden gate just off the Victoria Embankment. There she was met and greeted by the Middle Temple Treasurer, the Under Treasurer and their wives. They then turned and started to walk the full length of the garden to the "Queen Mother's Chair". (She had her own chair – always kept within the Inn. Nobody else was ever allowed to sit in it).

As they turned to make this walk, the crowd of guests parted, leaving a clear corridor for them to pass through. The American guests were clearly excited at the presence of the Queen Mother.

Most just watched this small procession make its way up the garden, many took photographs, some clapped. One American lady, in a very bright dress, got a bit carried away and broke ranks, stepping out in front of the Queen Mother, and spoke to her, at the same time offering her hand to be shaken.

The Queen Mother took her hand and gently shook it and quietly said a few words (don't know what they were). Then she smiled and moved on. The American lady held the shaken hand up in the air and shouted to the moving away Queen Mother:

"Gee Ma'am, I'll never wash my hands again!"

The Treasurer and his wife did not look pleased, amused or impressed.

The second incident concerns a young American gent of about 25-30 years old. He had chosen to ignore the suggested male dress code on the invitations, which was dark coloured lounge suits.

He had decided to be different and, by the looks of it, had hired a morning suit, with black top hat.

Of course, he stood out like a sore thumb, whether or not that's what he wanted, there's no way of knowing, but stand out he did!

He looked pretty pleased with himself and was smiling at just about everybody, because no doubt he thought everybody was smiling at him, but they were in fact trying not to laugh. The trouble was his top hat was quite a bit too big for him. As the afternoon wore on, it slipped lower and lower down his head until he could just about see from underneath it. Plus it bent the tops of his ears over. He looked a right ninny, and he didn't have enough sense to take it off.

But we all had to make allowances - after all they were Americans!

It seems that all the garden parties were a great success; indeed the whole American visit had gone well. There is no way of knowing what happened at Lincolns and Grays Inn, but the Inner and Middle Temples paid a bonus to all their staff to show their appreciation of a job well done. These bonuses were not on the same scale as today's bankers, but a modest percentage of their salaries.

The following day (after the party) it was back to the old routine. Catering equipment being collected, and the marquees coming down. Once they had cleared the site, it was clear up time.

You know what they say, "After the Lord Mayor's Show". Guess who was driving the dustcart.

50. The Last Goodbye

Well, that just about wraps it up. It's nearly time for me to lay down my pen and say goodbye (another goodbye). Anyway, I'm getting writers' cramp.

There's just a few I's to dot and some T's to cross.

As I think you will already understand, after leaving Wickens I never saw Nelly, Hetty, dear old George, Aunty, Mr Billings or Mr and Mrs Ashby again. But I did see Mr Michael just that once in the Inner Temple.

Nevertheless, my admiration for what they did for us kids has no bounds. I think I've made that clear.

All of my brothers and sisters have passed away, but I would like to think that Kitty and Jim would approve of my telling this story; but I'm not too sure that Jim would – he wasn't a great one for reminiscing.

The lady that I have kept referring to as Mrs Ashby became Dame Margaret Corbett Ashby in 1967. She lived to be 99 years old and died at the family home, Dane Hill, in 1981. But I'm afraid that I have no such details regarding Mr Ashby, although there is something that I've found out whilst doing some research for this writing. With the help of the Inner Temple librarian (who I keep in touch with), she found out for me that Mr Ashby was in fact a member of the Inner Temple and was called to the bar there.

What a strange coincidence that many years later I should work and live there for thirty-six years; I think it's most strange.

At the end of my thirty-six years, I retired. We moved out of the City and out of London altogether, back to the countryside. The move was to Rutland where we bought a really lovely three hundred year old cottage. That's where I am as I write this.

Right from the very start of this writing as I thought about the task ahead (a task that quite frankly scared me stiff), I made my mind up then that, if I saw this through to the end, my last few paragraphs would be about the lady that helped me so much – my dear friend, Mrs Ongar.

Back over the years, I have spent a lot of time wondering who she was, where did she come from? Why was she so important enough to be here in our country at that time? What happened to her? The questions go on and on and at this late stage there will never be any answers. Except maybe to one of them. Where did she come from? Maybe I am getting somewhere near to an answer.

You see, I never knew her nationality, but by using that word that she used to use to charm the rabbits (and me) – do you remember? "Malutki, malutki", well with some help from a lot of people we are more or less sure that it's Polish for darling or dearest; but this is still ongoing.

As to what happened to her, I've no idea whatsoever, but in my childish imagination at that time I saw her being sent back to her own country on espionage work. Then I thought of her being caught by the Germans; I had to stop thinking any further at that point.

As for the stutter that she helped me with. As I grew older and became more confident, it became less and less of a problem. During my National Service in the army it did give me a few sticky moments when short, sharp answers are often required. But I survived.

As far as I'm concerned it's gone, whether other people notice it now, I don't know, and I don't really care very much.

However, the stutter does return if I get over tired, ill or stressed over some problem. But when that happens I seem to hear her accented voice in my head softly reminding me, "Slowly, Geoffrey, slowly."

Geoff and Shelagh Sleeman, now well into retirement,
outside their 300 year old cottage in Rutland.

Acknowledgements

There is a quite interesting Horsted Keynes website which, along with the history of the village, covers the World War Two period. This includes the arrival into the village of the Heathbrook School evacuees in September 1939. There are photographs of when Her Majesty the Queen visited not only our new school in the village and other groups of London evacuees in the area.

Also, a mention for the Danehill Parish Historical Society. When they were approached and understood what we were trying to do, they, through their secretary Mrs Jill Rolfe, became very interested and helpful. We were sent two photographs and newspaper cuttings from their archives that we have been able to use. Their letters were most helpful and friendly.

Further thanks go to Margaret Clay, the Inner Temple Librarian who helped to research some parts of the book, Karen Verrills for typing the manuscript, and my family for their encouragement and help.

Finally, many thanks to my friend David Bland, and his son Paul at Little School Publishing, for helping me to put all of this together.